CONTENTS

Part One
Journey into the Otherworld

Part Two
Therapeutic Harvest

PAST LIFE DREAMWORK

ॐ

"*Past Life Dreamwork* is a serious book, and ranks among the very few that are worth carrying in one's briefcase, and sleeping on."

"I have just finished reading *Past Life Dreamwork* and I want to give it a five-star review. Aside from insights into her patients and ultimately herself, Sabine Lucas has helped me understand and contextualize dreams and patterns of dreams I have experienced over the past sixty years."

PAST LIFE DREAMWORK

Healing the Soul through Understanding Karmic Patterns

Sabine Lucas, Ph.D.

Bear & Company
Rochester, Vermont

Bear & Company
One Park Street
Rochester, Vermont 05767
www.BearandCompanyBooks.com

Bear & Company is a division of Inner Traditions International

Originally published in 2005 by iUniverse, 2021 Pine Lake Road, Suite 100, Lincoln, NE 68512, under the title *Bloodlines of the Soul.*

Library of Congress Cataloging-in-Publication Data
Lucas, Sabine.
  [Bloodlines of the soul]
  Past life dreamwork : healing the soul through understanding karmic patterns / Sabine Lucas.
    p. cm.
  Originally published: Bloodlines of the soul. Lincoln, NE : iUniverse, 2005.
  Includes bibliographical references and index.
  ISBN: 978-1-59143-075-9
  1. Reincarnation. 2. Dreams. 3. Karma. I. Title.

BL515.L77 2008
133.901'35—dc22

                                                                2007050888

Printed and bound in the United States by Lake Book Manufacturing

10   9   8   7   6   5   4   3   2   1

Text design and layout by Virginia Scott Bowman
This book was typeset in Garamond Premiere Pro with Schneidler Intitials, Gill Sans, and Avant Garde as display typefaces.

To send correspondence to the author of this book, mail a first-class letter to the author c/o Inner Traditions • Bear & Company, One Park Street, Rochester, VT 05767, and we will forward the communication to the author.

In loving memory of Jenny
And dedicated to the heroes of these stories

FOREWORD

Last night, following an ancient ritual to create a sacred writing place, I burned some *euzaerlik* in this room. For a Hindu to enter this Muslim ritual is to honor our common ancestors, and to pray for peace among us. Now, after the night and a day has passed, the sun is moving again toward the horizon in Zacatecas. In this setting, I find that the imprint of past lives on us is like the lingering euzaerlik smell . . . or like the whispers of the moon as it grazes Earth with its nocturnal blessings. Most people alive today fail to sense such subtle presences and thus remain largely disconnected from finer and, at times, more beautiful and important aspects of their lives, present and past.

Sabine Lucas's book—for me—carries the voice of an autobiography of a soul, where ancient bloodlines stream through monastic lives and mingle with those of prostitutes. In the fires of these, and many other lives, a woman was born in whom these various bloodlines have found a temporary resting place. Specifically, through well-examined night dreams and synchronistic events, the book reasserts that the ancient notion of reincarnation is simply not a philosophical possibility or a matter of religious faith but a reality that ought to be accepted, or at least examined on its scientific merits. *Past Life Dreamwork* reconfirms the existence of a karmic law that operates in the realm of life. In this process, the unexplained becomes explained and is connected to the larger context of life's currents.

Before I proceed further, given the subject and the present cultural environment in the West, a few remarks on my own background and, more importantly, on the nature of science and its practice seem to be called for. As a physicist, and as a scientific exile living in a remote desert mountain area, my life's task appears to be a search for the truth. I know it is beyond my present abilities to reach this ultimate goal, but certainly, glimpses of that realm are within reach of every honest effort. I consider it my calling to obtain these glimpses and share them with my fellow beings in order to inspire them and reconnect them to the universe in a factual and poetic manner.

The stated, larger task asks me to place honesty and critical examination of all phenomena at a primary focal point. Any theory, be it about the dark matter of the universe or the shadows of the soul, would then follow, but only as an instrument to place order in what otherwise would appear to be a random and unconnected set of occurrences and happenings. This desire to bring harmony, this urge to obtain coherent knowledge of the laws of Nature, must not be allowed to go beyond its proper role. That is, it must not neglect events and data selectively or otherwise, for if that is done, the chosen path does not lead to the secrets of nature or to science but stays within the realm of science fiction and the politics of science. While fiction and politics have respected roles to play in human affairs, they are no substitute for an uncompromised look into the heart of the universe.

If one takes the position stated above, this book establishes that human life neither begins nor ends at the biological birth nor at the biological end. It is, to use a physics example, like when particles and antiparticles collide, annihilate, and propagate as pure energy of light, and later, after finding a suitable environment, reappear as particles and antiparticles. The energy contained in this particle-antiparticle pair dissolves into pure light and reemerges later in the form of a newly created particle-antiparticle pair. Of course, the author, not being a physicist, does not invoke any such argument, which is only valid as an analogy anyway. Her argument and conclusion is based on data appropriate to the subject. In fact, the author of this book draws no conclusions; the conclusions simply dawn on the reader. Apart from this, what is important is that no karma is devoid of its consequences. The consequences, at times, may play their role in some future life, and not necessarily in the next life. Because implications of these matters fill the book, I call attention to the wider implications this may have for humanity.

Our Earth moves at about thirty kilometers per human heartbeat around our sun. This orbital journey occurs with a beauty and precision that has no match in human technological inventions. It requires no fuel stops and causes no exhaust. The ride is smooth, and no ticket is required for this adventure in space. It carries with it a renewable supply of oxygen and nourishment. It is showered by the life-giving warmth of the sun and by the inspiring silver light of the moon, which dances to the beat of a twenty-eight-day rhythm. Were all the light-bulbs on the planet to be switched off, one would be exposed to a celestial beauty of unparalleled inspiration; billions of stars and galaxies would exhibit their presence as twinkling light holes in the otherwise dark night sky.

Only a person without honor can accept such gifts without gratitude, but collectively, humanity is engaged in the most brutal rape and soiling of Earth and its local environment of the solar system. Earth's rivers are no longer the carriers of clear, life-giving water to quench our thirst. We are, without knowing it, constantly thirsty. I know how the river waters full of oxygen and minerals used to quench my thirst when I grew up in India fifty years ago. Today, the fish are dying all across the oceans in large areas known as dead zones, while plastic bottles float and are scattered all over the planet, insulting its beauty and its very existence. Similarly, most humans and other life-forms are slowly suffocating on fumes of car exhaust and industrial waste. The mantra of this age is maximization of profit, and only lip service is being paid to matters ethical and moral. By ethics and morality I do not mean such things as who sleeps with whom, but who speaks the truth and lives in truth. By ethics and morality, I mean a sense of dignity and respect for this planet and those who live and die on it.

By raising my concerns for the planet and the quality of life—despite all the glitter and the synthetic perfume—I wanted to bring to the reader's attention that *Past Life Dreamwork* raises a bloodcurdling question: How will the collective karma of the human race come back to us, and with what vengeance? Those who think they can buy a ticket for a spaceship to some new planet of paradise carry a deep illusion, a deep denial. According to the larger implications of this book, after dying on the way to the planet of paradise or when they are on it, again they will have to face the raped and soiled planet Earth in their next incarnation. This conclusion is so apparent that it is left to dawn on the reader, and on the collective inhumanity of this age.

D. V. Ahluwalia-Khalilova, Ph.D.

Zacatecas, Mexico

D. V. Ahluwalia-Khalilova is a physicist and astronomer who holds a Ph.D. in physics from Texas A&M University. He is a professor and senior lecturer at the University of Canterbury, Christchurch, New Zealand, and, at present, is focusing his research on a new quantum field theoretic construct that explains the darkness of dark matter and carries important implications for astrophysics and cosmology.

PREFACE

I have to warn the reader from the beginning that this is not a self-help book. Self-help books operate on the tacit assumption that we can manage and manipulate a situation and make things happen at will. They all contain recipes that show us how to do that. I, on the other hand, have to confess that I never had any control over the past life dream process that is recorded in this book. The spontaneous return of unconscious memories happens when a person is ready, regardless of whether he or she likes it. I personally decided, after having one particularly uncomfortable dream, that I had better accept what was happening to me, because otherwise I might miss the whole purpose of my life.

So instead of resisting the past life dream recall, I did my best to stimulate it. I attended a lecture series on dreams and reincarnation at the Jung Institute in Zurich and later consulted an internationally renowned Swiss past life reader and aura painter, the late Jenny Ganz. Apart from Jane Robert's *Seth* books*—for which I was the authorized German translator— Elisabeth Ruef's lecture series and Jenny Ganz's readings have been the

---

*For those readers not familiar with the *Seth* books, they are a series of seven books written by the American author Jane Roberts between 1969 and 1984 (the year of her death), wherein she channeled a disincarnate entity named Seth. In addition to the channeled material itself, she published many other Seth-related books of her own. In all of her writings she deals with psychological, philosophical, and metaphysical subjects such as the nature of reality, the origin of the universe, reincarnation, dreams, and creativity.

catalyst for my subsequent work. I am deeply grateful for having met Elisabeth Ruef and Jenny Ganz at just the right time. Without these unusually gifted, adventurous, and deeply caring women, my inner process would not have gotten off the ground, and this book would not have been written.

In general, and with regard to accuracy, Jenny's readings were clearly a match for Edgar Cayce's well-known life readings, although she never attained his level of fame. In my own particular case, over a period of two years she informed me of twenty incarnations and provided personal data, some of which could be validated by subsequent historical research. These incarnations were also confirmed by my own dreams. Yet I discovered over time that Jenny had tried to spare my feelings by omitting some very disturbing facts from her readings. She also never mentioned those lifetimes that were karmically responsible for the suffering I had to endure in the rest of my incarnations. To compensate for that, my unconscious has always tried to provide what was missing. Especially since I started writing this book, my dreams have aimed at rounding out the picture.

For instance, the brutal and seemingly unjust execution in the sixteenth century of the French Renaissance poet Maurice Scève, which is described in chapter 3, received a karmic explanation, even while I was writing this preface. I dreamed that I had been the Lord Chancellor of England in the fifteenth century at the time of the War of the Roses and had condemned people to "strange tortures, never heard of" as Shakespeare puts it in *King Henry VI*. I had no conscious knowledge of the Lord Chancellor's role during the Middle Ages and had to consult the Encyclopedia Britannica online.

The Lord Chancellor of England was the head of a special court that was not bound by common law. This meant that during the War of the Roses, the Lord Chancellor must have been following the orders of a succession of murderous noblemen and kings, including the royal monster Richard III. But karmically this was no excuse. Thus, what happened to the gentle poet Maurice Scève in Lyons, France, a century later turned out to have been merely a "measure-for-measure" payback for the Lord Chancellor's abuse of justice.

Because my past life dream therapy evolved from my own inner process, I have presented my story before presenting my clients' stories. This may serve as a reminder that, in the psychoanalytical tradition, one's work with clients has always been preceded by extensive work on the therapist's own inner self. Today, however, this original two-way treatment model has largely gone by the wayside, and it is no longer considered essential that a therapist examine his own unprocessed, unconscious material first. It is, of course, a lot easier to reprogram other peoples' behavior than to try and manage one's own unconscious. Personally, when I began helping my clients to integrate their past lives, I had eleven years of analysis behind me and ten years of solitary work with my own past lives.

Authors of books about past life regression often make the point that they have only regressed people to lives that are exceedingly ordinary, never to any that are elevated in any way. This is to give their work credibility, no doubt. But where is it written that past lives have to be working class in order to be credible? I have personally worked with individuals who, in past lives, were former European royalty; this past life material was completely convincing and verifiable. According to one of my own dreams, I have been royalty myself: a hapless empress in the ninth century. To counterbalance this, I signed the Declaration of Independence in one of my male lives nine centuries later. I have also been a beggar, gypsy, nun, monk, hermit, prostitute, performing artist, lawyer, and healer many times. It is precisely this colorful mixture of complementary life situations that makes our past life histories so interesting. The soul loves opposites, and even within one lifetime it is only through the union of opposites that we can find inner wholeness.

Besides, what would have become of all those famous and infamous historical personalities who never seem to find their way into these past life therapists' offices? Would a Napoleon and a Cleopatra not have had more karmic lessons to learn? Would their fame have been enough to beam them as stars into the heavens, Hollywood-style? Not very likely. I suspect they are right here among us, disguised as ordinary people.

ACKNOWLEDGMENTS

First of all, I would like to express my gratitude to those courageous four men who not only entrusted me with their stories but generously allowed me to share them here. In one way or another, they have all been actively involved in the creation of this book. They collected their dreams, shared their dream journals, chose their own pseudonyms, and conducted independent investigations into the authenticity of their past life material. Although they cannot be named for reasons of confidentiality, they need to be honored for making an invaluable contribution to this book.

In addition, I wish to give my heartfelt thanks to all those friends and helpers who made the previous, self-published edition of this book, entitled *Bloodlines of the Soul,* possible:

Lola Moonfrog, who believed enough in the importance of this material to generously provide the financial means for its first publication.

Joseph Dispenza, who accompanied the book through its long, drawn out birthing process by giving me professional advice, encouragement, and practical help.

D. V. Ahluwalia-Khalilova, Ph.D., whose scientific approval and deep understanding of my empirical research has given me faith in its validity.

Elizabeth Bishop, Ph.D., who encouraged me to write this book in the first place and continued to take a deep interest in it.

Eduardo Duran, Ph.D., who supported me as a friend and colleague throughout the writing process.

Bonnie Bisbee, who, in a spirit of friendship, shared some important writing secrets with me.

Soledad Santiago, who, as an author, gave me honest feedback when the book was still in its fledgling stage.

Claudia Honeywell, Monica Faulker, and Fred de Javanne, all of whom did editorial work on the manuscript for the first edition.

For the present edition, entitled *Past Life Dreamwork,* I am deeply indebted to Philip Miller, Ph.D., director of the Klau Library at Hebrew Union College–Jewish Institute of Religion, who recommended the book to Inner Traditions • Bear & Company, and to my caring editor, Anne Dillon, who, by gently but persistently probing into previously obscure passages of the book, greatly enhanced its clarity. Last, but not least, my thanks are due to those mysterious forces in the deep unconscious, who—in the dreamtime—continued to give me new insights into my own past life history and into the nature of reincarnation.

IDENTIFYING AND WORKING WITH PAST LIFE DREAMS

In view of the novelty of this material, some pointers and also some caveats may be called for. Identifying past life dreams, for the first time, is like discovering a hidden image in a picture. At first we see only the picture itself and search in vain for what might also be there. Then, when our vision begins to blur, the hidden image suddenly pops out, and now we are fixated on the popped-out image and do not see the picture itself anymore. In the same way, we can become fixated on past life material at the expense of other important dream material. To avoid this danger, we should keep in mind that, for most people, the vast majority of night dreams merely process daily events. Even archetypal dreams are much less common than is popularly believed. Both past life and archetypal dreams tend to appear in those critical moments of our lives when the collective unconscious opens to give us guidance and remind us of what we have been through before.

There are three types of past life dreams: the classic type, the informatory type, and the hybrid type. The classic type is so different from other dreams that it can only be mistaken for something else if one is prejudiced, either by religious beliefs or by religiously followed dream theories. This type is lacking all normal dream features, such as familiar places and people, symbols, and archetypes. Instead, it is realistic and factual and has the déjà vu feeling of half-conscious memories. Often, it has the markings of a different century and culture, and the dreamer may only be present as an observer on the scene.

The informatory type is even more unmistakable, because it is completely devoid of images and action. Instead, the dreamer is directly informed, or simply knows, that he or she was, for example, a revolutionary in Russia in 1918 who shot innocent people to death. This type of dream, if it can be called a dream at all, only occurs when the pathway to the eighth chakra—where our past life memories are stored*— has already been cleared through extensive past life dreamwork.

The hybrid type, which is the most common type, can be easily missed. If this were not so, and the other two types were more common, past life dreams would have been included in psychological dream typologies a long time ago. The reason why this type is so difficult to recognize is that it combines realistic and symbolical elements. It dwells in a twilight zone where boundaries are blurred and other interpretations are possible too, especially archetypal ones. Whenever I am not sure if I am dealing with archetypal material or past life material, I use the presence or absence of realistic and personalized elements as decisive criterion, because past life material is personal, while archetypal material is universal and numinous.

Most people dream about only one past life at a time—the one that gets in the way of their present life performance. Since this kind of past life is usually heavily traumatized, the therapist has to work mainly with the trauma. If, in rare cases, many past lives come up all at once in a series of dreams, a different psychological situation exists,

---

*I am personally convinced that past life memories are not stored in the brain but in the eighth chakra, a few inches above the head. If we choose to call this out-of-body place "the unconscious" rather than—as some of the Cayce people do—"the superconscious" mind, then it has to be, as Gina Cerminara in *Many Mansions* (New York: Signet, 1988) suggested, a deeper level of the collective unconscious.

which requires a different psychotherapeutic approach. I agree with the British medium Joan Grant, who assigns such flooding of past life material to the end of the reincarnational cycle. In her book *Many Lifetimes,* which she coauthored with her psychiatrist husband, Denys Kelsey, she compares the reincarnational cycle to an orange, whose segments represent individual lifetimes. At the beginning of the reincarnational cycle, according to her, we are aware only of one segment at a time. As we progress in the reincarnational cycle, our awareness of other segments grows, until at the very end, we finally see the whole orange. If a therapist has the rare opportunity to witness and facilitate such a past life synthesis at the end of a person's reincarnational cycle, his work becomes more analytical and, at the same time, more comprehensive. In addition to helping the client work through the past life trauma, the therapist has to find and point out the common themes, or "soul bloodlines" as I call them, that run like threads or veins through all this past life material. To know these bloodlines increases the client's understanding of himself in new and previously inconceivable ways. It also helps synthesize all of these lifetimes into a meaningful whole.

The proper integration of past life material is a psychological necessity, in my opinion, because without integration the past lives remain an ego-alien curiosity, which will be quickly forgotten, either because they cannot be related to or because they are too overwhelming. Only if the information is deeply absorbed and responsibly "owned" can it contribute to an individual's emotional and spiritual growth. This can only be done in processing sessions held over a shorter or longer period of time after the actual surfacing of the (often disturbing) material. And yet, no provisions or even suggestions for follow-up treatments have ever been made in any of the past life regressions I have personally experienced: from my week-long intensive at the Light Institute in Gallisteo to my week-long intensive with Joy Hinson-Ryder in Santa Fe to Roger Woolger's weekend workshop or Woolger-style courses at Southwestern College in Santa Fe, not to speak of Chet Snow's group progressions into future lives. Integration seems to be the Achilles heel of most—if not all—those regression (or progression) therapies, whereas in past life dreamwork, integration is a strength rather than a weakness. For here the unconscious directs the process naturally, spontaneously, and at its own leisurely pace. It usually allows enough time to therapeutically work through whatever the dreams have brought into consciousness.

In my past life dreamwork, I use the following methods that have proven to be supportive of the integration process: First of all, I look for the trigger in the client's present life situation that has brought these ancient memories to the surface. The unconscious thinks in analogies, so there is always a similar situation in the present acting as a "reminder" about the past. By linking the past to the present, it becomes possible to learn from past mistakes.

I always conduct and encourage historical background research, because it is very helpful for the integration process. Reading about the ethnic tradition and the sociocultural and socioeconomic context of a particular lifetime stimulates more past life dreams and memories about that lifetime. It also helps us understand the past life within its own historical and cultural context. This is very different from judging it from our present cultural and historical perspective. Thus murders, crimes, and acts of black magic, which we all have committed in previous incarnations, can be more easily accepted and forgiven.

A more personalized way of integrating past lives is to enter into a dialogue with the past life personalities. Just like the autonomous, part-personalities in the unconscious described by Jung, past life personalities have a mind of their own and can be contacted on inner levels. They also carry specialized knowledge and a great variety of life experience, which can be very helpful to us, especially in times of crisis.

Past life integration clearly has a physical aspect, because of the cellular memory that is involved. I recently dreamed that, in order to be integrated, a past life has to pass through "ten layers." I thought this might refer to the seven chakras and the three subtle bodies—the etheric, the emotional, and the mental. In any case, it would mean that the absorption of the material must take place on *all* energetic levels. Many past life therapists are aware of this need for a holistic approach and include some form of energy work in their treatments. If they don't, they should refer their clients to body therapists for complementary energy work.

People often suffer intensely when a traumatic past life resurfaces. It is important for the healing process that this suffering be bravely endured, and not rationalized or medicated away. To reexperience the previously unconscious feelings is the only way to eradicate them from the unconscious. Since the origin of this suffering is not based in the present, the client rarely gets much sympathy from family and friends. This puts a lot of responsibility on the past life therapist to provide the required emotional support. Above all, the client needs to be reassured that, although the integration process may take time, his patience will be rewarded in the end with a greater sense of freedom and wholeness.

I was a storyteller,
But they called me a witch.
I was a poet,
And they stoned and hanged me for it.
In spite of this, I am writing this book
Because it must be written.

PART ONE

Journey into the Otherworld

1

DREAM INITIATION

Listening to a Calling

Therefore an advance always begins with individuation,
that is to say with the individual, conscious of his
isolation, cutting a new path through hitherto
unknown territory.

C. G. JUNG

A DIFFERENT KIND OF DREAM

I am a man. I am standing with my back against a barn door in a medi-
eval European town. I am facing an angry mob that is throwing stones at
me. I am terrified and in pain. In order to buy time and get away from
my tormentors, I say I have to urinate. They let me step inside the barn so
that I can relieve myself in private. I am aware of taking my penis out of
my pants, but after that there is a blank.

Next I am being driven on an ox-cart through town. A red-robed
priest is by my side. I have collapsed on the wagon floor, sobbing uncon-
trollably, while deeply ashamed of my lack of composure. For until the
public mood had changed, I had been a celebrity in this town. "My God,
is it still like this?" I ask the priest, and he replies, "Yes, it is."

Five years of analysis and intensive study of my dreams had familiarized me with my inner figures enough to know that the man in my dream did not fit the Jungian model. No authority could have convinced me that this figure was simply an archetype, the template of the animus, a woman's inner male. He was too personalized for that. While in his body, I was keenly aware of his sensitivity, the complexity of his feelings, and his overwhelming sense of shame, which was rendered all the more poignant because of his social position in town. I was also aware that the time was that of the Inquisition, when red-robed priests accompanied accused persons on their way to the ecclesiastical court. Yet, there was timelessness in my brief exchange with the priest. This was revealed in our dialogue when I had asked him "Is it still like this?" and his answer was, "Yes, it is."

Essentially, not much progress has been made in the exercise of justice since the Middle Ages. People still get executed every day for crimes they did not commit, and social injustice is rampant everywhere. Just prior to this dream, my prospects for Jungian training in London had gone up in smoke for no better reason than the fact that two Jungian training institutions were in conflict with each other. The hopelessness I was experiencing at this time vaguely echoed what I had felt in the dream, but this did not explain the medieval scenario I had been part of. The only plausible explanation I could find was that I must have projected myself, in a stressful moment, into another lifetime.

As soon as I realized this, reincarnation, which as a philosophical concept had never interested me before, became a living reality for me. I never questioned it after that, which does not surprise me any more, after having traced the belief in reincarnation through the majority of my lifetimes. Literally overnight, my still unformed spirituality had found its way back into an ancient, well-worn riverbed.

All this came back to me in a flash two years later when, as a student at the C. G. Jung Institute in Zurich, I decided to attend a public lecture series on dreams and reincarnation. Dr. Elisabeth Ruef, senior training analyst, coeditor of Jung's Collected Works, and a personal friend of the Jung family, was going to speak on this controversial subject. For me this was a secret wish come true because I was still hoping that the mysterious dream experience I had had while living in England might come to roost in Jung's theoretical system.

It was a freezing cold winter. The evening lectures were held in the small auditorium of the old ramshackle institute, which had been declared unsafe at the last building inspection. In spite of this, the room was tightly packed, but more with auditors from the city than with candidates from the Jung Institute. This surprised me. Then only in my second semester, I was not yet in on the fact that the Curatorium, the governing body of the institute, had officially blacklisted reincarnation, along with magic and certain forms of parapsychology. Even Jung himself had not escaped censorship when, toward the end of his life, he had found psychological evidence for the existence of reincarnation. He had even written about it in his autobiography, *Memories, Dreams, Reflections,* but his family and his publisher, concerned for his reputation, had prevailed upon him to take it out. Although this might have been justified in the late 1950s, it was now twenty years later, and certain belief systems and spiritual practices of the Eastern religions had been absorbed by the Western mind.

In 1978 when this lecture series was taking place it had looked at first as if even the conservative Jungian school was opening up. Erlo van Waveren, a former analysand of Jung and a wealthy patron of the Jung Institute, had published an account of his past life experiences in a small volume entitled *Pilgrimage to the Rebirth.*[1] Jung, who in his later years had worked with van Waveren on this past life material, made him promise to keep it confidential. But seventeen years after Jung's death, van Waveren probably felt that he had protected his analyst long enough and that he needed to leave a legacy of his own. I met the tall, elegant, gray-haired author in the secretary's office of the Jung Institute, where I had gone to purchase his book. I asked him to sign my copy, and when I later looked at what he had written I was very puzzled by his remark, "Perhaps we will sing a duet." Only now, thirty years later, do I fully understand what this meant.

It was in the wake of van Waveren's book that Elisabeth Ruef—a strong-willed, scholarly, and deeply caring woman—decided to go public with her own research on past lives and dreams. However, if she had counted on van Waveren's book protecting her, she was mistaken. She later became the target of professional ridicule just the same.

Her interest in the subject had been sparked appropriately by a dream. In this dream, which she had had several years earlier, the American psychic Edgar Cayce, had appeared to her and had drawn her attention to past life dreams. When she began to focus on that, she detected past life material in many of her clients' dreams. Over time, she was able to isolate certain traits that set this type of dream apart from other dreams. Among these traits were realism, historical settings, and old-fashioned clothing. When she quoted some of those dreams, I felt a sense of relief. Suddenly I was no longer alone with my experience. Other people were having similar dreams, but most importantly, someone whose professional judgment I trusted had validated not only my experience but also my understanding of it.

When I left the institute at the end of the first evening's lecture, the streets were sparkling white with freshly fallen snow. Although an icy wind was blowing in my face I only barely noticed it because I was feeling almost euphoric. Some ancient soul memory was stirring in my unconscious and was on the point of breaking through, and during the night, it did.

I am rising up in cosmic space until the crown of my head touches God; then I start to fall. On my descent, I pass through different layers of atmosphere; one of them is turbulent and fraught with danger. But an invisible guide appears at my side and coaches me safely through it. At the end of my journey through outer space, I plunge headlong into the World Ocean.

At first I go all the way under, tasting the salty seawater. When I come to the surface again, I find myself adrift on the ocean waves, feeling small and insignificant, like a piece of cork. But soon enough, pulled by an irresistible force, I dive deep into the water again, only to resurface a little later. As this in-and-out movement continues, my body becomes increasingly lighter, and my immersion into the ocean less deep. In the end, I do not go under anymore, and my aimless drifting stops altogether. Instead, I am dancing and leaping across the surface of the ocean, which has become calm and shiny like a mirror. At the same time, I feel a pull from above, which is drawing me back to where I had come from—back to the Source, back to God.

This was the first in a series of visionary dreams that would reveal the laws of reincarnation to me. They provided me with the metaphysical background for more personalized information I was to receive later.

My dream of the fall into the World Ocean was so powerful that I didn't want to analyze it at first. It was one of those "big dreams" that are better left alone, because they tend to lose transformative power in the interpretation. Yet the contrast with the biblical story of the Fall would have been hard to overlook. While the Bible presents the Fall as a divine punishment for human disobedience and sin, nothing in my dream suggested that an infraction had taken place or that God was displeased with me. On the contrary, I appeared to be following higher orders when I embarked on my downward journey. Throughout the fall, I was divinely protected, and after diving into the World Ocean, my incarnations proceeded in an orderly fashion that seemed to be part of a greater plan. According to my dream, the soul refines itself in a paradoxical interaction with the low vibrations of the material world. The ultimate goal of this sublimation process is a state of "enlightenment" that literally makes our energy body lighter. Once we attain this exalted state, our soul can then be reunited with God.

It never occurred to me, at the time, to look for parallels in the mystical traditions, but I came across them later in the Gnosis, and especially in the Kabbalah, where the teachings about Jacob's ladder follow roughly the same pattern. Jacob's ladder is the Kabbalist's roadmap for the human soul's evolution. Kabbalist teachings also do not rule out the possibility that the Fall might have been part of God's plan.[2] When I first discovered the parallels between these teachings and my dream, I considered them to be merely coincidental. I thought that my unconscious had randomly chosen this image from a pool of possible representations of the archetype of reincarnation, but a recent dream made me think of another possibility.

In this dream, the larger-than-life face of a woman appeared to me, projected against a steep rock surface. The woman's features were homely, but kind. I knew her to be the wife of a Kabbalist, whose aim it was to bring more people into his spiritual community. Still half-asleep, I started communicating with the woman, and I learned that she lived in Toledo, Spain, in the thirteenth century. She gave her name as Hannah Azriel, or Ezrael. I also learned that her family was from Toledo, while her husband had come from Provence in France. Subsequently, I was able to validate most of this information. The city of Toledo is situated on a rocky plateau. In the thirteenth century it was a center of rabbinic studies, and an older Toledanic tradition of the Kabbalah came into being there at that time. Also, a famous Kabbalist named Azriel lived in Spain in the thirteenth century. He is known to have studied in Provence with Isaac the Blind, who was a mystic and visionary.

When Azriel later moved from Provence to Spain, he tried to popularize the esoteric teachings he had received, much to his teacher's regret. This corresponded with Hannah Azriel's desire to make the Kabbalah accessible to more people. After that, it occurred to me that what I had previously thought to be a collective, archetypal dream might really have been a remembered visionary experience of a mystical journey down Jacob's ladder that I had once had in Toledo.

Although at the time of the lectures, I had only been aware of the visionary nature of the dream, I had considered it important enough to send to Dr. Ruef. I was hoping that she would comment on it in her upcoming lecture, and she did. She used the dream to demonstrate to her spellbound audience that the unconscious remembers the whole reincarnational process. This stimulated my past life recall even more, and pretty soon I was supplying most of the dream material for Dr. Ruef's lectures on a weekly basis.

SIDE-EFFECTS OF THE SETH TRANSLATION

By the time the lectures were over, my past life recall had gathered a momentum of its own. My dreams kept finding new catalysts, such as the German translation of Jane Roberts's book *Seth Speaks,* which the Ariston Verlag in Geneva contracted me for. The book had been a bestseller in the United States, because it was without a doubt the most psychologically sophisticated and innovative trance material ever recorded. Thanks to its outstanding quality and depth, it later became a bestseller in the German translation, too.

To remain true to the author's intent, a translator must become the author's medium, in some respects. Since *Seth Speaks* was channeled material, I was becoming something like a medium of the medium by translating it. But what I did not realize until later was that by translating *Seth,* I was getting enmeshed with Jane Roberts's otherworldly realm in other ways as well. Some of my dreams began to include different realities. Most of these concerned life after death, especially in regard to suicide. I was able to observe a woman's inner process as she jumped from the top of a high-rise building. In midair she suddenly wanted to live, but by then it was too late. I understood that this was the reason why, according to folklore, the spirits of those who kill themselves are said to become earthbound. For when the survival instinct returns after the self-destructive act has been completed, it binds the spirit to the material world.

In another dream, I visited a suicide clinic, located in an old-fashioned villa. This clinic must have been on the astral plane, because

I knew that its director—a German doctor—was an old friend of my parents who had shot himself several decades ago. In the dream, I never saw him. But I did meet the psychiatrist who seemed to be exhausted and was lounging on the floor. I knew that in the Spanish Civil War he had been a conscientious objector who had committed suicide to avoid being tortured. Apparently, he was still recovering from the after-effects of this ordeal. There was also a third man, a psychological consultant who, to my surprise, turned out to be Ernest Hemmingway. He was the most active member of the clinic's staff, and the only one I had any dealings with. He showed me the chart of a thirty-eight-year-old client who had to be kept in isolation because he was raving mad. When I looked at this particular patient's case history, I realized that he had lost his mind in the trenches of World War I. In the dream I felt eager to help him, but when I awoke, I was shocked by the persistence of his delusions. Sixty years after his death, he had still not awoken from his nightmare!

In other dreams I was an apprentice to a guide whose task it was to help the deceased with the transition into the spirit world. I will always remember one precious dream where, under his directions, I materialized a gardenia for a young woman who had just died. It happened to be her favorite flower, and we created it to help her adjust to her new environment. While this dream had been uplifting, a later one dragged me down. I dreamed that I had to lend a color of my aura to a dead woman who, without it, could not rise from her grave. While this Good Samaritan act had felt completely natural to me in the dream, it terrified me when I remembered it in the morning. I thought of Marie-Louise von Franz's warning not to get too close to the dead in the dream state. And how much closer than that could I get? I feared this meant that I was going to die. Not knowing where else to turn in my distress, I sent these dreams to Jane Roberts for a psychic evaluation. To my relief, she saw them quite differently. She replied:

To me, your dreams represent your own desire to develop and grow—to expand your psychic, mental, and spiritual horizons. You must have picked up the idea that it was dangerous to do so, though; we think that such development is fully natural and a part of our human heritage that has been ignored or misinterpreted.[3]

After this reassurance, I lost most of my fear of the otherworldly realm. This happened just in time, because the translation of the reincarnation chapters in *Seth Speaks,* which I was about to begin, was going to be even more of a challenge to me. Most of what I found in these chapters I already knew from my dreams, but two statements in the book shook up some old belief systems.

The less threatening one of the two was Seth's reinterpretation of the anima and animus archetypes. Jung had explained these inner figures, which appear to us in dreams, as archetypal representations of our male and female recessive genes. The male component in the woman he called *animus* (Latin for "spirit"), and the female component in man *anima* (Latin for "soul"). I had always found this theory very convincing. But Seth, after suggesting that Jane Roberts familiarize herself with Jung's ideas, offered a different explanation for these inner figures. He explained them as past life selves, and it was the *composite* of them that he defined as being the animus/anima archetypes. Because this was corroborated by my own experience, it only required a minor theoretical adjustment.

The second statement in *Seth Speaks*—Seth's contention that our incarnations are simultaneous and that linear time is an illusion—rubbed me the wrong way. I mistakenly thought that this would eliminate cause and effect and deeply resented the notion that things might not be as I had always thought them to be. When I came across the relevant passages in *Seth Speaks* late one night, I closed the book in frustration and went to bed. This time, I thought, Seth had gone too far.

But falling asleep offered no respite from this uncomfortable idea. On the contrary, I was forced to confront it in two life-changing dream episodes that seemed to be taking place on two different dream levels in succession:

From a very high place, a deep, booming voice informs me that I am in my fourth incarnation. I say, "What nonsense! There were many, many more!"

With this in mind, I awoke. When I dozed off again, the dream continued on a somewhat lower level, which was, however, still uncommonly high:

I am standing in front of a transparent, rectangular container that is divided into four sections. It is filled with water, and innumerable deep-sea creatures in different shapes and colors are swimming around in it—all of them very lively. I know that these are my incarnations and that I am fully responsible for them. And now I understand what the voice had meant by "fourth incarnation." It had referred to these four sections: four reincarnational cycles, each one containing hundreds of simultaneous lives.

I open the flap that keeps the container closed. I want to convince myself that one of the creatures, which looks limp, is not actually dead. I know it is time for me to find a different kind of container for them—a large, round glass bowl, where they can all be together.

At this moment, the question pops into my mind: What can be done for the poor limp creature? The answer comes to me telepathically: it is my task to salvage it.

ACCEPTING THE CHALLENGE

The image of the past life container made it sufficiently clear that our lives are indeed simultaneous. Did this free me from experiencing them in terms of linear time? No, because in the three-dimensional world we live in, which the Buddhists rightly call illusionary, our brains are programmed to interpret a process that seems to unfold rather like the petals of a flower, as something that happens in chronological sequence. Therefore, although I knew better after this dream, I continued and will continue to treat past lives as a historical phenomenon.

Being held responsible for all of my incarnations did not seem to bother me all that much. I felt mainly relieved that my work in this lifetime had been so clearly mapped out. In terms of Jungian psychology, to integrate all my past lives meant taking the magnum opus—the integration of the deep unconscious—still one step further.

The deep-sea creatures looked very familiar to me. I had dreamed of them not very long ago, but then I had tried very hard to get rid of them. When I was dreaming of them a second time I saw, at the outset of the dream, a number of past life selves pass in front of my inner eye. The only one that stayed with me was the tormented man in the ox-cart in medieval Europe. I also recalled having dreamed the following:

I find a bunch of sea creatures backed up in my toilet. All of them are very lively. Before I flush them down, I particularly notice a small black eel and some fish.

Then I am outside my house, bragging to an unknown woman that I have gotten rid of all those pesky sea creatures in my toilet. She replies with a touch of sarcasm in her voice, "You are saying they are all gone. But this thing over there—is that nothing?" She points toward a very large fish that is lying on a bridge, gasping for air. I have to admit that the woman is right. I have flushed them only part way down.

In retrospect, I asked myself why previously it had been so important to me to keep these deep-sea creatures—my past lives—submerged. The answer, I found, was surprising: I was less afraid of the past lives themselves than of my teacher's reaction to them. To share these dreams with my analyst was taking too much of a risk, despite the confidentiality rule that applies—with some exceptions—to a training analysis, too. On the other hand, to deliberately keep these dreams out of the analytical process had felt dishonest to me. To avoid a painful conflict, I had tried to suppress the material altogether. However opportune this might have been, it had not been good for my soul. The image of the stranded fish on the bridge really said it all.

But my latest "golden dream," to use a Mayan term, had resolved this conflict for me on a higher level. In a golden dream, the gods themselves appear to the dreamer and reveal his life's purpose to him. If I had been called by the gods to integrate my past lives, no outer authority had a right to prevent that. But I did realize now the need for discretion. A medieval engraving of two alchemists that I found in Jung's *Psychology and Alchemy* showed this discretion to be essential to the work. In this picture, the *artifex* (alchemist) and his *soror mystica* (female helper) both hold a finger on their lips in a silencing gesture to demonstrate that the success of the magnum opus—the great work—depends on the alchemist's secrecy.[4]

From then on, my past lives had my undivided attention. This happened just in time, because this unconscious material was getting so close to the surface that just about anything could set it off. Sometimes it put so much pressure on me that I had almost fallen apart. On one occasion, a past life even became life threatening to me. This happened when I was reading Mircea Eliade's book *Shamanism*.[5]

This anthropological classic was on my reading list for the Jung Institute, which meant that it was considered safe. However, for me it was not safe at all. Late one night I was reading about the ritual practices of the Inuit shaman when, to my surprise, I became overwhelmed by emotion. My reaction to the material was so powerful that I could not read any further. A few hours later I dreamed that I was an Eskimo shaman. On the following morning, happy to still be alive, I recorded this dream, and what followed, in my dream journal.

Reading the book on shamanism conjured up vivid dream images. After crossing over to the "other side"—the spirit world—in a man's body, I notice that a young woman who does not belong there has followed me. She is in great danger and needs to be carried back into the world of the living. What complicates matters is that the border crossing itself represents an initiation. This means that she will be attacked by spirit beings. In order to save her, I will have to ward off the attack with my own person.

Waking up in the dead of night, I instantly knew who this woman was in her present incarnation: Katja, a young Swiss woman who lived with her husband in the apartment below mine. We had become fast friends, and she often surprised me with her psychic crossovers into my dream world. Sometimes she dreamed for me, and at other times we had parallel dreams in the same night.

Although I was deeply shaken by this dream and unable to go back to sleep, it never crossed my mind that the impending threat from the spirit world could follow me into the waking state. After tossing and turning for a while, I got up and took half a Valium to help me go back to sleep. Once I was back in bed, I discovered that I could not breathe. It felt as if something heavy were sitting on my chest, trying to squeeze the life out of me. In order not to suffocate, I had to practice a shallow, slow yoga breathing for almost an hour. Then, all of a sudden the weight lifted, and I was able to breathe normally again. By then I was so exhausted that I instantly fell asleep. My next dream took me straight back into the Eskimo life, but this time to an exhilarating experience.

I am back in the spirit world. I am walking along the flat, sandy bottom of the ocean. I come to a spooky house that is overshadowed by cypress trees.

Next I find myself in a large, cold, empty room. I am looking into a deep stone basin where a baby seal lies captive. As soon as he sees me, he takes a huge, joyful leap out of his prison. He has a happy smile on his face as he lands next to me on the stone floor, and I bend down to caress him.

According to Eskimo belief, times of starvation that are caused by a shortage of hunting prey are brought on by the sins of the tribe. Human transgressions anger the Mother of the Beasts, who lives on the bottom of the sea, and as a punishment, she keeps the animals locked up in her house. In order to put an end to the famine, the Eskimo shaman must first hear the confessions of his community and then go on a peace mission to the house of the Mother of the Beasts. He does this on a spirit journey that is fraught with many dangers. The freeing of the baby seal in my dream captured the happy moment of such a completed mission.

Still later that night, the shaman's relationship with the young woman of my dream was revealed to me in another dream.

I am poring over the biography of a woman, who had served a shaman all her life. Without thinking, she had followed him to the spirit world, as a faithful dog follows his master, and inadvertently she had put herself, and also the shaman, in mortal danger.

When I awoke the next morning, I found myself still in "dreamtime"—where past, present, and future merge. I could not make out whether the dangerous border crossing had occurred in my Eskimo life, in the here and now, or simultaneously in both time dimensions. I was also not sure if the mysterious asphyxiation I had suffered from was part of the shamanic experience or an allergic reaction to the Valium I had taken. But the dosage had been tiny, and I had never experienced an allergic reaction to Valium before.

Fortunately, a follow-up dream I had a few nights later made everything clear. After talking this incident over with a visiting analyst friend and medical doctor from Brighton, I dreamed the following:

I am in my bed. A ghost who is sitting on top of me makes rubbing motions on my chest with his hands. I wrestle with him for quite some time before I succeed in throwing him off. When the danger is over, I get up from my bed and exclaim, "Nobody tell me that ghosts are harmless. This could have ended in a respiratory paralysis!"

Jung made the observation that although our conscious senses have only a limited range of perception, the unconscious has an additional sense organ that is more sensitive, watchful, and finely tuned. He called this sensitive feeling antenna "subliminal perception." What it takes in during our waking hours, it feeds back to us in the dream state so we can better protect ourselves—provided we will listen. My subliminal perception had given me this feedback, albeit somewhat delayed. While the struggle for air had absorbed all my attention, this subliminal sense organ had registered the invasion of my aural field by a foreign energy body. This confirmed my suspicion that during that night, in a bleed-through from the Eskimo life, I had been astrally attacked by a spirit *as if* I were still the shaman.

THE LOFT ABOVE THE LOFT

My next significant past life experience occurred in the summer of 1980. Around that time I was starting to realize that my marriage with Robert, who had stayed behind in England, had quietly died. We had first met at a sherry party in 1966, given by the university where we were both employed. I was a language instructor in the German Department and Robert was a lecturer in the Geography Department. After becoming good friends, we had married in 1968 and spent nine uneventful years together. Although we were very fond of each other, there was no chemistry between us, and consequently, no intimacy. Since I was thirteen years younger than Robert, I had grown sexually very frustrated over the years. Thus, in 1977 when a "cosmic kick in the butt" transported me to Switzerland for my Jungian training, I had felt liberated from my puritanical prison. But I had not been able to face the fact that this might mean the end of my marriage. I had even managed to overlook a powerful omen that had occurred when Robert had driven me with my luggage to Dover. Without warning, his car clock had died and was incapable of being repaired. Clocks often die when people die. In this case, what had died was our marriage.

After three years of separation from Robert, when I was finally coming out of denial, a past life dream helped me finalize my decision to ask for a divorce. It was the last dream of its kind prior to my work with Jenny, whose past life readings would give my past life integration process a new direction.

Somebody sends me to a loft above the loft, with instructions to pick something up. I know this is a dangerous undertaking, because the loft above the loft is so ancient that it cannot support the weight of a human body. I climb up the steep flight of stairs anyway, but stop cautiously on the landing, waiting for something to happen. When a door is flung wide open to welcome me, I know that this is where my "ancestors" live.

Then a woman appears and places a faded white bridal gown in my arms with the comment, "That's what you always wanted, isn't it?" The tulle garment is held together by a sky-blue ribbon above the waistline. It has quite obviously been worn, because its armpits are stained with sweat from a night of ballroom dancing. I know that this is my bridal gown from my wedding with Robert—not from this life, but from another life. While I stand there with the garment in my arms, feeling at a loss as to what to do next, someone else steps forward from inside the loft. This time it's a man. He is dark haired, handsome, delicately built, and in evening dress.

After bowing gracefully to me as his only audience, he begins to recite a love poem in the strict metric form of a long-past era. All I would remember in the morning was the opening line: "Should love ever grow cold . . ." But in the dream, the poem says it all. It makes me realize that the return of the bridal gown means that my karma with Robert is over. I feel very relieved to know this, but my "ancestors" are even more relieved. They are getting ready to celebrate this occasion in style. Before I start back down the stairs, I watch their festive preparations for a ball. The dance floor is white and oval shaped, with a sky-blue border. For reasons I don't understand, but are most likely meaningful, it replicates the colors of the returned bridal gown.

Apparently my past life history with Robert had not been pretty, otherwise my "ancestors" would not have been celebrating the ending of it. But who were they, anyway? In my dream journal I wrote "ancestors" in quotation marks to indicate that these were no ancestors in the ordinary sense, for even in the dream state I had known that this lineage was not genetic. According to Erlo van Waveren, Jung had used similar terms for these past life figures in his confidential conversations with him. He had called them "psychic ancestors," "ancestral components," or "ancestral souls."[6]

More than twenty years later, while I was working on this book, a dream explained the difference between biological and soul ancestors to me. I woke up one morning with a verbatim definition in mind. Neither the style nor the wording of it felt familiar. It was almost as if someone had dictated it to me.

There are two different types of ancestors. One is of the soul bloodline and the other of the genetic bloodline. The latter determines mainly the physicality of a person, while the former determines the nature of his soul.

Cayce, as I subsequently found out, had come to the same conclusion. Even recent research on the human genome might support this hypothesis in a backhanded way. Biologists were surprised to discover that we have only one-third of the genes they had expected. Only half the human genome consists of genetic material, and this is immersed in an unknown matrix. One researcher, when asked about the composition of this unknown matrix of the genome in a PBS interview, disparagingly called it "stuff" and "selfish DNA." Later in the interview he even referred to "them" as "freeloading parasites" that "don't care about us," as if "they" were pesky bloodsuckers that did not deserve to live. To me, it seemed very likely that what genetic research found swimming in the unknown matrix of the genome were the selfsame creatures I had observed in the see-through container in my dream, knowing that these were past life selves. And contrary to the scientist's premature judgment, I have found them to be important components of our psychological constitution. Most of the time they are a resource for us, while at other times they are in need of our help.

The graceful, formally dressed man of my dream had pointed out the all-importance of love to me, while I was trying to make a decision. Although in the dream I had not been able to tell if he was a poet or only an actor, I had known him to be the official "representative" of my ancestors. Later, in the waking state, this designation seemed a little far-fetched to me, for who had ever heard of past life representatives? As it turned out, Cayce had. He was, in fact, quite familiar with them. He defined the past life representative as a person's most evolved incarnation, and he often recommended that his clients call on this inner figure for personal guidance.

The "loft above the loft" is the seat of my soul ancestors of this dream. Lofts are storage places for things we may not need at the moment but wish to preserve for possible future use. As such, the loft is a perfect symbol for the memory pool. If everyday memories are stored in the loft, then the loft *above* the loft must be the storage place for memories of a different kind.

My dream described an elevated, ancient, nonmaterial structure. Upon awakening, I imagined it in a "lofty" position, above the head in the outer layers of the aura. I later discovered that, according to ancient yogic teachings, an eighth chakra, or energy center, is located exactly in that location—a few inches above the head. Unlike the seven chakras of the body, the eighth chakra is nonphysical. Its purpose is to coordinate the physical chakras and to establish a connection between the mind and higher consciousness. Because it functions like a master computer that allows different energy frequencies to link up with one another, it appears uniquely equipped to replicate the memories of the brain at the termination of each life and preserve them for later synthesis.

Even more specific in this regard are the teachings of the old Inca shamans, which I came across only recently in Dr. Alberto Villoldo's bestselling book *Shaman, Healer, Sage.*[7] In the Inca tradition the eighth chakra is called *wiracocha,* meaning "sacred source." According to these teachings, this is the place where the "ancestors" live. The wiracocha hovers over our heads like a spinning sun until, at the moment of death, it expands into a luminous globe and moves down the spinal cord to extract information from the seven chakras. This information is then stored and purified in the wiracocha to be reused and recombined in future incarnations.

Thus the eighth chakra might well be a smaller, individualized version of the legendary Akashic Records that, nonphysical in nature and permanently preserved on an unearthly plane, are said to contain the history of every soul since the beginning of time.

2

PAST LIVES FROM
A PAST LIFE READING
Women on the Fringe

As long as a woman is content with being femme à
homme *she has no feminine individuality.*

C. G. JUNG

A TIMELY ENCOUNTER

The German Romantics praised the poetic quality of the unconscious almost a century before Sigmund Freud started to use dreams
as a psychological healing tool. The poetic genius of the unconscious
is not only reflected in the symbolic architecture of our dreams but
also in those meaningful coincidences—where dream and reality flow
together—that Jung termed "synchronicity."

My encounter with Jenny was just such a synchronicity. The perfect timing of our meeting, and the way her multidimensional perspective complemented my psychological one, was clearly the work of the
poetic unconscious. Because of the new insights she gave me, I was able
to take my inner work to a whole new level. Although Jenny has since

passed over into another dimension, in this retelling of the work we did together I am able to honor her invaluable contribution to my individuation process.

Jenny was a seer with a profound depth of psychological and spiritual understanding. She had the unique ability to accurately perceive and paint people's auras,* but even more unusual was that she could read the Akashic Records. This explained her international clientele and why she did not have to advertise. Unlike most psychics, she could pick and choose. If she did not like someone's voice on the telephone, she would just say she had no time.

Jenny had been recommended to me by a woman friend who was in a different training program. This woman was desperately in love with her therapist and was searching for an explanation for her obsession with this man. Jenny described the past life that was feeding this intractable love transference. Although this information did not put an end to my friend's obsession altogether, it did increase her understanding of it.

My reasons for seeing Jenny were more ambitious; I was looking for someone to help me integrate my past lives. The chances of finding such a person were against me, of course. I knew that many so-called past life readers tell stories that come straight from their own unconscious and have little to do with the past lives of their clients. Cayce is supposed to have said that of all the past life readers in the United States only a handful were able to give their clients authentic information. But the phonies are never found out, because most people have no way of telling the difference. Consequently, many people end up owning stories that do not belong to them. I was protected from this danger by my knowledge of dreams. I knew if my dreams did not respond to the reading, I had better ignore the reading myself.

Jenny lived in a sunny, one-bedroom apartment at the foot of the Zurichberg, one of the most beautiful and expensive residential areas

---

*Jenny's painting of my aura was later replicated exactly by an aural photograph.

in Zurich. But it was not Jenny who met me at the door. It was her watchdog, Goldie, an ill-tempered cocker spaniel bitch that owed her overweight condition to daily raids of the cat's food. Goldie was Jenny's shadow, I subsequently discovered. The dog vented angry feelings that Jenny would have been too kind to express. After a year of knowing Jenny, she and I became close friends. We attended a New Year's Eve party together, where Goldie took a bite out of our hostess's jeans for no better reason than the fact that Jenny intensely disliked the woman.

Jenny was probably in her sixties, although it was hard to tell because she looked ageless. Red hair framed a soft-featured, made-up face with penetrating, widely set, bright blue eyes. She only wore loose-fitting, ivory-colored garments, and on the rare occasions when, despite her Parkinson's tremors, she still went out, she would place a beret of the same ivory color on her red hair. Her youthful spirit and her mischievous, silvery laughter were simply irresistible.

At our first meeting, she bypassed the German and German-Swiss convention of addressing strangers with the pronoun *Sie,* and called me *Du,* like an old friend. She also called me *Liebes*—a term of affection. This was Jenny's casual style, and perhaps a leftover from the ten years she had spent with her former writer-husband in Washington, D.C.

Her small apartment was overloaded with East Indian art objects. Several large Buddha statues sat in meditative positions on the floor, while the walls were decorated with Tibetan thangkas. The remaining wall space was taken up by Jenny's spiritual library. This turned her small, modern one-bedroom apartment into an oriental shrine, and the mess one could see piled up in her kitchen through a half-open door did not detract from it one iota. Whatever Jenny was, she was not a provincial housewife—or a *buenzli,* as they call them in Switzerland.

Having greeted me at the door, she showed me into her living room. She offered me a seat on her sofa and placed a large thermos full of coffee and a mug in front of me. Then she disappeared into her bedroom to meditate, while I was drowning my anxieties in the coffee. Later, when she started confiding in me, I learned that this was an anxious moment for her as well. She never knew if she could read someone until she meditated on it, with the person being present next door. If it turned out that she could not make a connection, she would return the money that had to be paid up front and send that person home. Instead of thanking her for her honesty, some of her "failures" bore her a grudge for years after, but Jenny refused to make up stories just to keep her clients satisfied.

HEALERS AND PROSTITUTES

When I had downed my first cup of coffee, Jenny reemerged from her bedroom, seated herself across from me on a chair, and began to speak. The reading moved at a fast pace, which made it difficult for me to take notes; Jenny did not allow tape recorders. Ten lifetimes* passed in front of me in this first session: female and male, obscure and prominent. For the significant lives, which were almost exclusively male, she gave me names and dates.

My female lives were mostly nameless, and Jenny only vaguely alluded to the centuries and countries wherein they had occurred. This may have been due to a lack of education and ego identity of these women, most of whom had eked out a living on the fringes of society. Despite the vagueness of Jenny's description of my female past lives, I was later able to discern certain patterns in them. I called these "bloodlines of the soul," to indicate that certain personal characteristics and life themes are handed down from incarnation to incarnation, in a manner analogous to our genetic inheritance. Tibetans such as Lama Gehlek Nawang Rimpoche have observed the same individual patterns in the reincarnational cycle.[1]

It appeared from the reading that I had been of importance as a woman only once. That was during the golden age of Atlantis, when I

---

*The lifetime overview in this and the following chapter includes the material from Jenny's second reading two years later. She recounted a total of twenty lives.

had been an initiated and highly respected physician who had worked in a sacred manner for the benefit of humanity. According to Edgar Cayce, Atlantean physicians practiced holistic medicine.[2] They practiced surgery, along with psychology and many other treatment modalities like color, sound, crystals, and herbs, all of which are experiencing a comeback today. Atlantean physicians also placed great emphasis on the purification of body and soul. This holistic approach to healing has followed me around through many lifetimes into the present. It started a bloodline associated with herbal medicine and shamanism, one that would weave in and out of my male and female incarnations.

Another important soul bloodline of mine was prostitution. Four times in the course of my soul history I have explored sexuality in women's "oldest profession," covering a wide spectrum—from the religious to the profane—without ever ending up in the gutter, however. In Heliopolis during the Fifth Dynasty I was a sacred prostitute and temple dancer in the Temple of Ra, only practicing the *hieros gamos* (sacred union) with priests of royal blood. In ancient Greece, I was a beautiful, vain, and heartless hetaera, living in great luxury in halls of marble. In none of these lifetimes did I seem to have suffered from hardship or abuse, but in the sixteenth century my prostitution bloodline unexpectedly bottomed out. According to Jenny, that life has had such an impact on me that she had seen it in my aura when I came in the door. I even looked like that woman, which is unusual, since, according to my dream, we do not inherit physical attributes from our soul ancestors. "You were just a little more petite then," Jenny said, before she told me the gruesome story.

When I was in my prime, I had exclusively serviced the British aristocracy. My husband, Robert, had then been my pimp. I was not all that surprised to hear this, and neither was he when I told him about it. It might even have partly explained why he did not feel physically attracted to me in our present life. However, this lack of attraction seems to have been an ongoing problem between us. In an eighteenth-century life in France, when Robert and I were stuck in a prearranged, aristocratic marriage, I was so deprived of love that I drowned myself in a river. This finally put my previous dream about the loft above the loft into context: the gown that was returned to me in a ceremonial fashion was the gown I had worn at my French wedding with Robert. It also explained why my ancestors had a ball when my karma with Robert was finally resolved: we had continuously been together for the wrong reasons. Therefore, the warning in the past life representative's poem, "Should love ever grow cold . . ."

In whichever way Robert might have been responsible for my suicide in France, in our earlier life in England he had not been guilty of anything in particular. He had exploited me financially, but that is what pimps do. He had been powerless to protect me, but that was not his fault. The culprit in that life had been a member of the British aristocracy, whom Jenny described as handsome but cynical. He had been a regular client of mine who had taken a personal interest in me. I had been infatuated with him, which had blinded me to his character flaws. Therefore, when he had offered to invest my savings, I had naively handed them over to him. But instead of investing them, he had spent them on himself. For many months he had managed to string me along. When I finally demanded my money back, he turned the tables on me by reporting me to the authorities for allegedly stealing from him. In old England, the penalty for stealing was hanging, but he could not have taken a prostitute to court without exposing himself socially, so he had used his connections to the Lord Chancellor to have me put away in the Tower of London. Jenny said that I had gone insane after a few years of incarceration, but she refused to tell me how I died.

However, as she was saying this, my eyes fell on a half-eaten gingerbread man that was lying around on her dining-room table (it was the Advent season). Then I knew in a flash how I had died: I had been eaten alive by rats. Subsequently, I realized that the half-dead sea creature I had seen in the past life container was none other than this poor sixteenth-century prostitute. I also finally understood why I had panicked during a sightseeing tour of the tower in 1955. As a student of

English, I had been making the rounds of all the museums and cultural attractions in London. By the time I reached the tower, I was down to my last few English pounds. To buy an admission ticket was a financial sacrifice under these circumstances, but I thought I owed it to my education to visit the tower.

Having joined one of the tour groups, with a sinking feeling, I followed the guide down the steep, winding stairs. When he stopped at the level of the crown jewels to show them to the group, my eyes wandered down to where the staircase loses itself in foreboding darkness. Then I panicked. I turned on my heels and raced up the stairs as if my life depended on it. When I reached the open air, I threw my wasted admission ticket into a garbage bin, wondering what had come over me.

My bloodline of prostitution has not manifested itself as sexual promiscuity in my present life, but I do have a history of pleasing men. My Zurich analyst once observed that I have a tendency to flatter my lovers, while years before him, a professor at Heidelberg University had pointed out to me that I was prone to becoming a victim of men. Although I trusted the accuracy of these perceptive men's observations, I never fully understood this weakness in myself until I learned about my past life history in prostitution.

VICTIMS

Victimization is certainly one of my bloodlines, but not all of the victims were women. The man who was stoned by the mob in medieval Europe was also an innocent victim, as Jenny's reading and later my own biographical research ascertained. On the feminine side, I know of four such cases where I played the victim. One of them was a traditional teller of fairy tales in Ireland. Her life story was almost as difficult for me to digest as that of the London prostitute. Whenever I think of my past lives, I tend to "forget" this one, leave it out, flush it down the toilet— like the sea creatures in my dream. As soon as I start to remember it, I cringe. In Ireland I was a married woman without children. Jenny said that in the olden days, childlessness in a marriage was automatically blamed on the wife, even if it was the husband's problem.

But I loved children, and since I was a traditional fairy tale teller, the village children flocked around me. After a while, the mothers became jealous of the attention I was getting and accused me of being a witch. They prevented their children from visiting me, and eventually I was shunned by the whole village. Even my husband joined the witch hunt and abandoned me in the end. Totally isolated, scorned, and persecuted, I took my own life by drowning myself in a lake.

After what had happened in Ireland, it is surprising that I still love fairy tales. Whenever I was sick in bed as a child, I read every fairy tale I could get hold of—fairy tales from all over the world. Yet I could never memorize them like other children do, because of my unconscious associations. A freak incident that happened at the International Light and Sound Conference in Chicago in 2000 brought the Irish tragedy back to me in an instant. I was standing behind the lectern, ready to deliver a paper on dreams and strobic light therapy, when the overtired program coordinator became confused and introduced me as "a great storyteller." I was so stunned that I could not even correct her blunder, and I proceeded with my lecture as if nothing had happened. However, I have been wondering since then if this woman had been part of the Irish witch hunt.

Another such life was that of a young girl who, in the eighth century, had been raped by marauding Vikings and abducted from the English coast. According to Jenny, I had surrendered because I had no other choice. She said that those were sexually uninhibited times, and that I had eventually enjoyed the sex and the seafaring life. She described me as honest, bright, and intelligent and said that I was well liked by the Vikings but that my luck had run out when I had become pregnant. According to Jenny, the captain would not tolerate a mother and baby on board. Therefore, his crew had dumped us off along the coast in northern France.

Jenny vividly described my shame and despair as I had wandered the French countryside with my infant daughter, unable to make myself understood. Finally, a farmer had taken pity on me and had hired me as a maid. However, since I did not speak any French, I had not been able to negotiate the terms of my employment and had been badly exploited by him. This had made me resentful and bitter, but I had put up with the exploitation for the sake of my child. My child seems to have been very unusual. According to Jenny, she had been clairvoyant and had communicated with fairies, dwarfs, and other nature spirits. She also had a special rapport with animals, which I seem to have shared with her to some extent.

Although the farmer's wife had been jealous of me—probably not without reason—I had been allowed to stay on because I had been such a good worker. Jenny ended her account by saying that although this had been a very difficult life, it had been a good opportunity for me "to work off a lot of bad karma."

The karma on the Vikings' side must have been due to be cleared, too, because the two men who abducted me came back into my life. I met them at different times, on different continents, and under very different circumstances. Both of these men—one a Swede, the other an American—remembered the Viking abduction independently from each other and without any prompting on my part. In a sports hotel in the mountains of Canton Schwyz, Switzerland, where I gave a dream work-shop every summer, I met a Swedish millionaire named Alec. He was a tall, handsome, charismatic man who had become generous to a fault after surviving a near-death experience. I felt drawn to him, and he to me, but our relationship remained mostly platonic during the two years we knew each other. When I last saw him, he had just undergone a past life regression with a famous professor of hypnotherapy in Frankfurt. Under hypnosis, he had remembered the Viking life and also an Assiniboin life in Canada (which will be explored in the following chapter).

Alec's recollections of the Viking life gave a new, interesting twist to Jenny's story. As Alec remembered it, he had been the captain of the Viking ship that had abducted me. At sea, a rivalry had broken out between him and his first mate. Apparently, both men had been my lovers. Therefore, when I had become pregnant, nobody had been able to tell whose child I carried. To avoid a delivery at sea, they had taken me to their village in Scandinavia. The men had hoped that the baby and I could be integrated into their families, but their wives had not liked the idea, and I had not been able to adjust to their more primitive lifestyle. Thus, after I had given birth to a little girl, the women had demanded that the men take us back. Only then, Alec insisted, had we been dumped on the coast of France.

When Alec relayed all of this to me, I had been on the point of leaving for the United States and was quite certain that our karma had been cleared. Unknowingly, Alec had been making amends for his former actions by showing me much generosity and kindness throughout our relationship. However, when the first mate from the Viking ship came to me for past life therapy five years later, it was quite another story (see chapter 8).

PERFORMING ARTISTS

I had an equally strong bloodline in the performing arts, but only in my lives as a woman. In former centuries, performing artists were part of the social fringe, although society needed them, like the prostitutes, for entertainment. For me, this performing arts bloodline was primarily focused on dance. I explored dance as an art form—from the sacred to the profane—in several of my incarnations. As mentioned earlier, I danced as a sacred prostitute in the Temple of Ra in Heliopolis, with a golden scarab dangling from a necklace around my neck. In another lifetime I was a child temple dancer in Bali with silver bells on my anklets. In Japan, I was a geisha named Shoko-san (butterfly) whose artistic entertainment, of course, also included dance.

In a more recent incarnation I took dance to a higher professional level as a ballerina in the czarist ballet in St. Petersburg. That ballerina life, in which I died young of tuberculosis, left a residue in my present life. As an infant, I reacted to music by bobbing up and down in my crib. As a five-year-old, I danced ballerina-style on my toes, without ever having seen a ballet. My parents, who watched my Sunday performances with some amusement, never thought to offer me ballet lessons, so this past life talent fell by the wayside. However, ten years ago I got in touch with the Russian ballerina during a workshop. All of the participants in the workshop were given the task of massaging each other's feet. As soon as the woman I was partnering with dug her fingers into my big toe, the ballerina's face popped up as if on a television screen. I saw her oval face, her lovely, dark, almond-shaped eyes, and the chestnut-colored tendrils that had escaped from her chignon. Although nobody talked about cellular memory ten years ago, I thought it must exist, for how else could the image of the ballerina's face have been preserved in my big toe?

Jenny went into great detail in her description of my life as an actress in the King's Company in London during the reign of Charles II (1630–1685). I had been the best friend of Nell Gwynn, a coactress in this company who later became a national icon as Charles II's mistress and the mother of two of his bastard sons. Nell—or Eleanor, as Jenny consistently called her—and I had grown up in Soho, the London slums. We had both been illiterates, and Nell, despite her special role in the king's life, had always remained close to her common roots. For this reason she had been the only one of Charles II's many mistresses who was loved by the English people. Historians praise her for her "frank recklessness, generosity, invariably good temper, ready wit, infectious high spirits, and amazing indiscretion" and call her "the living antithesis of Puritanism."[3]

After becoming the king's concubine, Nell had been admitted to the inner circle of the court and had spent the rest of her life entertaining the king and his friends while scheming against her rivals. I seem to have been included in her new life, because, according to Jenny, we had both been at the king's bedside when he died, and both of us had remained loyal to him even after his death. I found it very revealing that I only featured in Jenny's story as Nell Gwynn's best friend. It seemed as if I had had no life of my own. The only personal comment that Jenny made was that I had been prettier than Nell. This conspicuous lack of identity only began to make sense when, despite my newly gained insights into the simultaneous nature of our lives, I listed my incarnations in chronological order. For after all, we operate in linear time, and at least within that paradigm there seems to exist an affinity, an interactive relationship between adjoining lifetimes.

In this case, this interconnectedness was particularly striking, for the actress's life had directly followed that of the prostitute. And under the deeply traumatizing and debilitating conditions of the prostitute's death, it seemed very likely that she had suffered a soul loss, which had caused her to be reborn without a sense of self in her next incarnation. As an actress, she could have easily covered this up. It might even have been a professional advantage, because it must have made it all the more easy for her to impersonate others.

Although Jenny had never met Ingmar, my lover in Zurich, in person, she suspected that he was a reincarnation of Charles II. If she was right, we might have been reviving old feelings that had to be shelved in the seventh century out of loyalty to Nell. Of all the men in my life, only Ingmar "knew" me, in the biblical sense of the word, but he also broke my heart. Not unlike Charles II, Ingmar lived in an open marriage and would not commit to any woman, including his own wife. Apparently, Ingmar still privately upheld the Habeas Corpus Act, the "writ of freedom" that Charles II had helped sign into law.

Ingmar was a scholar of international repute, with an exceptionally wide spectrum of professional interests. Shortly after Jenny told me about his connection with Charles II, Ingmar was invited to the United States as a visiting professor. He broke the news to me when we were at a conference together. That evening, he got so drunk that he briefly passed out on his bed. While he was in an unconscious state, I heard him murmur, "I don't want to get on that throne. That throne is too big for me."

A moment later, when he was conscious again, I asked him, "Do you know what you just said?" He had no idea. I repeated his words verbatim and offered to reveal his past life identity to him, but he did not want to know. Although he believed in reincarnation, he always shied away from the topic. Yet he acted as if he did indeed know his former identity when, a few months later, he gave me an engraving of a Scottish castle and said with a chuckle (for he never had any money), "I give you a castle."

SECTARIANS

The unconventional lifestyle of my female incarnations had a spiritual correlate. The religious sects I had belonged to in some of my lives were always at odds with mainstream religions that existed in the respective culture of the time. Several times throughout the course of history I had been considered a heretic and had suffered persecution. In all those cases there were overlaps with my victim bloodline. In Palestine, before Christ's time, I had—as a married woman—been part of a predominantly male Essene group that lived on the West Bank of the Dead Sea and believed in reincarnation. In ancient Rome, I had been an early Christian, who had lived and died in the catacombs. I might have believed in reincarnation then, too, for many of the early Christian church fathers, notably Origen, had held this belief.

In southern France in the twelfth century I had belonged to the Albigenses, also known as the Cathars. Jenny called the Cathars the spiritual successors of the Essenes because of the similarity of their beliefs. I suspect that I might not have been the only Essene who had come back as a Cathar. The Essenes might, in fact, have reincarnated in southern France as a soul group. The Cathars were mystical pacifists. While ordinary "believers in the true faith" were allowed to lead a normal life, their priests, who were called *les parfaits* (the perfect ones) for good reason, had to live up to almost impossibly high moral standards. They had to practice celibacy and were strict vegetarians. In order to be ordained they had to be initiated from the darkness into the light (in this order).

They traveled the countryside, providing spiritual guidance and healing to their community; they also administered last rites to believers on their deathbeds. Both sexes could be ordained, which showed that the Cathars were way ahead of their time. This alone would have been enough to get them into trouble with the Catholic church. However, they deviated from the church dogma in even more important ways. What must have been particularly threatening to Rome was that they did not accept hierarchical structures of any kind. They honored Christ as a prophet but not as the only Son of God. They believed in reincarnation and were convinced that Satan created the world. This pessimistic worldview became a living reality when Pope Innocent II (clearly a misnomer) created the fires of hell for these innocent people by burning them all at the stake.

According to Jenny, that's how I died. Yet there is no doubt in my mind that the burning of the Cathars had been less traumatic than the burning of the Jews during the Spanish Inquisition in the fifteenth century, or the burning of witches in the seventeenth.

Roger Woolger, who, like another expert on reincarnation Arthur Guirdham, had been a Cathar in a past life, believes that the *parfaits* taught a fire meditation that helped them leave their bodies as soon as the stakes were lit.[4,5] I find this hypothesis very convincing, not only because of the peace I felt on my visit to Cathar country in 1982, but also because of a dreamlike vision I had in a small hotel in the village of Yssat-les-Bains, near Foix. As I was falling asleep, after a long, tiring drive through the Pyrenees, I watched a group of Cathars walk in line to the stake, and they were singing. I still remembered the tune when I briefly awoke after this vision, but in the morning it was gone. Elisabeth Ruef later confirmed the singing of the Cathars on their way to the stake. Apparently, there is no terror that cannot be overcome and transcended by a loving spiritual community.

WANDERERS

Even though I had been martyred as a Cathar, and probably as an early Christian as well, martyrdom had not been my only response to persecution. In later centuries, a wanderer bloodline had emerged to compensate for my dangerous tendency to be an outsider. It had manifested itself in both my male and female incarnations. Previous victimizations might have taught me to value life more than possessions, home, community, and country and honed my instincts to recognize the last moment before disaster struck. To utilize this intuitive knowing in the service of self-preservation, one has to face reality and abstain from denial and wishful thinking. Denial is a powerful psychological defense, designed to help us survive difficult life situations, but more often than not it will get us killed.

It was after the Cathar burning, toward the end of the thirteenth century, when this new pattern first emerged in one of my female lives. My husband and I had been living under the tyrannical reign of a Visconti di Pisa on the island of Corsica. We had joined a group of rebels that had made their escape by boat and had taken refuge on the island of Sardinia. When my husband had died shortly after that, I had taken the veil in the church of St. Nicolas. About my life in the convent, I once had the following nightmare:

I am walking briskly through a plague-stricken medieval town. Left and right, people are collapsing, exposing horrible, stinking boils as they fall. I am returning from an errand in town, and I am on my way back to the convent, but when I reach a vaulted passageway, which is like a short, roughly constructed tunnel, the sick begin to throw themselves at me. They cling to my habit and beg me for a healing. In sheer terror, I try to shake them off.

When I finally manage to free myself, I know it is too late; I have already been infected with the plague. Thus, when I reach the convent, I do not speak to anyone. I grab a jug of water and a loaf of bread from the kitchen and sneak up the stairs to the attic, where I will remain for the rest of my illness. In the dream, I know the final outcome of this retreat: Christ will appear to me, and I will be miraculously healed.

In another female life, I was a wanderer by definition—a gypsy. This was my last incarnation, according to Jenny, which means that it still has a hold over me. In addition to the wanderer bloodline, three other bloodlines converged in this complex personality: the social outcast, the heretic, and the healer.

The gypsies, who as a nomadic ethnic group originated in northern India, have traditionally been regarded by the *gadjos*—the nongypsies—with fear and suspicion. On their journeys through Europe, gypsies have not been allowed to camp inside townships and typically were banished to dump sites and stone quarries. Although the gadjos consider them dirty, thieving, and heathen, they are nonetheless fascinated by the mystery that surrounds them. Gypsies do not feel bound by the laws of the gadjos, but this does not mean they are lawless. They merely have a different ethical code, which in some respects is stricter than ours. As nomads, they do not believe in worldly possessions, and as people who live close to the earth, they practice a nature religion that includes witchcraft and magic. Their healers and sorcerers have traditionally been powerful initiates who have known as much about medicinal plants, healing magnetism, and tantric lovemaking as they do about the mysteries of the soul. My ancient bloodline of holistic healing, which has surfaced time and again since Atlantis, found a fertile ground in this culture.

Before Jenny's readings, I had often wondered about my relationship with the gypsies as I had had many gypsy dreams that I could not explain. There had also been some memorable encounters with gypsies in Heidelberg and London. I seem to have a magnetic attraction for these people. Whenever a gypsy crosses my path, she will ignore everyone else and focus only on me. An unforgettable incident that happened in London years ago is a good example of this. I was sitting with a friend in an outside ice cream parlor on Baker Street when two gypsy women walked by. The moment they saw me, they made a beeline toward me. One of the women grabbed my hand, took a quick look at my palm, and said, "You don't have much luck with men, because you are too honest. And financially, you would be better off if you earned your money day-by-day [like a gypsy], instead of relying on a fixed income from an institution." Then they went on their way, without having asked me for money. What the gypsy said was only too true. I knew I had no luck with men, but I had never attributed this to being too honest. And regarding my financial situation, I was working at the time as a *Lektorin* in the German Department at Reading University and was earning about as much as a ticket collector on a bus. When I moved to Zurich a few years later to study at the Jung Institute, I was forced to live the way they suggested and had a much more enjoyable time.

Even more remarkable than the palm reading itself was the fact that the woman had not asked me for money. Gypsies always ask you to "cross your palm with money" before telling your fortune. According to the late gypsy expert Pierre Derlon, gypsies despise the gadjos—the non-gypsies—just as much as the other way around. To show their disrespect, they deliberately lie to them when they are telling their fortune. This has never happened to me. Gypsies have always told me the honest truth, just like this woman in Baker Street. Knowingly or instinctively, they have treated me like one of their own.

Although my gypsy life was important, I learned about it only piecemeal and rather late in the day. Jenny never mentioned it in her first reading, perhaps because it contained too much shadow material. Yet almost everyone else I knew who had gone to her for a reading brought back the same blood-curdling story—they had all belonged to a band of gypsies that had been stoned to death in Germany. In each case, Jenny had added as an aside, "You knew Sabine in that life." I had, therefore, taken for granted that I had been stoned to death in Germany with the rest of my friends.

Shelly, an American woman and a close friend of mine, received the most detailed information about that gypsy life from Jenny. On the eve before Shelly's reading, we were sitting in my tiny kitchen, chatting over a glass of merlot. Naturally, we were wondering if we had known each other before. But before Jenny had a chance to answer this question for us, my dreams responded to it. That night I dreamed:

A woman who does not look like Shelly, but who is Shelly, and I are in a classroom together. Her name is Elage Laclaig. The teacher calls on her, but Elage does not know the answer. After a while, the teacher calls on her again, but she still does not know the answer. It is becoming increasingly clear: Elage Laclaig is not learning her lessons.

Next, I am sitting with her before a large, hand-woven carpet. The image of a huge, towering tree is set against a sand-colored background. We both agree that the drab background needs more color, so Elage Laclaig takes a crayon and begins to cover the sandy background with green. At first I like the green, but then it starts to worry me. I say to Elage, "In the next wash, the green will bleed and the whole tree will be wiped out." But Elage, who never listens to anyone, continues to fill in the background with green.

Suddenly wide awake, I jumped out of bed to jot down the strange-sounding name. In the morning, when I woke up, I felt quite certain that Shelly had been a friend or relative who had consistently failed to learn from experience, but I did not know what the tree signified in this context. Could this have been a family tree that had been spoiled through her carelessness? I wondered. Two days later, after her reading with Jenny, Shelly returned with the following information: she and I had been sisters in the gypsy life. Our band had been stranded for some time in Saintes-Maries-de-la-Mer in southern France (this must have been during World War I) when some members had grown restless and had wanted to move on. The greener pastures they had in mind were in Germany, but Germany was not safe for us. As a nation obsessed with orderliness, the Germans had been hostile to the freewheeling gypsies long before they exterminated thousands of them in their concentration camps. France was a much better place for the gypsies, because the French aristocracy had traditionally protected them. Saintes-Maries-de-la-Mer, in particular, was a special refuge, because in this small fishing village the Marquis Baroncelli had been safeguarding the gypsies' annual spring gatherings in honor of their saint, the black Sara la Kali, for many generations.

In metaphorical language, my dream described a conflict between my sister and myself at a crucial moment in the band's history: as a woman who did not learn from mistakes, she had wanted to move on to greener pastures in Germany, while I had insisted on remaining in the relative safety of the sandy beaches of Saintes-Maries-de-la-Mer so that our family tree could be protected. I probably had a warning dream during the initial decision-making process. In fact, my present dream might even have been a replica of that former dream.

In any event, my warnings to my sister fell on deaf ears, and the band traveled to Germany.

According to Jenny, their arrival in an alpine village in Bavaria had coincided with a local farmer's wedding. Our men, who were accomplished musicians, had been hired to play at a dance. When the farmers had gotten drunk, they had picked a fight with our men and everyone in the band had been stoned to death. The family tree had been wiped out, just as I had foreseen it would be.

I had assumed that I had also died in this carnage, so I was taken by surprise when Jenny informed me in my second reading that I had remained in Saintes-Maries-de-la-Mer. It must have been very unusual for a gypsy woman to part with her band, but Jenny did not go into that. Neither did she disclose any details about my personal life. Instead, she focused entirely on the band's history and traditions. She said our home base had been Turkey (thus, Elage Laclaig was probably a Turkish name). From there, we had fanned out to Greece, Yugoslavia, Italy, Spain, and southern France, but we had always returned to our home base in the end. She elaborated on our pilgrimages to Saintes-Maries-de-la-Mer and to the Cathedral of Chartres, which harbors secrets that are known only to the gypsies.

Although I had lost most of my relatives in that incarnation, Jenny called this a happy life. While this might have been true for the beginning, it could not have been true for the ending of it. Even during the reading, I was aware of some inconsistencies and gaps in Jenny's account. While she managed to protect me from the shadow side of that life, it all came out several years later—mostly during a past life regression session at the Light Institute in Galisteo, New Mexico. Here is the rest of the gypsy story, as I recorded it after that session:

I am an initiated tribal healer with a great deal of herbal knowledge. Besides many other magical things, I know the recipe for a salve that can confer healing powers to a person. I also know how to make a love potion that will throw a man into sexual bondage. In addition, I have reliable clairvoyance. That's why I can be so sure of what to expect in Germany. To part with my band is a very risky thing, because the gypsies' safety lies in their numbers. Only my next of kin—my daughter, my son-in-law, and my two grandchildren—agree to stay behind with me in Saintes-Maries-de-la-Mer.

A few months after the parting, traveling gypsies bring us the news of the stoning that had occurred in Germany. We grieve so deeply for so long that my daughter's husband abandons us and goes in search of a brighter future. Without a male protector, we find ourselves in an even more vulnerable position. We also have to work harder to feed the family. Since I do not approve of stealing, we have to make an honest living. Thus, my daughter dances flamenco, while I tell the tourists' fortunes. (This is how gypsies in Saintes-Maries-de-la-Mer make a living even today.)

During one of my daughter's dance performances she catches the eye of the Marquis. Although he is married with a son, they start an affair. Instead of feeling morally outraged at the adultery, I welcome it as an opportunity to replace our lost male protector with a more powerful one. But the only way the affair can be made to last is by administering a love potion to the Marquis. According to gypsy law, it is forbidden to mix love potions for tribal members. On the other hand, it is permitted to sneak them to powerful gadjos, if the gypsies' survival depends on it. I therefore see nothing wrong in preparing a love potion for the Marquis, which my daughter pours secretly into his wine at their next tête-à-tête.

The magic works better than expected. The nobleman becomes so infatuated with my daughter that he spends most of his time with us. For the first time in our lives, we feel completely secure and protected. But our good fortune does not last, despite the love potion. It ends very suddenly when the Marquis decides to let us into a strictly guarded family secret: Only his father had been of noble birth, while his mother had been a gypsy. This makes him virtually one of us and turns me into a lawbreaker in the eyes of my own people. I cannot live with myself after that, and when the Marquise tries to solve her marital problem by having us poisoned and having our bodies thrown into the ocean, death comes as a relief.

A Gypsy Dream Group

Apparently, the group karma from Saintes-Maries-de-la-Mer was due to be cleared. Quite unaware of what I was doing on a conscious level, I provided the opportunity for such a clearing when I put a small dream group together in 1989. As the group process unfolded in the course of one year, the six group members began having gypsy dreams. Gypsy dreams are actually quite rare. I hardly ever come across them in my clients' dream material. I therefore thought it might be worthwhile to collect these dreams and see if they added up to a coherent story. When we had gathered enough material, I called a special gypsy dream session. Since some of the group members had friends who also claimed to have had gypsy dreams, I threw the group open to anyone who wanted to join us for that session.

At the appointed time, eight people had gathered in my living room.

One of the outsiders who had joined us was an internationally famous psychic and past life regression therapist. While sitting in a circle on the floor, we used the group members' dreams and the psychic's vision to piece a composite story together. The group story matched my own story. We were stunned to discover that all the main players from that lifetime were present in my living room. Some of us had been gypsies, others members of the local aristocracy. The former Marquis was now in a tormented relationship with my former daughter. They could neither be with or without each other. Both were independently wealthy. The Marquise, now a German woman on a spiritual quest, was residing with her former son, now a gay artist and gardener. The Marquis' father, the patriarch of the family, turned out to be the visiting psychic. My two grandchildren, then brother and sister, were now husband and wife.

After we had sorted out our past life identities and relationships with each other, I confessed to having mixed a love potion for the Marquis. At this news, the group became very emotional. People were crying as they lay in each other's arms, asking one another for forgiveness. When I apologized to the former Marquis, my body began to shake uncontrollably, which is a symptom of trauma release.

After this cathartic session, the dream group disbanded, because its unconscious purpose had been fulfilled. A few years later, I ran into the psychic, who reported having regressed at least forty more people to that same life. Apparently, we had all come together in Santa Fe to clean up the karmic mess we had left behind in Saintes-Maries-de-la-Mer. The dream group had provided us with a unique opportunity to acknowledge our wrongdoings and forgive each other. I, in particular, had been in need of making amends. Therefore, my unconscious continued to work on the karma even after the dream group had ended. One night I dreamed how to undo the magic of the love potion, which still seemed to be holding the couple in an unhealthy bondage. I passed on the recipe to my former daughter, leaving it up to her to use it or not.

I subsequently lost track of the couple for about two years. But one day the postman delivered a card with an invitation to their "gypsy wedding" on the lawn of the Audubon Society. When I arrived at the site, the bride, who was holding a flower bouquet in her hand, tossed it on a table and rushed to embrace me. "Without you," she said, "none of this could have happened." When I asked her if my recipe had worked, she smiled and nodded. It had, in fact, worked so well that ten years after the wedding the couple is still happily married.

Visit to Saintes-Maries-de-la-Mer

In 1982 I went on a past life pilgrimage to France, accompanied by my Swiss friend Henry who drove a red Alfa Romeo. Our itinerary took us, among other places, to Saintes-Maries-de-la-Mer. Owing to rather unusual circumstances, I had a firsthand experience on site of what it means to be a gypsy. This story began to unfold after we had paid our respects to the statue of the black Sara la Kali. She occupies a dark corner of the crypt in the old village church by the sea.

According to an ancient legend, after Jesus's death, the three Maries—Mary Magdalen, Mary Kleophae, and Mary Salome—together with their Egyptian servant Sara la Kali, were pushed by the Jews into the sea on a rudderless boat. Friendly currents guided the boat to the beach of Saintes-Maries-de-la-Mer, and ever since then, the legend tells, this little fishing village has been a place to worship the three Maries. However, it is not the three Maries but their black servant Sara la Kali who is the patron saint of the gypsies. The laces and jewels with which they adorn her are telltale signs that she is not a servant to them at all. The concept of service is alien to the gypsies. They are also not Christians. What Sara la Kali means to them has nothing to do with the Christian legend at all. They see in her the Egyptian mother goddess Isis in her dual aspect of the great magician (positive) and the great witch (negative).[6]

But Sara la Kali was not the only "heathen" relic I found in this old village church. Walking down one of the aisles, I came across an artifact that looked very much like a stone altar. It was leaning inconspicuously against a wall, and I would have missed it had I not been on the look-out for power objects. Henry, who is a hobby photographer, insisted on taking pictures of the interior of every ancient church en route. While he was busy doing that, I kept myself occupied by dowsing the churches for energy spots. Being energy sensitive myself, I was curious to know if the medieval master builders had also been aware of power spots and had built their churches on such sites.

Although my dowsing results were inconclusive in this respect, I discovered something else—sacred objects have an energy field, too. Of all the sacred objects I had subsequently located and mea-sured with my pendulum, this artifact was by far the strongest. It had a simple, even primitive design. A stone pedestal raised it to the level of my chest, and its square, flat top had an indentation in the middle—for offerings, I supposed. But there was no information about its origin, age, or purpose anywhere to be found. Still wonder-ing what this artifact was, Henry and I left the church. Outside, we were immediately surrounded by gypsies wanting to tell our fortune. I chose the least obnoxious one, and after she had finished reading my palm, I asked her in my broken French if she could tell us some-thing about the ancient stone altar in the church. I said I had dowsed it with my pendulum and had detected a very strong energy field around it. To my surprise, she was quite unaware of the altar's exis-tence, but now her interest had been piqued. She asked me to meet her at noon in front of the main church entrance so that I could show it to her. I was not expecting her to be there, but to my sur-prise she showed up at the stroke of twelve. She had not come alone, either. She had brought six gypsy children with her, most of them little boys. She must have told them about my dowsing, because they were all clamoring to have their palms checked for healing abilities. If the pendulum said "yes," they jumped up and down with joy; if it said "no," they said I was lying. (So I could not have been such a great authority on dowsing for them, after all!)

When we had finished dowsing, I took the gypsy woman with

her six children inside the church. When we came to the stone altar, the woman told the children to reach up to the top of it and make a wish. I was deeply shocked when they all asked for the same unobtainable thing: they wanted to have blond hair and blue eyes! In other words, they did not want to be—or look like—gypsies. By now, our little group had become conspicuous. This had not been my intention, because I believe in keeping a low profile when abroad. But the church-warden was already on his way to evict us noisily from the church for worshipping "that heathen stone," as he called it.

I was too stunned and not fluent enough in French to ask him what such an object was doing in a Christian church in the first place, and what kind of a "heathen stone" it actually was. Somebody later identified it as a Druid altar. There are said to be quite a number of them both inside and outside Christian churches in southern France. How did these altars get there? Celts had been settled in large parts of France long before the country was Christianized. So the Church must have done what they did so remarkably well: integrate the old faith into the new faith somehow, instead of destroying its ancient symbols and relics.

The humiliating experience of being chased out of the church with the gypsies triggered old, familiar feelings in me, and I wept for the rest of the day. The pain and shame I must have felt as a social outcast in my last life had suddenly surfaced and overwhelmed me again.

I cannot deny that the gypsies' nomadic lifestyle has left its mark on my present life. During World War II, my parents moved from place to place and I changed schools every time. Later, as a student, I attended three different universities, and after my graduation I lived in three different countries. Every time I moved, I had to start over. It never occurred to me that this was financially wasteful, because I was not attached to material things.

I also never attributed my vagrant lifestyle to a bleed-through from a gypsy life until I was about to buy a house in Santa Fe and the gypsies showed up in a dream. In this dream, a band of angry gypsies broke down the fence of my backyard and advanced toward me in a menacing manner. I knew they were feeling betrayed, because as a homeowner, I was finally joining the ranks of the gadjos. Several years later, after I had passed my INS exam prior to acquiring American citizenship, I had another gypsy dream. This time a gypsy girl offered to sell me pansies and irises without stems. The German name for pansy is *Stiefmuetterchen,* meaning "little stepmother." The iris, on the other hand, is named after the Greco-Roman virgin goddess who builds the Rainbow Bridge. This flower choice was symbolic, of course. The gypsy girl was making fun of me. The irony became even more blatant when she offered to send me the flowers in monthly shipments and charge them, American style, to my credit card. In the dream, I politely turned down her offer, because I have come to realize, as I get older, that I do need a stem, and even roots, for my flowers.

3

MORE PAST LIVES

Men of Power

Power rests on the kind of knowledge one holds.
CARLOS CASTANEDA

OPPOSITES

Jung found that the human psyche is organized in pairs of opposites. In the relationship between the conscious and the unconscious mind, he saw compensatory processes at work that aim to maintain a state of inner balance. The same psychological opposites are also active in our reincarnational patterns, as the Jungian past life therapist Roger Woolger first observed in his book *Other Lives, Other Selves.*[1] According to him, the tension of opposites is helping humanity to become conscious of itself. Although most of my female lives were spent on the fringes of society, a certain amount of polarization could be discerned; but where the opposites really stood out was in the difference between my female and male incarnations.

Although (as it seemed at the time), my male lives had been fewer in number, they had been much more powerful than my female lives.

If the women described in the previous chapter had been part of these men's psychological constitution, it endowed the men with an unconventional anima, or feeling side, thus complementing their culture, their education, and their intellect to secure them a place at the hub of society. The dichotomy between marginal (female) and central (male) modes of existence, which is typical of my incarnations, was even reflected in my parents. My father was conservative and socially prominent, my mother outrageous and eccentric (see chapter 5). A tarot reader and an iridologist both observed the split this had created in my psyche. The tarot reader was startled by the polarization he found in my male and female cards. While the powerful Emperor card represented my male side, my female card was one of the weakest in the lesser arcana. It showed two homeless people, one on crutches, staggering barefoot through the snow.

The iridologist found the same opposites in the irises of my eyes, which he described as being equally strong. On the male side, he found the same archetypal emperor energy that the tarot reader had seen in the cards. He spoke of my many lifetimes of intellectual leadership as a man. On the female side, on the other hand, he saw a tendency to give myself away and fall into depression. This inner tension had first been spotted by my father's hobby—astrology. I had known from childhood that I was bearing the cross of a Venus-Mars square, which renders a woman's relationships with the opposite sex, and also with her inner male, particularly difficult.

If one pictures society as a circle, with concentric rings and a center point that represents ultimate worldly power, then my female lives were positioned on the outer circumference, and my male ones in or near the center. Wondering what higher purpose this might serve, I realized that this arrangement enabled me to view human existence from opposite angles—one looking outward from within, the other looking inward from without. While shame and humiliation had often been my lot in my incarnations as a woman, my male lives had compensated for this with public recognition, honor, and social status. Repeatedly, as a man, I had worked with other progressive minds on projects that furthered human evolution.

QUINTUS MUCIUS SCAEVOLA, ROMAN SENATOR AND AUGUR

An early exponent of such work was Quintus Mucius Scaevola, the augur, who lived at the time of the Roman Republic from 159 to 88 BCE. Jenny gave me the exact name and dates for him.* Scaevola was a prominent jurist and a member of a distinguished family of scholars, who created the Roman law on which the legal system of continental Europe is based. Scaevola was a follower of Panaetius of Rhodos, who founded a school of Stoic philosophy that emphasized morality. The Stoa stressed the importance of sense control for the development of three virtues: thoughtful action, fortitude in suffering, and justice in human intercourse. The ultimate goal of this philosophical school was the attainment of an emotionally detached form of wisdom.

Scaevola appears to have embodied that, at least in his old age when he became the mentor of the young Cicero. The public offices that Scaevola held in the course of his life were that of a senator, a governor of the Roman province of Minor Asia, a one-term consul, and an augur. This meant that he held more power and shouldered more responsibility than most. As consul, he was (along with the pro-consul) the parliamentary ruler of the Roman Empire. As governor of the province of Minor Asia, he ruled over a suppressed and exploited people. And in his office as augur, he mediated as a priest between Jupiter, the highest Roman God, and the State. There were, at any given time, nine Roman augurs (Cicero was later one of them) who made up a college of priests. They were elected for life, chosen from the most distinguished citizens of Rome. They could be recognized by the purple borders on

---

*I have completed Jenny's data whenever possible with information from historical sources.

their white togas and by the staff they carried as a symbol of their authority.

Whenever an important political decision had to be made, the augurs pitched their tent on a hill outside of Rome and observed the signs of nature: bird flight, feeding patterns of consecrated chickens, and elemental forces like thunder and lightning. Such observations were then interpreted and reported to the senate, which based its decision on these divination results. Cicero later honored his childhood mentor by making him one of the interlocutors in his treatises *De Amicitia* (On Friendship), *De Re Publica* (On Matters of State), and *De Oratore* (About Speech Making). However, Scaevola does not say much in them and seems to have been mainly content with playing the role of a listener. This tallies with his reputation of not having been much of a public speaker except for one notable occasion when he defended himself in front of the senate against a libelous accusation. His self-representation must have been very effective; he was elected consul the very next year. His contemporaries knew him as a charming man who was tirelessly active in the service of the State and highly respected for his sense of justice. He cultivated close friendships with other prominent Roman citizens and sat with his guests on a round bench in his garden, or in a circle on the lawn, to emphasize equality during the time of the Roman Republic.

Despite Scaevola's impeccable reputation, he must have had flaws that were not visible to his upper-class friends who shared, after all, the same collective shadow. The truth is that no one could rise to a position of power in ancient Rome, even during the times of the Republic, without being ruthless to some extent. Likewise, nobody can be the ruler of an empire at any given time without accumulating a proportional amount of karmic debt. This is something that modern politicians who so eagerly run for office never seem to think about.

I suspect that despite Scaevola's sense of justice, a good bit of injustice was performed in his name. Thus, in a past life regression I remembered that as governor of Minor Asia I had felt perfectly justified to have Turks thrown to the lions if they refused to bow to the Roman gods. I also helped create a legal system that defined slaves as "things" and wives and children as "property of the husband." Although this was an expression of the spirit of the time, it does not make it any more humane.

Apart from Scaevola's chauvinism, which is offensive to me as a modern woman, I do feel close to him as a person. It is not difficult for me to recognize him in myself. We both prefer listening to talking, and have a basically quiet demeanor. His augury, which amounted to the interpretation of synchronistic phenomena, is closely related to my interpretation of dreams and other unconscious manifestations in my work as a depth psychologist. His love for Stoic philosophy had been rekindled in me at an early age when an older friend had presented me with an anthology of the writings of Seneca, Epictetus, and Marcus Aurelius. Scaevola's pragmatism, a quality that I was famous for as a child, seemed to have gotten lost when I became romantically involved with the opposite sex. However, during my time at the Jung Institute, when I was deeply immersed in the world of the unconscious, Scaevola appeared to me in a dream to remind me of ordinary reality.

He is gray haired, distinguished looking, and middle-aged. He slips under my bedcovers, and as he lies next to me, he holds up his left hand to identify himself as Scaevola, for scaevola *means "left-handed" in Latin. He has not come to make love to me, either, but to give me a piece of sound advice. "It is not what you do in your dreams that matters," he says, "but what you do in real life."*

MAURICE SCÈVE, PRINCE OF THE RENAISSANCE IN LYON

The next male life that Jenny elaborated on had occurred more than five hundred years later. In that incarnation I was the French Renaissance poet Maurice Scève, who spent most of his life in Lyon as a spiritual and cultural leader. He was connected with Scaevola through a bloodline of justice. Like his Roman soul ancestor, Scève was born into a distinguished family of jurists, on or about 1500. His father was the president of the court in Lyon, and Maurice, as the only son of four children, was expected to carry on his father's work. He studied law in Italy and returned to Lyon with a doctorate of jurisprudence in his pocket. As creators of the Roman law, the Scaevolas might well have been his role model during his student years, because it seems to be more than a coincidence that he changed his family name from Sève, to Scève. By Latinizing his name, he made it sound more like Scaevola. He even signed some of his Latin poems "Mauricius Scaeva," which is remarkably close in sound to Mucius Scaevola. It is almost as if he had known of his soul connection with the Roman jurist.

However, by the time Mucius had come back as Maurice, his former passion for jurisprudence had either left him or his awareness of the dark side of justice had grown (see the preface). He might also have needed to develop different aspects of himself. Anyway, after satisfying his father's ambition, Maurice had never practiced law. Instead, he had chosen a private life where he was free to give creative expression to his many talents. He was, by nature, a true Renaissance man. Apart from writing poetry in French and Latin, he was a translator of Spanish literature, an architect, a painter, an astrologer, and a musician. To live in a perfect cultural environment furthered his multicultural interests. While under Protestant rule, Lyon was the center of French humanism and the place where the first Lutheran Bible translations and other books blacklisted by the Catholic Church were published. In other words, Lyon was a place for alternative thinkers.

It was also a major center of the arts. In the history of literature, Scève is known as the "prince of the Lyonnaise Renaissance," because he was the pivot of it all. Jenny especially mentioned the fact that during the royal visit of King Henry II in 1548, Scève orchestrated the whole spectacular ceremonial celebration. In the prime of his life, he must have felt very blessed. This was implied by a recent dream, in which I said to a friend:

The Renaissance was a very, very rich time. God was holding my hand.

The handholding had felt very physical in the dream, and when I awoke, I was surprised to find that my hands were folded in prayer.

Despite Scève's growing fame, he remained sensitive, gracious, and modest. He has been called *modeste jusque à coquetterie* (modest to the point of coquetry). He founded a school of poetry, which is considered to have been the forerunner of nineteenth-century French symbolism. When Jenny told me that Scève was famous for his spiritual love poetry, I immediately recognized him as the soul ancestor who had recited the love poem to me on the loft above the loft. Even Jenny's description of him matched the appearance of the man I had seen in my dream. She said he was dark haired, delicately built, graceful, and handsome.

However, on a sixteenth-century portrait of him, which is on the book cover of his love poem collection, *Délie,* he has a sad and anxious expression on his face. This is consistent with the sentiment of his poetry and with his life story. Like his fourteenth-century role model, Petrarch, Scève had a lifelong platonic love affair with a married woman, the poetess Pernette de Guillet. Like the better-known Loise Labbé, she belonged to his poetic circle. While his undying love for her might have been one of the reasons why Scève never married, the celibacy, which he is said to have practiced, cannot be explained with this love alone. When I began to remember additional lives after Jenny's readings, I found a very austere, monkish bloodline running through my male incarnations. I know of four lives spent as a monk in Christian, Buddhist, and Jain denominations. The austerity might have been needed to counterbalance the hedonism in some of my female lives.

After Pernette died from the plague in 1545 and Scève lost two of his closest male friends to political persecution (one died in exile, the other was burned at the stake)—all in a period of two years—his tendency toward depression and social withdrawal became more pronounced. He spent longer periods of time in a monastery on the Isle de Barbe, an island in the river Rhone outside Lyon. One biographer speaks of suicidal tendencies toward the end of his life, and it is certainly true that he expressed death wishes in some of his later poems. His anonymous signature, *non si, non là* (not here, not there), suggested that he dwelled in a borderland between life and death.

Jenny stated with great certainty that Scève was born in 1510 and died in 1564, while literary historians can only speculate about these dates. In addition, nobody knows how he died and where his remains are. He seems to have simply vanished, leaving no grave, no memorial, and—what is most unusual for a renowned sixteenth-century poet—no epitaphs behind.

In 1564, which according to Jenny was the year of his death, the city of Lyon was struck by two disasters at once. The Catholic army invaded and reconquered Lyon, and simultaneously the plague broke out. The ensuing social chaos is hard to imagine. Thousands died of the Black Death and were dumped into mass graves outside of town. Scève is supposed to have been among them, but this hypothesis only masks the embarrassing fact that nobody knows what happened to the "prince of the Lyonnaise Renaissance."

Jenny said nothing about his death either, but as I mentioned before, she often withheld information that she considered would be too upsetting to me. On the other hand, I did not need to be told, because I already knew from my dream what had happened to him. I knew that he had been stoned by the mob, before being arrested and taken to a Church tribunal by the Inquisition. Mercifully, my dream had ended before he had been sentenced and executed, but it turned out to be only a temporary reprieve. Fifteen years later in Santa Fe, I dreamed of the execution itself. If Jenny's dates are correct, Scève was fifty-four years old when he died.

When I was fifty-four, I developed a problem with my throat. A tightening of my gullet made it difficult for me to swallow. I thought I had a tumor and feared the worst. When a medical examination revealed no abnormalities, I felt greatly relieved, but the symptoms persisted nevertheless. I continued to suffer until one night the underlying, unconscious memories surfaced in a dream. I dreamed that two thugs were constructing a makeshift gallows for me inside a barn. I stood by, fervently praying. Then they hanged me before I could finish my prayers. Once I realized that I had relived Scève's death in this dream, the tightening of my throat disappeared and never returned. I later read in a book on the Spanish Inquisition that a death by hanging, before one was burned, was granted to those as a special favor who had the money to pay for it.

Why was a depressed, spiritual recluse like Scève singled out to be tortured and executed like that? I wondered about this for years until I arrived at the following explanation: The Catholic Church considered most of the publications that had come out of Lyon, especially the Lutheran Bible, as heresy. From there to declaring the plague a divine punishment was only a short step, and from there to looking for someone to blame was an even shorter step. As "prince of the Lyonnaise Renaissance" and a renowned man of letters, Scève was held responsible and blamed for the plague. This enraged the mob so much that they could not wait until the Inquisition arrived and proceeded to stone him. Like the scapegoat in the ancient Jewish custom, Scève was loaded with the "sins" of the community and publicly sacrificed.

Synchronicities in Lyon

On that memorable past life journey through France that I had taken with my friend Henry, Lyon was our first destination. I was impatient to find out how the exposure to my old haunts would affect me emotionally. Based on the information Jenny had given me, I had preconceived ideas about how I would feel in certain places. These proved to be wrong every time. In Lyon, I expected to feel elated, because I had been a celebrity in that town. Too late did I remember the terrible price that had been attached to that fame.

The time of our arrival in Lyon was so synchronistic that it sent shivers down my spine. As soon as we parked the car in the town center, we realized that the city was preparing to celebrate the five-hundred-year anniversary of the Lyonnaise Renaissance. We entered a tourist bureau, hoping to get information about Maurice Scève. Was he still known in Lyon? I asked the travel agent. Of course he was. Were there any historical sites connected to him that we could visit? There was no gravesite, said the travel agent regretfully, but his family home was still standing. Although it was in private hands, it was open to the public. Then she gave us directions.

The former Scève residence looked small and insignificant from the outside, but it was actually spacious and rambling. A long, gloomy corridor cut through the gray, medieval two-story building, connecting the main street with a parallel one. As soon as we entered and started walking down the corridor, I had a sense of foreboding. I felt trapped like an animal in a cage and could not get through the building fast enough. But at the other end a chilling surprise awaited us. A brass plate was nailed over the exit, commemorating members of the Resistance who had been rounded up by the Gestapo in this very building during World War II. Thus another synchronicity had occurred: the Gestapo had captured members of the Resistance in the very same location where Scève had been captured five hundred years before by the Inquisition—the medieval precursor of the Gestapo. Unbeknown to the good citizens of Lyon, history had thus repeated itself.

When the sightseeing was over, I collapsed in the hotel room. I found myself in a timeless place, where the atrocities of the sixteenth and the twentieth centuries flowed together into one hellish pool, and for hours I wept bitter tears. We had to leave Lyon the very next day, because I was falling into a depression. Was it my own or Scève's despair that was creeping up on me? It was impossible to tell. Before we turned our back on the city of Lyon, a third synchronicity occurred. Or was it just by chance that we went to the city archive instead of the public library? When asking for recent publications about Scève, we were shown a short article about his poetic circle. A previously unknown fact had just come to light: Shortly before Scève's mysterious disappearance, some of his friends had been publicly stoned. I was grateful to receive this confirmation just before leaving Lyon, because if Scève's friends had been stoned, why would Scève himself have been spared?

It is difficult to detect the greater design behind Maurice Scève's savage ending. It is even harder to understand how a man of his cultural and spiritual sophistication would choose to be reborn as a prostitute in London in his next life. But according to Jenny's timetable, he did. Perhaps his sexuality had been so deeply repressed that he needed to wallow in it for a while, or he might have secretly longed to *be* a woman, after longing *for* a woman most of his life. It might also have been necessary for him to experience working-class poverty after living a sheltered, upper-class life. Probably all of these factors contributed to this choice, plus—as I realize now—karmic necessities (see the preface). In terms of human justice, the only way that such a degradation of a pure human being makes any sense is if one assumes that the opposites have to assert themselves from one lifetime to another. One reassuring thing about this teetering course toward liberation is that once a level of personal development is attained, it never seems to get lost again. Scève is a shining example of that. Although he went through purgatory at the end of his life and descended all the way into hell in his following incarnation, he retained his status as my most highly evolved past life self. Thus, five centuries later he could appear in my dreams at a critical time as my soul guide and spiritual advocate.

My connection with Scève is too deep for words. When I first read a personality profile of him I burst into tears, although I was on a Zurich tram and people were staring at me. It was as if I had looked in a mirror and had seen his face superimposed over mine. Later, I realized that the sudden burst of creativity I had experienced as a teenager had been his and that the school essays I had birthed with tremendous effort from a deep unconscious place had also been his. For reasons I could never understand, my essays had all sounded archaic. I also inherited Scève's main psychological problem, which inspired much of his poetry.

He had a "phantom lover" complex, in terms of Jungian psychology. To have a phantom lover complex means that one is chronically pining for an unobtainable love object. Although this is a tormented state, it has the hidden advantage of shielding one's love from reality. While Scève remained in this state all his life, I eventually pulled out of it.

BUTTON GWINNETT, SIGNER OF THE DECLARATION OF INDEPENDENCE

A century and a half later, I had another male incarnation. My name was Button Gwinnett; I was born in Gloucester, England, in 1735, the second son of a clergyman. The genealogy on both father's and mother's side was old and distinguished. There were also strong family ties on the mother's side to the Welsh aristocracy, which Gwinnett's unusual Christian name Button (originally a family name) is owing to.

Yet his life history was somewhat out of line with my previous male incarnations. He descended from the level of exceptionally high personal standards, which his soul ancestors and even his genealogical ancestors had maintained, to the level of a somewhat flawed, although adventurous, dynamic, and complex human being. The artistic bloodline he inherited receded into the background, while the political and the lawgiver bloodlines from the Roman life resurfaced in him. At the same time, a new bloodline of commerce began to emerge when Gwinnett entered the business world.

Without any past life experience in commerce or an upbringing that would have prepared him for this line of work, he did not stand much of a chance. He apprenticed as a merchant in Bristol—probably with an uncle—and married the daughter of his business partner, who was below his social status although financially well off. If, through this marriage, he had hoped to place his business on a solid foundation, he had not taken his spending habits into account. When Jenny told me about this lifetime, shortly before my own departure for the United States in 1983, she did not explain why Gwinnett immigrated

with his wife to the American colonies and settled in Georgia sometime in the 1760s. The reasons for this unusual move for a member of
the English upper middle class, married with three small children, I
later inferred from a passing remark made by his biographer, Charles
Francis Jenkins.[2]

Jenkins said that Gwinnett had gone deeply into debt with his
overseas trade while living in Bristol, but his patriotism did not allow
Jenkins to draw the logical conclusion that the future signer of the
Declaration of Independence might have been on the run from the
authorities when he departed for the colonies. Yet this is the most plausible explanation for his leaving his family of origin and his home country behind. Even in Dickens's times, people were thrown into debtor's
prisons. And James Oglethorpe had founded the colony of Georgia,
where Gwinnett eventually settled, specifically as a refuge for the poor
debtor classes in England.

What did Gwinnett look like? A contemporary remembered him
like this:

> He was about six feet in height, and his person was properly pro-
> portioned, lofty and commanding. Without possessing remarkable
> eloquence his language was mild and persuasive. His manners were
> polite and his deportment graceful.[3]

According to this description, his appearance was that of perfect
gentleman. More individualized features link him to Scaevola's lack
of eloquence on the one hand and Scève's gracefulness on the other.
Gracefulness is an unusual attribute for a man, but it seems natural,
rather than effeminate, if one considers that both of these men had a
strong female bloodline as a dancer. Gwinnett's cultured family background, the style of his letters, and the Latin motto he selected for the
seal of the state of Georgia—*pro bono publico*—all speak of a classical
education. Even without a bloodline in law and politics, this educational
background alone would have singled him out for a leadership position

in a colony of illiterates and near-illiterates. Thus from very humble beginnings as a storekeeper, he rose in a very short time to be a land-owner of 3,750 acres, a planter, a slave owner, a politician, a delegate to the National Congress, and governor of Georgia.

The first public office that Gwinnett held was, interestingly, that of a justice of the peace. By agreeing to play this role, he tapped in to the bloodline of justice, which runs through five of my male incarnations. His political orientation is said to have been ultra liberal by the standards of his time. He was the leader of the radical or popular party in Georgia. His best friend and cosigner, Dr. Lyman Hall, therefore called him "a Whig to excess." This is consistent with the fact that the constitution for Georgia, which was drafted under his guidance, was the most liberal of the southern states.

Although Gwinnett has been criticized for being a dilettante in politics, his rapid rise to prominence, the instant respect he won at the National Congress, and his reincarnational history tell a different story. As a soul descendent of the Roman statesman, Mucius Scaevola, he was without a doubt the right man at the right time to promote the idea of the republic in the American colonies. He must have been what those of us, who do not think in terms of reincarnation, would call "a natural" in this field.

By contrast, Gwinnett was not "a natural" in business. There he made all the mistakes of a beginner without ever seeming to learn from them. The same financial foolhardiness that had brought him to the brink of disaster in England followed him into the colonies, where he wasted a second chance to stay out of debt. He might have had, what I would call, "a psychological past life takeover." In such cases, a past life personality, instead of being harmoniously integrated into the totality of the present self, takes over most of the ego functions. Oblivious to the individual's real life situation, it proceeds as if the past life conditions still prevail. A person who is "possessed" in this manner by a past life self can become deflated or inflated, depending on the nature of the past incarnation.

Gwinnett was inflated. In his past life as a Roman senator and consul he had been a wealthy landowner. When this past life was triggered in him through his new involvement in politics, it overwhelmed him with old feelings of entitlement. He started to act more like a member of a wealthy Roman family than the son of a poor English clergyman that he really was. Jenkins, looking at Gwinnett's behavior from a biographer's standpoint, states it quite clearly:

> One of the outstanding characteristics of the man was his sanguine temperament, as shown by his financial operations. Fortune was always just within his grasp and always eluding him. He hopefully undertook new ventures and assumed overwhelming burdens in expectation that he could carry them.[4]

Gwinnett kept his fantasy of wealthy land ownership going by paying his old accounts with funds from newly acquired creditors, according to Jenkins. Behaving very much like an addict or like a manic-depressive, he purchased more and more land on credit. By borrowing from Peter to pay Paul, he created a complex and stressful social environment for himself. Since he overextended his energy resources, he was often unable to live up to his commitments. Twice in his career as a justice of the peace he had to be taken by force to court hearings that he had been trying to dodge. Through his unreliability and financial untrustworthiness he made many enemies, although according to both Jenny and Jenkins he had an equal number of loyal friends.

His most serious karmic mistake was undoubtedly his purchase of St. Catherine's Island and his concomitant role as a slave owner. St. Catherine's was one of the "golden islands" nestled along the coast of Georgia. In 1739, General Oglethorpe had allocated these islands to the Lower Creek Indians as hunting and fishing grounds. Although Gwinnett was not the first contract-breaking landowner on the island, he joined the ranks of faithless colonizers through this purchase. However, no blessings went along with this morally questionable acquisition. He was neither able to keep up his mortgage payments nor live there in peace. Seafaring marauders and British marines were constantly preying on his livestock and crops. Although he eventually lost the ownership of the island, he managed to lease it until his death.

In spite of all his problems, Gwinnett's political career took off like a rocket, and as it did, a very different side of Gwinnett emerged. He became highly responsible and even self-sacrificing in his new public role. By reviving the bloodline of Mucius Scaevola's stewardship of the republic in himself, he struck a vein of solid gold. Therefore, his best friend and cosigner, Dr. Lyman Hall, could say about him after his death: "The man was valuable, so attached to the liberty of this State and continent, that his whole attention, influence and interest centered in it."[5] While he was still alive, his sudden rise to power was experienced by the conservatives—and even by the moderates in his own party—as a threat. Thus he found himself surrounded by envy and resentment.

Gwinnett had one mortal enemy whom Jenny mentioned by name. This was General Lachlan McIntosh, a Highlander who was universally hated by his subordinates. When I found his portrait in Jenkins's biography, it gave me the chills. I knew that long-nosed, bony face and that icy-cold stare only too well. McIntosh's clan had come over in 1736 with General Oglethorpe and had been in Georgia ever since. Gwinnett, on the other hand, was a newcomer, not only to the political arena, but also to Georgia and the American continent. Twice Gwinnett was defeated by McIntosh when he competed with him for command of the Georgian troops. How unsuited Gwinnett was for a military position can be gleaned from the fact that he had to borrow a gun before he rode off to the Continental Congress.

Lachlan McIntosh also had a brother, George, who was a politician and fellow member with Gwinnett in the Council of Safety. When Gwinnett was appointed president of the council after the popular Governor Bulloch had died under mysterious circumstances, George McIntosh refused to sign the new governor's commission, saying that Gwinnett would be the last person in the world he would choose. Gwinnett, stung by the insult, responded with a threat: "By God, then, this will be the last day you and I will ever sit together in Council."[6]

It is clear that the McIntoshs hated Gwinnett, and vice versa. Their dislike of each other went far beyond the animosity that traditionally exists between the Scots and Brits. Gwinnett had a disenfranchised female side, and a big male ego to compensate for it. This put him at a disadvantage when it came to handling a personal slight with integrity. Thus, twelve days later when an opportunity for revenge came along, he promptly seized it. Congress had instructed him to take George McIntosh into custody, because he had been identified as a traitor. Gwinnett gave this a cruel twist by throwing him into the common jail and putting him in irons. This impaired the prisoner's health and rebounded on Gwinnett by turning the public mood against him; less well-disposed colleagues called him a dictator from then on. George Walton, a cosigner and another enemy of Gwinnett's, mockingly compared him to Alexander the Great and predicted: "This great hero that has set our country in a flame cannot last long."[7]

Walton's prediction came true. A military expedition to Florida under Gwinnett's command miserably failed and undermined the public trust in him so deeply that he was not reelected. Shortly after that when Lachlan McIntosh called Gwinnett "a scoundrel and lying rascal" in the assembly, nobody called him to order. This left Gwinnett with no choice but to wipe out the insult by challenging the general to a duel. It was fought with pistols on May 16, 1777. The combatants aimed at each other's knees from a distance of only ten feet, with the intention of painfully injuring but not mortally wounding each other. But Gwinnett, whose thighbone was shattered above the knee, died of gangrene three days later, while McIntosh recovered from his wound.

Of Gwinnett's political achievements only one survived: his signature under the Declaration of Independence. Georgia's independence, which he had represented, was lost a year after his death when the British conquered the poorly protected state to rule it for another three years. Several constitutions subsequently replaced the original one, which had been mostly Gwinnett's work. The original constitution had one basic flaw: it allowed slavery, despite the statement made in the Declaration of Independence that all men are created equal.

I often quote the I Ching in my practice because of the wisdom and beautiful nature imagery it contains. Here one hexagram comes to mind that perfectly illustrates the futility of Gwinnett's life: The thirtieth hexagram, called "The Clinging," deals with what is required of a great man if he wants to bring light into the world.[8] The main requirement mentioned is perseverance. Others are compliance, voluntary dependence, and recognition of the limitations of human life. The changing line in the fourth place then illustrates, through an image, what happens if these basic requirements are not met:

> Its coming is sudden;
> It flames up, dies down, is thrown away.

The commentary elucidates this metaphor further by delineating the character profile of a man who answers to this description.

> Here the image used is that of a meteor or a straw fire. A man who
> is excitable and restless may rise quickly to prominence but produces
> no lasting effects. Thus matters end badly when a man spends himself too rapidly and consumes himself like a meteor.

This is exactly how Gwinnett's early biographers saw him, according to Jenkins. They likened his career to a meteor, which, rising out of the east, flamed with ever-increasing brightness across the zenith and plunged swiftly into darkness. Gwinnett's light was, in fact, so completely extinguished that nobody knows for sure where he is buried. A headstone that had once existed disappeared and, according to a newspaper story, later showed up as a bar top in a grog shop in Savannah. In contrast with this postmortem abuse, Gwinnett's autographs are now more highly priced than those of his more famous, more levelheaded, and therefore more long-lived colleagues. History is full of paradoxes.

Dream Memories

The kinship I presently feel with Gwinnett is restricted to his love of adventure and freedom. I might have had more in common with him when I was younger and less responsible than I am now. Yet I have had six dreams about him since coming to the United States—more than about any other past life—and I cannot get rid of the feeling that I am in this country at least partly because of the karma he created. When I first heard about him from Jenny, shortly before I left for the United States, I felt somewhat alarmed. I immediately suspected that my journey to America, which I was undertaking for personal reasons, might turn out to be a karmic cleanup mission.

This suspicion was later confirmed by a dream, which I had shortly after buying a small grassland ranch with many oak trees in Cathey's Valley, near Yosemite Park. The ranch was in the middle of nowhere, just like St. Catherine's Island had been, and I noted with some perplexity that even the names of the two locations had a similar ring to them. The only difference was that I purchased the ranch with my father's money, instead of buying it on credit as Gwinnett had done. I even paid cash for it, against the advice of my American friends, who said I was stupid not to take advantage of the tax break of a mortgage. Then one night, I had the following dream:

I have rings on all my fingers, except for the little finger on my right hand. I am now placing a ring on it. It is a man's signet ring. It has a square, light blue stone, with two white etchings on it. The word "Republic" is engraved in the center and a small star in the right hand corner. I feel embarrassed when I wake up. I also know that this is Button Gwinnett's ring.

My embarrassment was partly due to the fact that I had put a man's ring on my finger, and partly because it was Gwinnett's. I had not read Jenkin's biography yet and only suspected that the signer might have done things I would not be proud of. But I knew when I awoke that by putting on Gwinnett's ring in my dream I had made a commitment to clear his karma.

A few months later I dreamed of Gwinnett again. I had been spending large sums of money on remodeling the ranch buildings. I had also gone into culture shock and was beginning to question the wisdom of relocating to the United States so late in life.

I am inspecting the front of a building. It has a neoclassical facade and is several stories high. It was built when the United States was founded. I have already invested a lot of money in the restoration of this building, including the insertion of a new crossbeam to keep the structure from falling down, but the restoration is far from complete, and the building may not have a solid foundation. I ask myself whether it's worth saving.

On a personal level, the dream expressed doubt about the prudence of my financial investment. On a collective level, it reflected my concerns about the condition of the republic that I had helped to create two centuries prior. Two other dreams about Gwinnett, which are dated almost a decade later, contained no references to my present life at all, which is unusual. Rather, I had both dreams in response to the 4th of July. The first one I had on July 3, 1991.

I am a man. I am walking with a male friend along a wooded footpath on a hillside. We are looking down on a public building, which is in the valley below us, where something important has just taken place. Reflecting on the deeper meaning of this event, I say to my friend, "It seemed as if we were rebelling, but we were really right on time . . ."

When I dreamed this, I had no conscious knowledge of where the

Declaration of Independence was signed. Only later did I compare the geography of the dream to that of Philadelphia. The wooded footpath might have been on Chestnut Hill. From there, we might have been looking down on the Pennsylvania statehouse on Chestnut Street, where the Declaration of Independence was signed. I felt that if the place was real, then my remark was also real. But what was it referring to? The official reason for the Declaration of Independence is common knowledge. It is supposed to have been the last step in a colonial uprising against unfair taxes imposed by the English Crown. However, after this dream I started to wonder if there had been additional reasons for declaring independence that cannot be found in history books—reasons only known to the signers of it.

I remembered having read that many of them were Freemasons. Perhaps that's where I had to look for an answer. Sure enough, when I turned to Manley P. Hall's classic, *The Secret Teaching of All Ages,* I found it. In reference to the Declaration of Independence, Hall stated: "It cannot be doubted that the secret societies of Europe conspired to establish upon the American continent a new nation, conceived in liberty and dedicated to the proposition that all men are created equal."[9] The decisive words, "God has given America to be free," were uttered by a mysterious stranger just before the Declaration of Independence was signed. Another stranger, called "the Professor," had earlier advised Washington and Franklin on the design for the national flag. Once independence had been declared, both men vanished without a trace, which, unless they were murdered, suggested a European connection. Besides, parallel freedom movements such as the French Revolution were in preparation in Europe when the Declaration of Independence was signed. Thus the Freemasons might have decided that it was time for the Western civilizations to leave their childlike dependence on royal parental figures behind and mature toward a more adult state of responsible self-representation. When the American founding fathers were approached with this idea, they had been willing to give it a try.

The second significant dream I had in the following year; I titled it "Dream Thoughts" in my journal, because there were no images in this dream. But these were not my own thoughts, either. Rather, they seemed to be Gwinnett's thoughts after signing the Declaration of Independence.

Paradoxically, we have chosen democracy against the will of the people who wanted to stay dependent on England. In a similar fashion, we have chosen equality for all on the basis of slavery. Contradictions . . . One should resist the sound of the drum and not lose touch with one's own inner truth.

Here, a different side of Gwinnett came to the fore. Although his character was flawed, he seems to have been an aware human being. According to another one of my dreams he was even a humanitarian. The "Dream Thoughts" show a certain uneasiness with the blatant contradiction between the content of the document he had just signed and what was being practiced in Georgia and the southern states. He also distanced himself from the public sentiment, which called for military action as part of the independence movement. The expression "sound of the drum" belongs to Gwinnett's time when the soldiers were called into battle that way. It also describes the hypnotic spell of the war propaganda during the Revolutionary War. In Philadelphia, an American Indian delegation of the Six Nations had appeared before the Continental Congress. In order to impress the delegation, a flashy display of the superior colonial military power had been staged. Perhaps there had been too much saber-rattling for Gwinnett's liking, who was, after all, a clergyman's son. Military defense was clearly not a priority for him, or for the State of Georgia he represented. This is clear from the following statement in a letter by General Howe to Button Gwinnett: "It gives me Sir, great anxiety to find your State so destitute of almost every Military requisite, and deficient in every necessary provision for the Soldiery."[10]

The "inner truth" that Gwinnett did not want to lose sight of seems to have been the concept of freedom, which was the driving force behind the Declaration of Independence. Beyond its universal significance, freedom had also a very personal meaning for Gwinnett. For him, it meant never having to face the threat of being confined to a debtor's prison again. To protect his freedom, Gwinnett had left England in the prime of his life, with his family. To protect his freedom, he had gone one step further and severed his ties with his homeland. To take preventive action instead of letting things run their course was in keeping with his wanderer bloodline. It was typical of this bloodline, which had first emerged in a female life in the thirteenth century, to choose migration over incarceration, adaptability over tradition, and freedom over enslavement whenever the alternative presented itself. Yet Gwinnett was still too hierarchical and racist in his thinking to grant the same freedom to people of color, like the African slaves he owned, or the Creek Indians, whose older rights to St. Catherine's Island he conveniently ignored.

SOMNA, SPIRITUAL LEADER OF THE ASSINIBOIN

It seems like a logical consequence of Gwinnett's racism that after his premature death he was reborn as an American Indian tribal leader. "You always become the thing you fight the most," says Jung. However, Gwinnett did not immediately reap the karma he had sown (by taking St. Catherine's Island away from the Creek Indians). This had to be dealt with in two subsequent incarnations—in the lives of individuals who were displaced from home and country due to persecution and war. What seems to have been more urgently needed for the evolution of Gwinnett's consciousness at this point was a lesson in the equality of all human beings. So Gwinnett had to incarnate as a member of a race, the Native Americans, whose rights he had violated out of ignorance. The irony of this lesson was that he had a much happier life and was more highly respected as a leader of so-called savages than he had ever been as a governing member of the supposedly "superior white race."

According to Jenny, his name was Somna, and he belonged to the Assiniboin tribe. The Assiniboin are Plains Indians by origin. They belong to the linguistic and cultural lineage of the Sioux. Sometime during the mid-seventeenth century, they had a falling out with the larger tribal group over ritual practices. This made them move northward into the prairie. Jenny saw them peacefully settled on the wooded banks of the Saskatchewan River. She called the river by its old Indian name, *sis sis saskatchewan sipi,* which she translated as "great, angry water." Since Jenny took the name from my past life memory bank, it would naturally have appeared in its original form. Jenny said that the tribe had lived in a relatively safe territory during those "still good times before the white settlers had overrun the whole country." This was the time when the English Hudson Bay Company, founded by a Royal Charter in 1670, had trading posts all along the Saskatchewan River. Thanks to this Royal Charter, the area remained a refuge for the tribes until the second half of the nineteenth century, when the Canadian government took over the region, the railway was built, and the settlers began to flood the countryside.

It was typical of Jenny's readings that if I had lived in tribal consciousness, she focused on tribal customs rather than on my personal life. This reflected, no doubt, my lack of self-interest, as compared with tribal interests, in this particular incarnation. Thus all Jenny told me about Somna was that he knew how to interpret sand paintings, which would have been the task of a medicine man or a holy man. Eventually, however, I received more information about Somna from two independent sources. This makes this Indian life one of my best-documented ones.

One of these sources was again my friend Alec, whose past lives had repeatedly intersected with mine. As I mentioned before, he had accessed these memories in a past life regression in Frankfurt, Germany. According to Alec, we both had belonged to the Assiniboin tribe—a tribe nobody has ever heard of in Europe. I had been the son of the tribal chief. Because of a tribal emergency, which I could later identify as a smallpox epidemic, I had become chief as a twelve-year-old. Later, I had been trained as a medicine man. Whereas Alec had rivaled *over* me as a Viking, he had rivaled *with* me for the attentions of another woman in this Indian lifetime. Rivalry seemed to have been one of the issues that Alec had been struggling with, incarnation after incarnation. Apparently he was still working on this issue, which I could tell by the grim expression on his face when he mentioned in passing that I had been the winner in the Assiniboin life.

My second source of confirmation of this Assiniboin lifetime was from a Mohawk medicine woman who went on a spirit journey for me. She returned with the information that I had been an Assiniboin medicine man or holy man in a past life in Canada. According to her, I had known everything about the Medicine Wheel and was supposed to remember all the details of this healing tradition in my present life. Years before she told me this, I had chosen the Medicine Wheel as a topic for my diploma thesis and had built a Medicine Wheel next to my home wherever I happened to live at the time. Since my Medicine Wheels had power, a Mescalero Apache medicine man felt obligated to initiate me into the Medicine Wheel tradition in the summer of 1989.

Moving from a position of leadership in the white man's world directly into a leadership position in the Indian culture taught me important lessons about the responsible use of power. My next male incarnation, as the owner of a bank and chairman of an international trading firm, showed that this lesson had been well learned.

Jenny gave me much detailed information about the traditions of the Assiniboin, most of which I have been able to verify since coming to America. Even a curious detail she mentioned proved to be accurate in the end: tribal members used to decorate themselves with golden platelets (they were oblivious to their monetary value). I had never heard of this before and was ready to discard this piece of information as the only outright error in Jenny's readings when I came across a reproduction of a nineteenth-century oil painting of two Indians—one

Assiniboin, the other Yankton—on the cover of the Swiss anthropologist Hans Läng's book, *Kulturgeschichte der Indianer Nordamerikas.*[11]

Assiniboin and Yankton, which are closely related tribes, traditionally lived in the same geographical area. In the painting, the Assiniboin was dressed in an elegant deer hide costume with a Medicine Wheel or shield painted on his chest and sky-blue trimmings on his sleeves. The Yankton, on the other hand, was bare chested and decorated with body paint. He wore golden platelets on a string around his neck and golden bracelets on each arm. When I read up on the mineral deposits in the province of Saskatchewan after this, it turned out that there are gold fields on the north shore of Lake Athabasca.

Jenny talked at great length about the Assiniboins' nature religion. Many of their rituals honored the sun as the giver of life. Sunrise and sunset were celebrated on a daily basis with ceremonial dances. At dusk, the people prayed for the sun to rise again the next morning, and at dawn, they gave thanks for its return. Kinnikinik, the Indian tobacco, was only smoked in a sacred manner. Peyote was also used in ceremony, but it was not ingested as it is today by members of the Native American Church. Jenny gave me a lively description of the Assiniboins' version of the peyote ceremony: The elders would sit in a circle on the ground while the medicine man would light a fire in the center. Accompanied by background chanting and drumming, the medicine man would throw the peyote on the fire. As the elders inhaled the developing smoke, they would become clairvoyant and clairaudient and would enter states of bliss.

Jenny mentioned tree burials during the winter when the ground was frozen solid, and also the Assiniboins' reverence for the gray geese. These migratory birds, whose eerie cry can be heard over Saskatchewan in early autumn and again at the onset of spring, were part of the Assiniboins' ancestor cult. They were believed to be ancestor spirits who were sending their relatives messages from the skies. I tried to verify this belief with a friend, who is a well-known and widely traveled American Indian psychotherapist and scholar. He told me that the

Assiniboin still revere the gray geese today, but they no longer know why. This disconnect must have been due to Christian interference with the native religion. Since the Jesuits condemned any ancestor cult, particularly in animal form, only the *reverence* for the gray geese survived, while the meaning of it was forgotten. However, as my past life reading shows, it did not get lost altogether; it survived in the ethnic unconscious of those who were incarnated as Indians when this belief was still intact. Christian interference also destroyed the North American tribe's widespread belief in reincarnation. Jenny's assertion that the Assiniboin held this belief has since been verified by anthropological research. According to a comprehensive study published by the Toronto University Press in 1994, most of the North American tribes, including the Assiniboin, believed in reincarnation in pre-Columbian times. Today, only individual tribal members still hold this belief.

Jenny called my Assiniboin life a very happy one. I have no reason to doubt that. The best way to connect with the general feeling of a past life is by visiting the place where it was lived. If there was trauma involved, the *spiritus loci*—the genius of the place—will bring it to the surface. In 1990, I drove through Saskatchewan on my way back from British Columbia, where I had built a Medicine Wheel for the Reiki community on Red Mountain. As I looked down from the highway on the forested banks of the "great angry water," I felt nothing but inner peace.

The unproblematic nature of this life might explain why I have never dreamed about it. This does not mean, however, that Somna is not around. In the summer of the year 2000, I was invited by Indian friends to support them at the Sun Dance on the Pine Ridge Reservation. The moment I stepped off the plane, I walked into a cloud of sweet grass scent, the source of which I could not detect. During the night a voice said to me in a dream:

The Spirit of the Sun Dance is welcoming you, though your Indian friends don't believe it.

They didn't believe it, even after I told them the dream, because for most Indians past lives and dreams are not a living reality anymore. Yet occasionally, a medicine person will sense this past life figure in me, as a jeweler in Taos Pueblo did a few years ago.

After crossing the creek that runs through the plaza, I entered a small jewelry shop; I was wearing a T-shirt with a Dream Catcher print on it. A middle-aged Indian woman was standing behind the counter, with a smile on her gentle face. It was not a businesslike smile, but a very personal one—a rare sight in Taos Pueblo. Then, instead of inviting me to look at her jewelry, she said, "The Medicine Wheel suits you well." Thinking she meant the Dream Catcher on my shirt, I thanked her and added in my irritating, know-better German way, "But this is not a Medicine Wheel. This is a Dream Catcher." "I know," she replied patiently, and not giving up on her smile, she surprisingly added, "I am a medicine woman."

SIR ALBERT ABDULLAH DAVID SASSOON: BANKER AND PHILANTHROPIST

Somna could not have lived beyond his mid-thirties, because he was born again in 1818 in a very different part of the world—the Middle East. Jenny gave his name as Sir Albert Abdullah David. No one would have suspected that, in this long-winded East-West name combination, the actual *family* name was missing, but so it was. Twenty years after the reading, one of my clients combed through London archives in search of this Jewish banker and eventually found him under the family name Sassoon. A detailed account of this young man's detective work and what we uncovered in the course of his therapy will take up the last two chapters of this book; but for now I will stay with Jenny's reading. She described Abdullah, later Sir Albert, as a man of international repute—a banker, a philanthropist, and a Jew. Judging from the dates she gave me, this was my last male incarnation. Abdullah, as I like to call him, was born in 1818 in Baghdad and died in 1896 in

England. The month of his birth is not on record, but Jenny said he was born in August.

Abdullah was the eldest son of a family of wealthy Jewish merchants who had to flee Iraq for religious reasons. After a brief exile in Persia, the family immigrated to India and opened a banking house in Bombay. Jenny said that Abdullah's father had been a great banker and philanthropist who had given to the needy, irrespective of race, creed, or caste. When Abdullah later became the head of the family, he followed in his father's footsteps. Jenny described Abdullah as serious and reflective. Even as a small boy, he had liked to help others, and when he became the owner of the bank, he did much more for the poor than just tithing. Eventually, in recognition of his beneficence, he was knighted by Queen Victoria and awarded honorary British citizenship. This had been his heart's desire, Jenny said, and he spent the rest of his life in England.

It is fascinating to see how Gwinnett's mind-set had been transformed by the American Indian incarnation. After that lifetime, all of my male soul ancestors' racial prejudices were gone. Also, thanks to the superior business training he received from a stalwart father, Abdullah became a responsible businessman. Biographical research later revealed that he was still a lavish spender, but his family wealth and business skills more than compensated for that. Jenny did not explain why Abdullah had moved from East to West—from Bombay to London— later in life. I subsequently speculated about this, as I tried to make sense of this incarnation. I pictured Abdullah as a somewhat unrealistic humanitarian who gave away more than he had. Since this is one of my own character flaws, it was easy for me to project this onto him. I was almost certain that the bank had gone under. I had even remembered the name of the bank—Bank of Bombay—before my first visit to India. Both these hunches were later validated.

On the other hand, my conclusion that the folding of the bank had been Abdullah's financial ruin turned out to be very far from the truth. Projecting Gwinnett's character flaws on Abdullah, I had wrongly assumed that the banker, too, had been on the run from his creditors. I had pictured Abdullah as a senior citizen, aging alone in a foreign country and spending his days on a bench in Hyde Park, feeding the ducks. My Hyde Park fantasy had actually an element of truth in it, because he did live in that fancy part of town, but—as I later discovered—he had more important things to do than feed the ducks.

What generated all these fantasies was my inability to properly relate to Abdullah. Of all my past life personalities, he felt the most alien to me. I could not imagine ever having been him, and certainly not as recently as the end of the past century, when my grandmother was in her prime. Although I was proud of his philanthropy, I disliked his preoccupation with money. I am a math illiterate myself. Since first grade, when I was shamed by a teacher in front of the class for not being able to add and subtract fast enough, I have been dyslexic with numbers. Paperwork drives me crazy; I have been known to toss valuable documents into the garbage when I have had to deal with too much of it at once.

The only characteristics I seemed to have in common with Abdullah were my aversion to penny-pinching, my seriousness, and my penchant for being reflective. But where, I wondered, had his other skills and abilities gone? Were they, perhaps, dormant in some dark corner of my unconscious, waiting to be reawakened like Sleeping Beauty? Or had my soul, seeing that these abilities had already been fully developed, decided to send the life force into other, still underdeveloped parts of myself? Was the soul perhaps like a tree that drops its ripened fruit in the autumn to free up the life force for the growth of new branches? Or was this just another manifestation of the play of opposites between lifetimes? I still wonder about that; however, my inability to relate to Abdullah was completely reversed when I got to know him better later on.

4

INTEGRATION

An Internal Process with Practical Consequences

Join the male and the female and you will find what is sought.

MARIA THE PROPHETESS

THE NIGHT AFTER THE READING

Before I left Jenny's house in the evening of that memorable day in November 1980, she told me to work on my past lives for a year. She said that after I had integrated them, she might be able to give me more. But more past lives did not bear thinking about at that very moment, for I felt disorientated enough as I stepped out into the street. Hoping that a walk through the crisp autumn air might help me find my way back into the present, I passed up the tram and walked home. But when the walk was over and my apartment door had closed behind me, I panicked. All of a sudden, spending the night alone felt intolerable. So I called Katja and asked her to come over. She and I had been neighbors before I had moved to a less expensive part of town. In my past life as Eskimo shaman, she had been my constant companion, and we were still connected through our old psychic pathways.

When Katja arrived by taxi half an hour later, we skipped the usual small talk and came straight to the point. She seated herself on the oriental leather cushion across from me, and I proceeded to give her my past life report. She listened attentively until I got to the part having to do with the Tower of London. Then, without a warning, she slipped off the leather cushion and fainted. When, a moment later, she regained consciousness, I heard her whisper, "The torches, the torches . . ." I then remembered them, too, but how could Katja have known about them? I thought she must have been tapping in to my unconscious, as she had done often before. Therefore, instead of exploring this any further, I said it was time to go to bed. It was actually long past bedtime, but once the lights were out I found myself tossing and turning. Fears of what I might dream kept me awake. What I was particularly afraid of were memories of the Tower of London. To keep them from invading my sleep, I programmed my unconscious to wake me up as soon as they surfaced. This made me feel safe enough to finally be able to fall asleep.

During the first REM phase, I watched a playback of a series of past life events. What I experienced can only be compared to the panoramic life-review of the dying. The pictures swept past me at such a pace that it was impossible for me to retain them. Only one image stayed with me: the marble statue of a man standing in a public place. Was this ancient Rome? Was this Scaevola, the lawmaker? A split second later, I heard a bloodcurdling scream rise up from a place underground. This was what I had feared: this came from the Tower of London. Fortunately, before the sound could be followed by images, I found myself sitting upright in bed; the self-suggestion had worked. I stayed in the upright position until, overcome by fatigue, I fell into a deep, dreamless sleep.

I awoke the next morning with the clear image of a very peaceful scene before my inner eye. It was the nightscape of Lake Zurich, with the water's surface as smooth as a mirror and the dark banks speckled with twinkling lights. I thought this must be a symbol of the dark matter of my soul, illuminated by thousands of sparks of consciousness kindled in the course of all my lifetimes. I was enjoying this peaceful scene, still half asleep, when I heard muffled sounds coming from the other side of the bed; Katja was crying. "Katja," I asked, suddenly wide-awake, "what is the matter?"

As it turned out, Katja had dreamed about the Tower of London. The terrifying images, which I had managed to suppress, had come to her instead. But these were not my images—they were her own. In her dream, we had been locked up in the tower together. She described at great length how we had languished in a dungeon on the bottom of the tower while a rat had built its nest on the rafters of the low ceiling above us. We had been unable to tell day from night in this eternal, pitch-black darkness—except for those occasions when the light from the guards' torches had penetrated the blackness around us. This usually meant that they had come to drag us out and rape us in a dark, dank corner. During one of these brutal assaults, Katja had killed a particularly sadistic guard. As a punishment for her crime, the other guards had beheaded her. Although this had been a horrible death, it had been merciful compared with mine, which was still waiting for me in the rafters of the dungeon.

Since Katja had died before me, she had no personal memories of how my life had ended. She clearly remembered, however, the good times before our incarceration. She was able to describe in great detail the expensive mahogany furniture and the red velvet fabrics in my luxury apartment—the place where I had lavishly entertained the British aristocracy. I seem to have been very popular with my noble customers, who had showered me with expensive gifts. Katja and I had been best friends at the time when my lover had stolen all my savings. Since she was my confidante, he had considered it prudent to have her put away as well. That's how we ended up in the tower together.

When Katja had finished her tale, we were both crying. We were holding and consoling each other, as we had often done in the sixteenth century in moments of despair. While this four-hundred-year-old wave of emotions swept over us, we lost all sense of time and place. We even lost our identities. When we were finally ready to return to the present, we had spent almost twenty-four hours in dreamtime together.

TRAUMA HEALING

This was the grand opening of the second part of my journey, where I dealt with the trauma and integrated the past life material that Jenny had given me. Although I was ready for this work, I did not have a clue how to go about it. Fortunately, my unconscious did. It first set a trauma-healing process into motion and later arranged the integration itself. I only had to balance things out. I had to make room for my past life selves, while keeping them from taking me over.

Past life integration always begins with trauma work. Since trauma leaves energy blockages behind, no healing can occur until the trauma is resolved. "Trauma is a straightjacket that binds the mind and body in frozen fear, but it is also a portal that can lead us to awakening and freedom."[1] This powerful statement made by the trauma expert Peter Levine applies equally well to past life trauma.

The prostitute's gruesome ending followed me around. I could feel the woman's terror all day long, although I was never quite identified with her. In the raw emotional state I was in, I often burst into tears at socially awkward moments. To protect me, the self-regulating function of the psyche started a dream-trauma-healing process. Although in the course of it, I had to face all those images that I had avoided before; the exposure to them was regulated according to how much I could take at any given time. It began with a powerful, multilevel dream that seemed to filter down from higher dimensions.

I am turning the pages of a thick photo album, admiring the photographer's work. The picture of a wooded, cone-shaped mountain, taken from above, attracts my attention before I realize that it is only one in a series of photographs that show a developing rainbow aura around a mountain-top. In the first picture, the mountain is surrounded by a single, rainbow-colored circle. In the following picture, another such circle is woven into the first one. In subsequent photographs, more and more rainbow circles are interwoven with each other to form a multicolored wreath.

Next, Robert and I are on a hike. We stop to look at a different page of the same photo album. I point out the picture of a dark fortress to him, which is taken again from above. "Is this a fort?" I ask Robert. He nods, with a somber expression on his face. I must have held the album close to the ground, because suddenly a rat leaps onto the open page. When it lands on its back, with its legs up in the air, I think at first that it is dead. But then I see it moving. As soon as Robert sees the rat, he puts his arm around my shoulder and leads me away from the photo album, which now lies open on the ground. Then he helps me up a slope to a plateau from where we can safely watch what happens next.

We see a young woman rise from the dying rat on the photo album. Her face is beautiful, but dark and brooding; she is dressed in the long, flowing, earth-tone robes of long-ago fashions. At first I am scared of her, but she reassures me with a friendly nod that I have nothing to fear. Then she turns her back on us and begins walking in the opposite direction. I feel relieved, because this means that she will not be our road companion from now on. After this, Robert and I climb over a low wall, which has magically appeared for our protection, scramble down the slope, and continue on our way.

The photo album, as a storage place for images of the past, often symbolizes the past life memory bank. But this dream differs from other past life dreams in so far as two parallel past life related processes are taking place at the same time—one on the level of the divine, the other on the human level. In some mythological traditions, the gods dwell on the mountaintop. In others, the mountaintop is the place where man meets God. Thus Moses had to climb up to the top of Mount Sinai to receive the Ten Commandments from Yahweh. In ancient Rome, the augurs had to pitch their tents on a hilltop to divine Jupiter's intentions. And until this day, the American Indian has to go to a lonely spot in the mountains for his vision quest. In the Old Testament, the rainbow was a peace offering from Yahweh. It was his pledge, at the end of the deluge, never to destroy his people again. In my dream, the rainbow symbol was intertwined with the symbolism of the circle and the wreath. While the circle signifies wholeness, the wreath—which is also a circle of a kind—represents crowning and victory. This combination of symbols was very auspicious. To me, each rainbow circle represented one integrated lifetime. Since the rainbow circles were woven into a wreath, I saw this as a promise that the integration work I had started would be divinely protected and eventually crowned with success.

The blessings from above gave me the strength to face the fortress in the next picture. I seemed to have trouble recognizing it, because I asked Robert to identify it for me. "Is this a fort (d)?" I inquired. What "fort" (d) means, depends on its spelling and pronunciation. With a hard dental consonant *t* it designates a fortress; with a soft dental consonant *d* it means a crossover place in the river. In real life, tower and ford are closely connected, because the tower is situated on the River Thames. In addition, the ford, as a crossover place, is a universal death symbol. This explains why, for this deranged woman, ford and fortress had become indistinguishable from each other. "Fort" had meant "ford" to her, and both had been associated with the rat. That's why the rodent had appeared so suddenly on the open page of the photo album.

However, this was the turning point where the trauma healing began and the past life story started to change: The rat was now close to death, while the prostitute reemerged unharmed from its body. Robert, the prostitute's pimp—who had been helpless to stop her from being thrown into the tower in the first place—now had the power to protect me. And most importantly—Robert and I both experienced a parting of ways with the prostitute. Until then, I had been completely unaware that I had been carrying this desperate, crazy woman around with me all my life.

I am sure that the rat had played a major role in this woman's psychotic hallucinations. The rat is synonymous with a treacherous man, and she was sharing her dungeon with many of them. In her psychotic fantasies, the sinister rat and her sinister lover, who had "ratted out" on her, had most likely merged into one. Residues of this identification can still be found in my dreams today, where male predators have been consistently symbolized by rats.

While the first dream in this series had shown me the rat only from a distance, the next dream led me into a direct confrontation with it. However, previous to this confrontation, and most likely for my protection, I had been introduced to the Atlantean physician in myself, who can be seen as a representation of the healer archetype.

I am in a spacious, primitive building, like a barn or shed with a dirt floor. An unknown woman who is a great authority on healing says to me, "You know all about healing, of course. After all, we practiced together in the oldest hospital of humanity." Then she prepares a tray with medicine for some patients. She fills a tall glass with a fluid that has the color of blood-orange juice. Before placing it on the tray, she pours half of its content on the dirt floor as an offering to the gods.

Next I take the tray out of her hands, stick a knife into the now half-empty glass, and carry it over to another building where three women are laid up together in a sickroom. One of the patients has her face bandaged up like a mummy. All three of them are in such a deeply dissociated state that they are unaware that I have entered the room. I quietly place the tray with the medicine and the knife on a bedside table and leave. I seem to rely on the patients to know what to do with the medicine.

Next I am lost in a vast underground vault. A rat suddenly drops from the low ceiling and attacks me. Although I am able to defend myself, it manages to sink its teeth into my right hand, causing a small, bleeding wound. After that, I manage to shake it off and escape from the

*underground vault. When the heavy iron door closes behind me, I know
that the rat will not be able to follow me outside.*

*Next I am eavesdropping on a formal dinner party, where people
are seated at a banquet table. Ingmar, my lover, is one of the guests. He
is accompanied by an ugly woman. While I am watching him and his
female companion, I feel reminded of my bite wound, which is in need of
attention. I leave the dinner party and go in search of the ladies' room.
When I find it, I hold my hand under cold running water until the
wound is cleaned out.*

The "great authority on healing" who made me remember my healing work in "the oldest hospital of humanity" was either my past life
self or an important teacher I had in Atlantis. The ritual spilling of the
medicine has parallels in other ancient traditions that are still being
practiced by ethnic societies today. The food offering of the Pueblo
Indians to the Kachinas before each meal is one such example. Another
is the ritualistic tradition that European farmers follow when they offer
the first fruits of their harvest to God. What motivates these offerings
is the notion that without his blessings, we are not able to benefit from
his gifts. In regard to healing, Jung always emphasized that it can only
be done *deo conscendente*—"with God's permission."

The blood-orange color of the medicine suggested some sort of
blood sacrifice. Blood is the very essence of life. There is an Arabic
saying, quoted by Cirlot, "Blood has flowed, the danger is past."[2] This
expresses the central idea of all sacrifice, that the offering appeases
the powers that be and wards off punishment. The knife is a symbol
of sacrifice, too, but in this context it might pertain more specifically
to Atlantean surgical practices. Jenny said that I practiced medicine
with "long forgotten methods" in Atlantis. According to Edgar Cayce,
Atlantean refugees helped establish so-called Temples of Sacrifice in
Egypt (presumably modeled after similar Atlantean institutions) where
surgical procedures were performed. One purpose of these procedures
was to prepare "individuals for definite services by removal of those

things that would cause one to become different-minded because of the relationships to the activities in a pre-existence or pre-period of materiality."[3] In modern psychological parlance, we would be talking about energy blockages caused by past life trauma.

Radical "surgery" was certainly needed if a soul wound such as mine was to be healed. The three women (in the sickroom) represented three personality fragments of the prostitute. When she had gone insane, her dissociation had probably progressed in two stages. Her personality would have split in Dr. Jekyll and Mr. Hyde fashion first. She would have remained in this state until the rats had attacked her. Then, in order to escape from the horror of being eaten alive, she would have dissociated completely by leaving her body. The woman with the bandaged face personified this final step of her dissociation process. Most likely, what her bandage was hiding was a horribly disfigured face. Residues of this terrible trauma are still present in my physical body; I have had lifelong problems with my throat, eyes, and teeth.

The next scene in the underground vault took the trauma-healing process one step further. Here, too, the original experience was being favorably altered. I was able to defend myself, contracted only a minor wound, and, most importantly, I could escape. The heavy iron door that kept the rat inside was a clear sign that I was developing adequate defenses. However, I was not out of the woods yet; the rat was not dead, and it was sure to attack me again, given the right circumstances.

The final dream episode connected the past life trauma to Ingmar. Although Ingmar had not been the one who had "ratted out on me" in the sixteenth century, he was, in my present lifetime, opening up this old soul wound again. The dream hinted that Ingmar's "ugly anima" might be to blame for that. But, according to this dream, I was getting stronger and was starting to take care of myself, in spite of it.

In the wake of the trauma-healing dream process, a self-defeating relationship pattern was breaking up. This pattern had been firmly in place since my childhood, when my parents, two strong personalities, had pushed me into the Cinderella role. Under their self-serving tutelage,

I had learned early on to accept the conditions of others without asking questions. Later, this attracted men into my life who took advantage of my compliance and had no regard for my personal needs. Since this dysfunction had started with my parents, it was not surprising that the next rat, the next male predator, to appear in my dream was my father. My eighty-year-old father, who had retired late from a highly successful government career, was trying to fill the vacuum in his life with my achievements. He phoned me every day from Germany, always expecting progress reports, but was never satisfied with my achievements. It was beginning to wear me out, and one day, in a fit of rebellion, I hung up on him—for the first time in my life. That night I dreamed:

I am struggling for a long time with a rat. Finally, exhausted and covered with wounds, I manage to kill it. This frees me up for my true partner.

This was the last time I dreamed about a rat. Apparently, the hold that male predators had over me was now broken. It was only natural to hope that the "true partner" would manifest as a real man in my life. This turned out to be an illusion, however. For me, the only "true partner" was within.

This dream series, as a whole, represented a step-by-step past life trauma resolution process. It followed the exact same pattern as other trauma-healing dream processes that have been researched and written about for some time. The fact that trauma can get healed through dreams was first observed by J. A. Hadfield, a British psychiatrist, who worked with shell-shock sufferers from World War II.[4] Some of these veterans went through an almost identical dream-healing process as the one that is described above. Those dream series always began with a replay of the original traumatic event, with the dreamer in a helpless position. Then, gradually, the dreams would improve. The situation would become less threatening, and the dreamer would find more effective means of coping with it. This would continue until, in the end, the dreamer would finally be in control of the situation. After this, the nightmares would stop.

The same self-healing process was observed many years later in the nightmares of combat veterans who had fought in the Vietnam War. Jungian analyst Harry Wilmer worked extensively with these veterans and studied thousands of their dreams.[5] Some of the veterans that Wilmer worked with experienced the same trauma transformation in the dream state as the survivors of World War II who had been treated by Hadfield. In cases where a dream trauma resolution occurred, the psychological condition of the veterans also improved. What remained largely unexplained in this research was why some people had healing dreams and recovered while others remained stuck in their nightmares.

AN UNAVOIDABLE SACRIFICE

I seemed to be one of the lucky ones, but the dream trauma-healing process was only the beginning of a much more demanding transformation process. To prevent a re-wounding, my relationship with men had to change. Ten years of analysis had made absolutely no difference to my propensity for attracting disastrous love affairs into my life. Perhaps this problem was so treatment resistant because the tragic life patterns of Maurice Scève and the London prostitute were interwoven in my unconscious.

My feelings for Ingmar were very conflicted at this point. Consciously I wanted to get closer to him, while my unconscious was determined to separate us. Today I fully understand why this separation was an inner necessity—it was time for me to forge a union between my polarized male and female sides. Yet a shared common ground between such opposites could not be found as long as I was stuck in a pattern of female victimization. Since my relationship with Ingmar was getting in the way of my reaching the next stage of my inner development, it needed to be removed. My unconscious tried to achieve this by giving me one nightmare after another.

The first dream in this series of warning dreams haunted me for months. At the time of the dream, a visually impaired man was in therapy with me. He was incredibly brilliant, highly educated, and he intimidated everyone with his fierce determination not to let his physical handicap stop him from living a full life. He had only one weakness: in addition to being physically blind, he was blinded by his feelings. This made it difficult for him, despite his penetrating intellect, to accurately assess the character of the significant women in his life. When I started dreaming about this client on a regular basis, I knew I was in trouble. The blind man was holding up a mirror to my own blindness in regard to Ingmar's shadow and the hopelessness of the overall situation.

I have been waiting all day for my blind client in my new home. He seems to have gotten lost. When he does not arrive by ten o'clock at night, I go looking for him in the streets; but I never find him.

Instead, I arrive at a chapel where the clock shows that it is still ten o'clock. Now, I remember that I am supposed to meet my friend N. from the Parapsychological Society at this time in this chapel. She has kindly offered to act as a mediator between an oracle named Laura and myself. I hand her a piece of paper where I have noted down two questions for her to present to the oracle:

1. Am I with the right partner?

2. Am I in the right profession?

In response, a woman's face appears in stone relief in three places of the chapel walls at once—each face with a slightly different expression. While I am drawing N.'s attention to the faces in the wall, the oracle booms out, "You have suffered more than is humanly possible. Don't ever do it again!" This is repeated three times before Laura's hollow voice, which seems to be coming from the crypt below, fades out in a hair-raising groan.

N., who tends to be critical of psychic readings, has no comments about the oracle, but she explains that Laura ignored my second question because I already know the answer to it.

The dream acknowledged that, after the recent trauma healing I had undergone in the dream state, I found myself in a different place (a new home). Unfortunately, this had not cured me of my emotional blindness, as the inclusion of my blind client in the dream shows. Since the tenth hour came up three times, it had to be an essential part of the dream message. The tenth hour has to be understood in connection with the symbolism of the eleventh hour. If the eleventh hour represents the last moment before time runs out at twelve o'clock, then the tenth hour signified that I was getting dangerously close to that last moment. In addition, since the oracle came from the "house of God," (the chapel) it carried extra weight.

Thanks to this dream, I finally knew the British prostitute's name—it was Laura. I was amazed at Laura's transformation after the trauma healing was complete. She seemed to have joined the underworld gods by turning into the triple figure of Hecate, the Greek goddess of pathways and crossroads traveled by night. Hecate, who was usually depicted carrying torches, was said to rise in triple form from masks placed at the junction of crossroads. The parallels between this myth, the torches in the Tower of London, and the triple masklike faces in my dream were striking; so was Laura-Hecate's connection with my "crossroads" situation.

Did I heed Laura's urgent warning? Yes, but only in the beginning. My diary speaks of several serious attempts to break up with Ingmar in the following months. But after a while, my determination wore thin, and I yielded once more to the pressures of inner and outer seduction. It took me yet another year on a roller coaster ride between hope and despair before I was able to free myself. What finally pushed me over the edge were several dreams predicting a fatal illness. I suspect that this is how the soul economizes its resources: if we do not follow the blueprint intended for a particular lifetime, it scraps the mold and starts over. When I sent off my final farewell letter to Ingmar, I knew that although I was hurting, Laura was rejoicing. For after years of procrastination, I had kept my initial commitment to her; I had salvaged her by saving myself.

Laura was the only one of my past life personalities who had to undergo this kind of trauma healing. Most likely, this was due to the fact that, despite many tragedies and shameful deaths, none of my other past life selves suffered a soul loss like Laura. Although the Cathar woman was burned at the stake, she went to her death spiritually united with her sisters and brothers in faith. And although Maurice Scève was stoned and subsequently hanged, this only happened to him at the end of an honored and privileged life. From my present perspective, I can see very clearly how profoundly Laura affected my female bloodline. Although she did nothing wrong herself, the soul damage she had suffered overshadowed all my subsequent female incarnations. My male bloodline, on the other hand, did not seem to be outwardly affected by this. The men continued to lead productive and prominent lives as if nothing was wrong on their feminine side. However, the anima is inward; she represents a man's emotional side. So there is no way of telling to what degree Laura's soul wound might have impaired these men's capacity to love and to feel.

INTEGRATION

After the trauma had healed and my behavior pattern had been adjusted, the integration of my male side moved to the forefront in my dreams. Since there is no basic difference between the integration of past life material and other unconscious material, I was well prepared for this task by my Jungian training. The word "integrate" comes from Latin *integrare,* meaning "to restore, to reunite." According to the *Oxford English Dictionary,* "to integrate" means "to complete by addition of parts." The German *Duden* offers what is, psychologically, an even more pertinent definition by emphasizing the assimilation of these parts into a greater whole. In order to properly integrate our past lives, we have to assign them a functional place in our wholeness.

While I was trying to accommodate my newly emerging male bloodline by making changes to my life, Scève, as representative of my soul ancestry, directed the integration process from within. He and Laura were opposites in every possible way. In Jungian terms, they were each other's shadow. Yet as reincarnational neighbors, they must have been connected in some way. This was also suggested by a truly remarkable duplicity of names: In actual fact, the real-life Scève had laid the foundation for his fame by discovering the tomb of Laura, Petrarch's beloved, in Avignon. Some names refer to each other across lifetimes. Thus Mucius Scaevola became Maurice Scève, elements of Nell Gwynn's name showed up in Button Gwinnett's name, and Scève's discovery of Laura's tomb turned into the living entombment of another woman named Laura (Scève in his next incarnation). Are these coincidences, or the fingerprints of the evolving soul?

On my personal journey, Scève spurred me on, while Laura held me back. Whenever important decisions had to be made, Scève appeared to me as a soul guide and personal advisor. At other times, he was the legal representative of my soul ancestry. He was, after all, also a lawyer, but first and foremost he was a poet. Once, when I was not sure if I should allow a friendship with someone to turn into a love affair, Scève showed up in a dream and advised me to sit "between Plato and Petrarch." At first I was puzzled by his pronouncement, until I realized that this was where he had sat himself most of his life, between two platonic role models—one philosophical, the other emotional.

The last time I dreamed about Scève, he represented me at an otherworldly court, which evaluated the results of my past life integration process. However, this life-changing inner event had been preceded by the following dream where both my courage and strength had been tested:

I am to cross a narrow footbridge that spans a deep ravine. I know that whoever reaches the other side has cleared his karma and integrated all his lifetimes.

I am fearful, although I see others cross over unharmed. From the other side, they beckon me to follow them. Then, I begin to cross over myself. As soon as I set foot on the bridge, it turns into a footpath, which is imbedded in a strong holding structure. This makes the crossing safer than expected.

When I reach the other side, I have to climb a steep flight of stairs. A young girl, who had been walking two steps ahead of me, suddenly turns around and throws herself at me. By clinging to my skirt, she tries to keep me from climbing farther. The only way I can get rid of her is by casting her ruthlessly aside. Having freed myself from her, I reach the top of the stairs.

Looking behind and underneath me, I see that the bridge has disappeared. This means that there is no turning back. I can only move forward now. What lies ahead of me is a high plateau with wide horizons, and I know that this is the way to freedom.

In order to reach a place of freedom within myself, I had to pass three different tests, like the hero in fairy tales. The first one was a test of faith. By following the example of others, I was able to trust enough to risk the dangerous crossing, and once I trusted, the crossing became much easier than I thought. The second test examined my determination to reach a higher level of consciousness. This was symbolized by the climbing of the stairs. The staircase itself was in good repair; no steps were missing. This meant that the pathways to higher consciousness had been strengthened by years of inner work. The last test tried my ability to act ruthlessly toward regressive tendencies in myself, represented by the clinging young girl. In Jungian psychology, this aspect of the child archetype is known as the "infantile shadow." It is a dark side of the child archetype, which is rarely talked about in contemporary psychology, although it impedes everyone's personal growth and is presently on a collective rampage, especially in the United States. It avoids responsibility, blames others for its own mistakes, and wants to stay dependent on others forever. The late Marie-Louise von Franz, the world's foremost authority on fairy tales and Jung's personal assistant for many years, drew attention to this dangerous aspect of the child archetype years ago. The only effective treatment she knew for this pesky infantile shadow child was exactly what I had done in my dream—to ruthlessly cast it aside.

Freedom means different things to different people at different stages of their lives. What it meant to me at that time was to be free of my projections on men. It meant that I no longer had to feel that something was missing in me, which only a man could provide. At this important turning point of my life, Maurice Scève helped me over the last hurdle.

I am resting on a couch on the ground floor of a multistoried house. At the sound of a bell, I hear someone come down the stairs in a hurry. When the person appears in my field of vision, I recognize him as a man I know very well. It is a slightly built, dark-haired, formally dressed man. Without paying much attention to me, he rushes out the front door. I know he will represent me at a high-level court that has gathered for the purpose of evaluating the progress of my past life integration process.

In anxious anticipation of the verdict, I follow him into the courtyard that separates my house from the courthouse. Here I wait for some time while the court is deliberating. Finally, a deep, resonant male voice pronounces the verdict, in poetic form. It is an adaptation of a famous two-liner, taken from the first part of Goethe's Faust. The original two-liner reads:

> *Was du ererbt von deinen Vaetern hast,*
> *Erwirb es, um es zu besitzen.*[6]
> *(Your forefathers' legacy*
> *must be earned to be owned.)*

This had been changed to:

Was du ererbt von deinen Vaetern hast,
hast du erworben.
(Your forefathers' legacy
you have earned.)

This meant that the integration of my male soul ancestors' legacy was now complete. I had become a whole human being.

I recognized the voice that pronounced the verdict as the same voice that had previously informed me that I am in my fourth incarnation (as described in chapter 1). There was clearly a beginning and an end to this process that had been shaped and formed by a creative higher mind into a cohesive, meaningful story. My personal contribution to the integration process had been fairly minor. Half of the time I had to be dragged along like a stubborn mule bent on grazing on the edge of a ravine. Scève had been the mediator between this higher intelligence and my blind ego. And with God's grace, which had been present from the very beginning as a rainbow wreath over the mountaintop, I had made it.

Dream Postscript

Jenny had given me twenty lives, and in the course of two decades I had remembered six additional ones. This added up to twenty-six incarnations. A dream I had in Sedona five years ago therefore came as a total surprise. Sedona, a charming little town in northern Arizona, is known for its vortices (earth energy centers), which are said to enhance people's psychic abilities. For this reason, Sedona has become the favorite haunt of meditators and would-be psychics, just like Glastonbury in England. What I had not known before this visit was that Sedona has something else in common with Glastonbury. It is supposed to have a place, somewhere in the mountains, where the veil between the worlds is particularly thin. I learned this from some locals the day after I had dreamed about this very place.

I am standing in front of a wide, wrought-iron gate, somewhere in the hills of Sedona. The gate is overhung by the branches of large, green shade trees on my side of the fence. Although the gate is locked, I am able to see through its vertical bars into the otherworld. It looks more desertlike over there than on my side of the fence, but I am less interested in that place itself than in the information I am receiving from there. This information is very specific: I have integrated forty-seven lives.

The dream woke me up in the middle of the night so that I would remember it in the morning. I found this information very perplexing but knew that it was meant to be shared in this book. According to this information, I had integrated twenty-one more lives than I had been aware of. But how could that be? This question kept me awake for hours. The explanation I eventually found was that the integration process might continue on unconscious levels once a "critical mass" of information has been consciously absorbed. The bloodlines might serve as conductors in this integration process. In other words, if enough lifetimes of the same bloodline have been consciously integrated, the rest of the lives of the same bloodline are automatically integrated on unconscious levels. For instance, if I confronted all the problems of my main bloodline that were involved with the issue of justice, by integrating the lives of Scaevola, Scève, and Laura, I might not have to go into the Lord Chancellor's life and other lives containing a similar theme. The eleventh hexagram of the I Ching (Peace) has a perfect image for such interconnectedness of past life themes in the unconscious: ". . . in pulling up ribbon grass one always pulls up a bunch of it, because the stalks are connected by their roots."[7]

5

WITCH MOTHER
AND EMPEROR FATHER
Past Life Roots of Parental Abuse

You cannot separate the just from the unjust and the good
   from the wicked,
For they stand together before the face of the sun as the
   black thread
and the white are woven together.
And when the black thread breaks, the weaver shall look
   into the whole cloth,
and he shall examine the loom also.

KAHLIL GIBRAN

A NEGLECTED ONLY CHILD

Jenny's readings had been a powerful stimulant for my past life recall, which began before I met her and is still ongoing. After my dream about the past life container, a continuation of this process was to be expected. But not until recently have I been able to face my karmic history with my parents. It could have happened years ago, had I not gone into denial each time my unconscious had made an attempt to throw some light on the family karma. Twenty years after my parents' deaths, this book has finally forced me to confront this aspect of our relationship.

I was born into an upper-middle-class family in Germany before World War II. I was an only child. My birth had been life-threatening to my mother and me, because her pelvis had been too narrow for my head. And when a professor of medicine at the university clinic in Dortmund had extracted me at the last moment with forceps from her womb, it had almost torn her apart, while I had almost been strangled by my umbilical cord. It was nothing short of a miracle that we both survived this ordeal, which in retrospect appears to have been a symbolical reenactment of a mutually destructive past life pattern.

My father was a civil servant, a university-trained engineer, and a prolific inventor. He was so honorable that one Christmas in postwar times when we had no food to put on the table, he turned down a Christmas goose, which had been offered to him as a bribe. My mother was the very opposite. After the war, she kept us fed by wheeling and dealing on the black market. She was the classic femme fatale: intelligent, provocative, beautiful, sexy, and stylish. I cannot count the times she told me that in medieval times she would have been burned as a witch. This gave me nightmares of witches, from early childhood on. Her relationship with my father resembled the humiliating enmeshment between Marlene Dietrich and the professor in the film *The Blue Angel*. My mother had constant extramarital affairs. My father was aware of this on some level but chose to ignore it on another. They were in disagreement over many things, including the politics of the Third Reich, but in collusion when it came to depriving me of basic life necessities like underwear and clothing.

Meanwhile, my mother was siphoning off all the housekeeping money into her luxury wardrobe. I learned never to ask for anything, express wishes, or make demands, because if I did, I was ridiculed and shamed. Although my father stood up for fairness at his workplace and was an active member in the labor union, he was incapable of showing fairness to his own daughter. At the age of thirty-three, I fell ill with colitis. My parents experienced this as a personal insult and severed their connection with me until I recovered on my own. Considering that I was their only child, a loyal daughter, and a good student, the treatment I received at their hands was incomprehensible. On the other hand, it did make sense in the context of my downtrodden female past life history. As a woman, I had been burned at the stake, driven into the catacombs, raped and abducted, wrongly accused of being a witch, and thrown into a rat-infested dungeon to rot.

A CASE OF KARMIC REVENGE

I was therefore going to end the chapter "Women on the Fringe" on a note of self-pity when a dream reminded me of a past life that I had swept under the carpet more than a decade ago. I had first accessed this life in a hypnotic regression on Joy Hinson-Ryder's massage table. The late Hinson-Ryder was a brilliant past life therapist and a teacher of Chris Griscom, who later did past life regressions with Shirley MacLaine. Hinson-Ryder very effectively combined past life regression with deep tissue massage, highly dramatic opera music, and ritual (she exorcized past life entities on a regular basis). I trained with her for three months, and although she taught me a lot, I found her technique too physical for me. After this experience, it became very clear to me that my access to past lives as well as my therapeutic work with past lives is through the "royal road" of dreams.

What I had experienced in my regression had been so similar to the Red Dog story in Lynn Andrews's book *Medicine Woman*[1] that I had instantly discarded it as a case of kryptomnesia—as an unconscious memory of something I had read. I had even considered the possibility that, at the time, I had made the story up for the benefit of Hinson-Ryder who, I knew, loved exotic stories. But when my recent dream brought up this past life again, so many years later, I knew I had to take it seriously.

It was particularly significant that this reminder came at a time when I was about to make a sweeping statement about the victimization of my female bloodline and the historical disfranchisement of women (of which my bloodline seemed to be an example) in the pages of this book. Instead of indulging me, however, the dream pointed a finger at me and dropped the responsibility for all my misfortunes back into my lap. The following text is based on my notes, taken after the past life regression:

The first thing I see, as I drift into a semitrance, is the grinning face of a jaguar. I am in South America. I am a Mayan curandera, *a healer, but also a* bruja, *a sorceress. I cure the sick with herbal concoctions. I have also been taught by my teacher, an older bruja, how to "skinwalk," or shape-shift into an animal.*

When my apprenticeship with her is over and I have become a healer in my own right, she turns on me. She sees me as competition and regrets having shared her knowledge with me. So she tries to take back what she had given. She steals the healing crystals that are buried under my rosemary bush and undermines me in every way she can. Her ultimate triumph is to steal away my lover. With her sorcery, she sucks his soul out of his body and turns him into a mindless sex slave. I become so enraged by this that I use what she has taught me against her; I shape-shift into a jaguar and tear her to pieces.

It spoke volumes that, at the end of the past life regression, I had felt no remorse. On the contrary, I was grinning like the jaguar had been at the beginning of the session. Still identified with the bruja as I was emerging from the hypnotic state, I had self-righteously felt that the bitch had only gotten what she deserved. But unfortunately, with this one deeply satisfying act of revenge, I had burdened my female bloodline with negative karma, which had to be paid off in many lifetimes. This karma was still unresolved when I was born—this time as the daughter of my old enemy as it turned out. For when Joy Hinson-Ryder had asked me after the session who the teacher reminded me of, I had blurted out, without thinking, "My mother."

This instant identification had been due to the fact that my relationship with my mother had gone through the same reversal (as in the past life) when I had entered my teens. Rivalries are common between narcissistic mothers and their daughters, as every psychotherapist knows. As soon as the daughter becomes viable as a woman, the mother sees her as competition and begins to undercut her in subtle ways. In my case, the undercutting had been more blatant than subtle, although, for the longest time, I had been oblivious to that. I had taken it simply for granted that I had no underwear as a child unless my grandmother provided it and that in my student years I had to rely entirely on hand-me-downs from my mother's wardrobe. Unconsciously, I had drawn the conclusion that she was deserving and I was not. While my mother had blamed this on my father's stinginess, he had cynically argued that he could not afford to clothe both his expensive wife and me. In reality, of course, they had been in collusion together.

However, my love for my mother had been so strong that every potential eye-opener had sent me into denial. This had continued until, in my early twenties, I had been confronted with the fact that she had taken some of my boyfriends to bed. She had boasted about these conquests to my then fiancé, who had promptly relayed the information to me. To confide this to someone so close to me had seemed like the ultimate provocation, and I almost had no choice but to get my father involved. Since my mother was not working, her marriage was the only security she had, and to try and undermine that would have been the perfect revenge. But to my own surprise, I did nothing. I did not even confront my mother with her betrayal. I simply cut my losses and moved on.

For many years to come, I would attribute my lack of action to a combination of cowardice and compassion. To a certain extent, this might also have been true. But the real reason was only known on my soul level at the time: I had resisted the temptation to fall into the trap that my mother had unconsciously set for both of us. Had I avenged myself as before, my share of the karma would have been doubled. At the same time, a window of opportunity to reach the next stage in my soul development would have closed for this lifetime, and perhaps for many lifetimes to come.

THE ENEMY'S JANUS FACE

Twenty years after my mother's death, I have finally forgiven her. True forgiveness cannot be therapeutically programmed or speeded up, as I learned in my work as a therapist. It requires an existential leap, which can only be taken when our hearts and minds are ready. I took this leap when I realized that our enemies are Janus-faced: one face is hostile, the other kind. These "petty tyrants," as Castaneda calls them, can bring out the best or the worst in us. Whether it will be our best or our worst is entirely up to us. The following dream, which drew attention once more to my past life as a bruja, deepened my understanding of this duality as well as of my karmic responsibility for the injustice I had suffered:

I share a bedroom with my mother. Our beds are positioned on opposite sides of the room, so we face each other lying down. My mother set the alarm early, but I turned it off, wanting to sleep late. When I finally wake up, a strange woman is in my mother's bed. I get up and walk over to her. I feel irresistibly drawn to a piece of paper that is lying next to the alarm clock, on the stranger's bedside table. As I come closer, I see that it is a list of all my female incarnations, including names and dates. The list is in my own handwriting. When I pick it up to look at it more closely the woman snatches it out of my hand and turns it over. "But you must look at the other side," she says reproachfully. The other side is blank, except for a drawing of a jaguar's grinning face.

Next, I am with the same woman in my back garden. I climb up a ladder into my old pear tree while the woman is looking on. In real life, this pear tree has disappointed me year after year by bearing only worm-eaten fruit. When I reach the top of the ladder, I let go of my footing and try to pull myself up into the branches. But I soon realize that I have gone too far and that I have to come down again. As I begin the descent, the woman gives me instructions. "When you get to the bottom end of the ladder," she says, "you will come under attack, but do not lose your sense of direction. Remember your point of gravity."

Having awoken from this dream, I dozed off again for a moment. When I awoke the second time, I remembered a detail I had previously forgotten: a cover sheet had been attached to the list with a handwritten note on it, which said that the karmic list had been "a task."

At the beginning of the dream, my mother and I were sharing a bedroom. Here the bedroom—in other contexts, a place of resting and dreaming—had clearly sexual connotations. For not only in the bruja life but also in my present life had I shared lovers with my mother, against my will. She had tried to alert me to this early on (the alarm), but I had preferred to remain unconscious of it. When I had finally woken up—in the dream as in real life—my mother had felt like a stranger to me. But the stranger in my dream, unlike the one in real life, was a wise woman who knew that behind my difficult female incarnations had been the black magic killing of the older bruja. While the stranger confronted me with this crime, the cover sheet on the karmic list reminded me of the fact that my suffering had been for a reason: I had to learn to turn the other cheek. This was the only way the black magic murder could be atoned for.

The climbing of the ladder was a metaphor for how I had gradually elevated myself to a position of hubris as a bruja. The pear tree is a feminine symbol because of its uterus-shaped fruit. The fact that I associated this tree with the one in my garden, which had only born rotten fruit, showed that my lives as a woman had also been rotten. But the dream left no doubt whose fault that was. My hubris had simply been followed by an *enantiodromia*—by a swing of the pendulum in the opposite direction, in accordance with spiritual laws. Fortunately, the stranger had taught me to survive on the lower rungs of the ladder. She knew from experience that helplessness calls in the predators. They "smell" it and go for the vitals. Our only protection in such a vulnerable position is to remain centered, no matter what happens to us.

Subsequently, I spent many lifetimes on the lower rungs of the ladder and—as the stranger predicted—I was brutally attacked. At least once, in my life as Laura, I lost everything: my human dignity, my freedom, my mind, and even part of my soul. Yet in subsequent incarnations I was able to recover it all. Presently, I am ready to step off the ladder altogether. I am no longer interested in feminine power, nor in its opposite: feminine powerlessness. Something calls me away from these opposites and hierarchical structures symbolized by the ladder to the shared common ground of the androgynous soul.

INCESTUOUS PAST LIFE BLEED-THROUGH

While the bruja legacy rendered a normal mother-daughter relationship virtually impossible for my mother and me, another past life interfered with my relationship with my father. That interference was of a different nature, however. Instead of being due to negative karma, it had been caused by a past life bleed-through. In a past life bleed-through, our ego functions are temporarily taken over by a past life personality. We unconsciously confuse past and present and our behavior becomes maladjusted to the present reality. In my father's case, it led to an isolated incident of sexual abuse of his only child.

I was only two-and-a-half years old at the time and was still functioning mostly on a preverbal level. It must have happened during the week when my mother was in hospital to have her tubes tied and my father was alone with me in the apartment. When she returned, I was supposed to have spoken my first coherent sentence, which was, "Mummy, never go to hospital again. Always stay with Nuti." (Nuti was my baby name.) In her absence, I had developed a fear of umbrellas (the stick that inflates) and sleep problems. Whatever had happened between my father and me in my mother's absence put us both into shock and led to a mutual withdrawal. Although the incident itself was forgotten (at least by me), its rippling effect lasted a lifetime. I reacted by feeling physically repulsed by my father, whereas he refused to hold me or let me ride on his shoulders, as fathers normally do. In fact, he more or less ignored me until I reached school age, when he began to show some interest in my academic performance. During the war, my mother and I were separated from him for several years, which put even more emotional distance between us. By the time the war was over and we were reunited as a family, I was in my early teens. At this age, which is so crucial for the development of a healthy female sense of self, my father got into the habit of making me feel like a frump, compared to my mother.

It didn't occur to me until I was in my late thirties, married, and in analysis in London that my father's demeaning behavior toward me might have been a defense against unacceptable feelings. At that time, he came over from Germany for a visit and showed some interest in my analysis. My father was then in his early seventies. One day, when we were talking about my childhood, he said, "You have always been jealous of your mother, even when you were very young, because she had everything and you had nothing."

"Why did you allow this happen?" I asked, appalled by the cynicism of his statement. But it got worse.

"You weren't important enough to me," my father coldly replied. "I had my hands full with my work and my marriage."

"Why did you give life to me, then?" I almost shouted at him.

"That had nothing to do with it," was his truthful answer.

In the wake of this devastating exchange, my father had two dreams, which he shared with me the next morning. One of them showed that the discrimination against me, which he consciously took for granted, was really a huge problem for him on unconscious levels.

He dreamed he was stuck in a submarine on the bottom of the ocean. The entire world had disappeared. Only my mother and I were present with him in the submarine. The only way he could free himself from his underwater prison was by finding the archimedian (equidistant) point between my mother and me.

Despite his mathematical genius, my father never found the archimedian point between his wife and daughter. Consequently, he remained emotionally isolated and unconscious of the pain he caused me. However, in order to find the archimedian point, he would have had to get to the core of the problem and face the early sexual abuse, which his second dream was referring to.

He dreamed I was sitting as a three-year-old in a taxi that was slowly rolling away from him. He was trying to catch up with me, but a herd of goats got in the way. As the distance between us kept growing, he knew that he would never see me again.

I knew enough about dreams, even then, to be able to come up with an interpretation. I gleaned from my father's dream that when I was three, an inner separation between him and me had occurred, which was connected to sexual interference of some sort (the herd of goats). But I had no idea what this actually *meant*. Twenty-five years ago nobody, not even my oversexed London analyst, was on the look-out for signs of sexual abuse appearing in dreams. Freud had closed the door to that by explaining memories of this kind as oedipal fantasies of the children. And even if not all psychologists swallowed Freud's child-hood sexuality theory hook, line, and sinker, they still shared his opinion that such memories are mere fantasy.

Consequently, I considered only two possible interpretations: either my father had had sexual feelings for me that had kept him at a distance, or he had been so overly sexually involved with my mother that he had lost sight of me altogether. Of the two possibilities, the second seemed to be the more likely one, considering how our relationship had evolved. Because of my failure to understand specifically what the goats were referring to, I missed this rare opportunity to ask my father what had happened between us when I was three. But would he have told me the truth? It was not very likely. Fathers rarely admit to sexually abusing their children.

THE SECRET IS EXPOSED

Thus the incest remained buried in my unconscious until eight years after my father's death when Joy Hinson-Ryder dug it up. Joy held a doctorate in occult sciences and had been a professional dancer in the past. With her kind of background, she might have seen telltale signs in the way I moved during the dance exercises that always preceded her past life regressions. Once she identified the problem, she regressed me to the sexual abuse. Although the experience had been real enough at the moment, I later thought that I had made it up. I used the same defense I had used before when, during a past life regression, we had found the battle of the brujas at the root of my mother-problem.

Our karmic history with our parents appears to be a secret we keep from ourselves at almost any cost, because our survival depends on it when we are young. The speed with which every new insight into the family karma would vanish into my unconscious again was very telling in this respect. I tricked myself over and over with my rationalizations and doubts. Yet there is also a counter force in the unconscious that strives to make us conscious of our problems. And consequently, three years later, the incest question returned. What caused me to take it off the shelf was a documentary I had been watching on PBS.

It was a documentary about the sexual abuse of children in a day-care home and the trial that followed. As I was listening, spellbound, to the children's testimonies, my suspicion grew that what I had experienced during my age regression with Joy Hinson-Ryder had been authentic, after all. But in order to be quite certain, I needed a dream to validate that. Before I went to bed that night, I therefore asked my unconscious for a straight answer. The unconscious responded with a dream that told me what I needed to know, rather than what I had wanted to know. By uncovering the problem-causing past life with my father, it traced the incest back to its origin.

I am with an unknown male helper. We are reconstructing a past life together. In this life, I am a woman with very little freedom. My actions are prescribed by conventions and regulations. I am married to a much older man, whom I obey. His first wife had died, and I am his second wife. My husband is king, and I am his queen. In a tone that is charged with ominous meaning, I say to my helper, "And then there were sons from the first marriage, of course . . ."

Next I am at the State funeral of my husband. The pallbearers are carrying the king's hearse, in step with Gregorian chanting. The overall feeling is one of great sadness.

When I awoke, the Gregorian chanting was still in my ears, although as a Protestant it was not familiar to me. Several years later, however, while watching the funeral of Pope Paul on television, I recognized it instantly as the Litany of the Saints. Still half asleep, I asked the queen for more information and received it. This was in the eighth and ninth century, and Charlemagne was the key figure. On the basis of these data, I could identify the king quite easily by consulting a reference book. The king I was married to was not Charlemagne himself, but his only surviving son, Louis I, nicknamed the Pious (778–840), who was the only heir to his father's vast Carolingian Empire. He owed his nickname Pious ("fair" was another one) to a "moral purge" of the court that he had ordered as soon as he had ascended the throne.

Louis was emperor of the Germans and king of France. In his first marriage to Irmengarde he had three sons: Lothair, Pepin, and Louis the German—the sons I had been referring to. A year before Irmengarde's death, when Louis was only thirty-nine years old, he divided his empire between his three sons. This might have been Irmengarde's dying wish, but already a year after her passing, in 819, Louis remarried. His second wife, Judith of Bavaria, was (as my dream had hinted) seventeen years younger than he. She was of lower birth than Irmengarde (a countess versus a duchess) but strong-willed, very beautiful, and highly educated for her time. According to some historians, her emperor husband was in her power, and she is considered to be a controversial figure. In addition to a daughter named Gisela, she gave Louis a fourth son, Charles the Bald. It seems to have been due to her influence that the emperor decided to secure Charles his fair share of the Carolingian Empire, which could only be done by repartitioning it. This caused Irmengarde's sons to rebel. For the remaining years of the emperor's life they waged a relentless war on him and on Judith.

Within a period of ten years they defeated and deposed their father twice. The first time they sent Judith to a nunnery, the second time into exile in Italy, but each time Louis was reinstated by an independent council and Judith was allowed to return. Louis the Pious died in 840 in Germany, and Judith died three years later, age forty-seven, in France, which was under the rule of her son Charles. Although the two main players were now dead, the family feud continued, and when it was finally over, Charlemagne's European empire had ceased to exist.

SUSPICIOUS FORGETFULNESS

After I had finished my background research, there was no doubt in my mind that my father had been Louis the Pious and I his second wife, the unfortunate Judith. Our character profiles still matched those medieval ones in some significant ways. My father was still patriarchal and a champion of morality—outside his own family. I, on the other hand, had become again the victim of family discrimination. An entry I made in my dream journal the following morning showed how aware I was of all its implications.

Why did I have this dream? It actually does confirm my suspicion regarding the sexual abuse. It also explains why it happened. It was a bleed-through from our previous life, which happened at a moment when my father was under great stress, because his wife's fertility was being undone.

By revealing the background story of the incest to me, the dream contributed to my healing. Without justifying my father's actions, it helped me understand why he had acted that way, and by doing so it made it easier to forgive him. I could even explain the violation now in terms of Jungian psychology. My father had suffered an *abaissement du niveau mental* at a time of confusion and stress. In this mental state, the ego temporarily loses control and gets overwhelmed by unexpected impulses from the unconscious. In such a state of diminished accountability, my father had treated his baby daughter as if she were still his wife. His subsequent emotional withdrawal, which I had experienced as a rejection, had really been for our mutual protection; it had kept him from becoming a habitual child abuser.

It is difficult for me to admit that, having seen all this so clearly, I let it slip into the unconscious again. Although it is normal for conscious content to become unconscious again, this "forgetfulness" was not within the range of normality. I even went so far as to congratulate myself on never having been royalty in my past lives at all! Proud of my active involvement with democratic forms of government in my male incarnations, I had tried to cast myself in the role of an anti-royalist. However, such "cosmetic makeovers" were usually undone by my unconscious in the process of writing this book.

Usually, a current dream would free me of my misconceptions, but in this case, the old dream simply resurfaced. I came across it "accidentally" while I was searching old dream journals for other dream material. When I found the dream along with my comments, I actually blushed. How could I possibly forget something of such psychological significance? As far as I knew I had accepted the sexual abuse. So where was this "forgetfulness" coming from? I began to suspect that the disappearance of this whole memory packet in my unconscious had less to do with the incest itself than with something in Judith's life I did not want to look at. When I contacted her on an inner level, I heard her say over and over "Never any peace, never any peace . . ." She sounded like a distraught woman.

This was hardly a surprise, since Irmengarde's three sons had made her life and the emperor's life a living hell with their warfare. Moreover, by denying her son Charles his birthright to part of the empire, they had treated him like a royal bastard, which must have been very humiliating for her. On the other hand, Judith was clearly no innocent bystander in this heartbreaking, unnatural family feud. By pursuing her own interests and those of her son at the expense of the royal family she had married into and the Carolingian Empire over which they ruled, she must have drawn a full measure of karmic debt upon herself. It had obviously been enough of a debt for me to become "forgetful" about that life.

On the other hand, against this historical backdrop, my father's submarine dream seemed more profound than I had previously thought. It meant that his trouble with the archimedian point was actually over a thousand years old and that he was even now—after all those incarnations—trying in vain to create an equal distance between himself and his loved ones. When asked for a definition of old souls, a well-known psychic replied with a smile, "Old souls are slow learners."

PART TWO

Therapeutic

Harvest

6

CLOSING THE CIRCLE
A Christian Monk at the Crossroads

*Jesus said, "If you bring forth what is within you, what
you have will save you."*

THE GOSPEL OF THOMAS

A CELIBACY PROBLEM

Having survived all the pitfalls of the past life integration process myself, I felt well prepared to guide others through similar ordeals. I did not advertise that fact, however. For years it felt professionally safer to work behind the scenes. I was listed in the Yellow Pages as a Jungian analyst, and it did not take me long to discover that certain therapeutic encounters do not depend on advertising. Every time one of those special clients would choose me, apparently at random, out of the telephone directory, I would chuckle to myself and think, "God has his finger in the Yellow Pages."

Ironically, the first person who was in need of past life work had been referred to me by the Catholic Church, although not, of course, for that reason. This client was Brother Anselm, a Christian monk. I sensed from the moment he walked through my door that he was a true man of God. His humble and gentle demeanor and the aura of tranquillity that surrounded him seemed strangely inconsistent with the inner turmoil he was in. He was having problems with the celibacy vows he had taken as a young novice. Now, in his mid-thirties, they no longer made sense to him. In fifteen years he had broken those vows only once when, a year previously, he had fallen in love with an Indonesian nun. He had learned from this experience that a loving relationship with a woman was essential to his well-being. Instead of taking a cavalier attitude toward his vows, like so many others, he had decided to look deep within himself for an answer to the question that was tormenting him: Should he be a monk or not? His plan was that after doing inner work with me, he intended to make a decision and then tell his superiors where he stood.

Years of selfless service in third world countries had amply tested his faith. Only recently had he asked for permission to return to the United States so that he might lead a less stressful life. His superiors had gone along with his wishes and put him in charge of a small spiritual community in northern New Mexico. When I met him, he had settled down into a contemplative, simple life, and was doing his daily household chores "in a prayerful way," as he said.

It is a time-honored Jungian tradition to ask for a recent dream in a client's first session. This so-called initial dream, which may occur either immediately before or shortly after the first contact, often indicates the direction that the inner process will take.*

The first dream Anselm reported placed me in a difficult position because I instantly recognized it as a past life dream. What was I to tell a Christian Brother about this?

---

*In the writing of this book, I have religiously stuck to representing my clients' dream reports exactly as they wrote them down. I do this not only out of respect for them but also in the interest of the accuracy of what they are trying to convey. They write their dreams down while they are still half asleep and close to their unconscious. This closeness has to be preserved even for the benefit of the readers, because it speaks to their *own* unconscious. The somehow unfinished writing style is a by-product of the dominance of the right-brain function and the original closeness to the unconscious.

A little girl was to be executed with some four men. I didn't know what her offence had been, but I was impressed that it was so serious as to warrant this kind of execution. As she was loaded into a kind of chamber that looked like the exoskeleton of a beetle, she was crying pitifully. The chamber had a small window. Gas was released inside.

After the chamber was loaded, it was turned on its side and the door was shut. When it was tipped, the gas was released. I looked through the window just far enough to see a jet of gas shooting inside the chamber, but I didn't look so far as to see anyone inside. The whimpering of the little girl stopped. The executioner, wearing a gas mask, then went to open the chamber. I felt pity and compassion for the little girl. I wish there had been some way to save her.

Two features clearly identified this as a past life dream. The first was its realism, the second the dreamer's observer position. The latter can be seen as a psychological defense that distances the dreamer from the disturbing event. In *Past Lives, Future Healing*, Sylvia Browne describes using the observer role as a technique in her past life regressions.[1] In critical situations, she orders her clients to get into the "observant position" to protect them from getting retraumatized.

In the dream state, however, we instinctively know how much we can take. We shield ourselves by letting the "film" break just in time, or by getting into the observer position from the beginning. But even in the observer role, we experience an overwhelmingly empathic response. We are torn between wanting to hold up the course of events and knowing that any such attempt would be futile. Anselm expressed this dilemma in the phrase, "I wish there had been some way to save her."

There was also the link that always exists between a past life replay and a present day problem. Anselm was expecting to be severely punished for the vows he had broken with the pure, loving heart of a child. But how could I tell a Christian monk that he had dreamed of a past life? Christians officially stopped believing in reincarnation when Emperor Justinian anathematized it in 553 CE. So I kept my thoughts to myself, hoping that the dream would remain an isolated incident. I also knew, should he have more dreams of this kind, I would have to raise the question of reincarnation with him, even if it brought his therapy to an untimely end.

Anselm's unconscious, however, would not let up. In the very next session he mentioned a physical problem that had troubled him all his life—a consistent pattern of passing out whenever he had to stand in line for a mass vaccination. In school, his classmates had labeled him a sissy because of this, and he had endured endless teasing. This fainting was medically inexplicable and persisted into the present where it continued to be a source of embarrassment to him. I immediately noticed a connection between the previous week's concentration camp dream and his fainting spells. In my mind's eye I saw a long line of emaciated Jewish prisoners in their striped uniforms, fearfully waiting to be experimented on, and one little girl—the one in his dream—fainting with fear.

This time I could not avoid the subject of reincarnation, but I approached it as cautiously as I could. "I know you are a Christian monk," I began, "and that you don't believe in reincarnation, but I cannot help noticing a connection between the little girl in the gas chamber last week and the fainting spells you are mentioning now." Here I paused and waited for his response. There was a moment of silence between us, during which I gazed at his placid face, trying to guess what he was feeling. Then he said simply, "I am open."

PAST LIFE SEXUALITY

Without this openness, Anselm's therapy would have gone nowhere, because the integration of past lives happened to be on his unconscious agenda. Why this was so became clearer as time went on. Anselm needed his past life resources to find his way out of his present dilemma. But no matter how open he thought he was, his fear of heresy was equally strong. It created a conflict in him that blocked his dream recall for two weeks. Then, all of a sudden, the floodgates opened and his past life memories began to pour out. It started with a series of American Indian dreams.

In the place where I grew up, I am helping a man do simple plumbing work and dig trenches. While he and I are standing there, we see a group of people go by. One is a tall Indian man who had just had an attractive house built in the area. The Indian and his friends are talking animatedly. The group is on its way to see the new house. The Indian's name was Hapiru; he was apparently well to do.

Here, pipes were being laid through which energies from his American Indian lives could be conveyed into his present life. Hapiru clearly had what Anselm was lacking: a social life. In addition, he was wealthy. Names to which we have no associations, especially uncommon ones, usually belong to past life selves. Thus one of Anselm's Indian names had probably been Hapiru.

Two nights later, Anselm dreamed of an Indian again, but this time he was the Indian himself.

I am an Indian. I go out on a quest. Last year, a circle had been completed, as in old times. This year the circle is incomplete; it is only completed at the time the grapes are grown.

Anselm's associations to this dream took us back to his love experience, which a year ago had seemed like the answer to his search for wholeness. The dream made it very clear that, without this fulfillment, his life would never be complete. At the same time, the door was left open for the circle of life to complete itself again. In fact, the dream suggested that it would be only a matter of time before this happened. The closing of the circle depended on the ripening of the grapes, which indicated that a maturation process was involved.

Grapes were one of Anselm's favorite dream symbols. It ran like a leitmotif through his dreams and seemed to carry some of his soul essence. On the one hand, grapes belong to Dionysus, the Greek God of wine, and, on the other, to Christ. Thus grapes have two aspects: ecstatic intoxication and self-sacrifice. In Anselm's dream, both these aspects were present, because for him the physical union with a woman was ecstasy as well as sacrament. He had not been taught this in the seminary, of course. But it was an inner knowing that he had carried over from his American Indian lives. The more he lost confidence in certain Catholic doctrines, the more he believed in the sacredness of nature and of the circle of life.

Anselm's next dream was also about Indians, but this time the sexual content was explicit.

I am with an older Indian woman; we are in some way flying through or over her land—reservation land. There is a mountain with incredibly beautiful colors and rock formations. I feel ecstatic. I ask her if these are the Sandia Mountains. She says, "Yes they are." I realize it is an area I have never seen before; it is the backside of the Sandias, and this is the Ibarra Indian Reservation. The Ibarra tribe.*

Then her son—a man perhaps in his twenties—is with me. We see a bass fiddle skidding on top of the water of a stream. The fiddle then comes to us, as if being presented to us.

The next scene: I, the son, the mother, and another woman (the mother's friend) are in their house. The house is made of stone, and gray slate slabs are put together in intricate patterns. The house is very large and beautiful. It is then as if the bass fiddle turns into a young woman in the house. The young boy is with the young woman, but he does not know what to do. He lies down on a stone bed. The mother, who has been nearby, comes forward and begins to speak. The boy thought he was to "play" the instrument. The mother says, "to play," means to "make love."

---

*An Ibarra tribe is unknown in northern New Mexico, but a sixteenth-century Spanish explorer, Francisco de Ibarra, allegedly traveled from Mexico to what is known today as New Mexico.

She then begins to laugh uproariously, good-naturedly. These people are not ashamed about these things; it is all very natural for them.

The mother is corpulent, but has an interior beauty, desirability, and wisdom. Other Indians come and go quietly and don't disturb us.

In matters of sexuality, Anselm was a neophyte. Unconsciously, he was looking for role models appropriate to his innocence. He found these neither in the Christian religion, with its confusion of sex and sin, nor in the soulless bed acrobatics of the technological age. He found it in the tribal traditions that take the sacredness of all natural phenomena for granted. The scene where the mother instructed the boy, who was lying "on a bed of stone" (that is, petrified with fear), in the art of lovemaking, could well have represented an authentic memory. Some of the Indian tribes encouraged sexual play at a very early age. The metaphor of the woman's body as a musical instrument that a man must learn to play is both poetic and true. Although the maternal Indian woman initiated Anselm into the secrets of lovemaking, it was really the dream itself, with its beautiful nature symbolism, that taught him.

A fourth, very short dream from the same time period completed this Indian dream series, which was centered on sexuality. Anselm dreamed the following:

I am an Indian and am in need of an intravenous feeding or transfusion. I see the needle, and it is long. Another Indian inserts it gently into my left wrist area.

Although Anselm had started to integrate his Indian past lives, he was still lacking the red blood of passion. Years of celibacy and asceticism had somewhat weakened his masculinity. Therefore, an energy transfusion was needed to nurture that part of him back to life. His first dream about the laying of pipes in Hapiru's presence had already implied that past life energies were going to be redirected to him, but here the transfer was actually occurring. It seemed that his Indian incarnations were the carriers of a certain type of masculinity that was compatible with his own. Although this masculinity was brave, it was also much softer than the one embodied by white Americans. The blood transfusion, as it occurred in the dream, was highly symbolic. The long needle was a metaphor for the phallus, and since another male was inserting it into his left, or feminine, side, this act represented a symbolical impregnation.

In Anselm's waking life, this was reflected as an irresistible attraction to the Indian Cultural Center in Albuquerque where he would spend hours listening to the heartbeat of Indian drums. When these self-healing efforts began to bear fruit, Anselm fell in love with a young woman. Although this relationship turned out to be only short-lived, it helped to strengthen his masculinity.

A PAST LIFE ROLE MODEL

From then on, Anselm's Indian dreams faded into the background, and a bloodline of rebellion came to the fore. Its emergence was timely, because he had broken his vows once again. What surfaced first was the exemplary life of a black spiritual leader in Africa who had resolved his inner conflict of obedience and rebellion with courage and integrity. Anselm dreamed this man's life history in chronological order. This was unusual, because past life memories tend to appear in topsy-turvy fashion. The first dream in this series recalled the black man's boyhood.

The setting is like a main street in an old Wild West town. A group of young Negro boys, all the same age and even uniform height, come out of the buildings. They are dressed up in some sort of brownish military uniforms with caps. Some have flags in their hands. They begin to sing songs; their voices are beautiful, moving. Their voices are so beautiful, in contrast to their uniforms and intent; it is a pitiful scene, and I begin to cry. They are trying to be like the whites.

The obedience to authority figures, who seemed to belong to a different "race" of men, had repeated itself in Anselm's life. This explains why he wept while witnessing the loss of individuality in these young boys. He was really grieving for himself, for his own personhood that had gotten lost when he entered the Church. But there was hope, for in the black man's life this scene was only the beginning, and not the end of the story. Childlike obedience later turned into rebellion, as Anselm's next dream showed.

Military (white) come into the black area or neighborhood. There is one black man in particular who is nonconforming, and the military is harassing him—shooting at the ground very near him.

Although the targeted man represented Anselm's past life self, he was, at the same time, also his present self, expecting to be "shot at" by the Church for violating monastic rules.

While the two previous dreams had been predominantly realistic and memory based, the following dream—the last in this series—contained a mixture of realistic and symbolical elements. It portrayed the black man in the prime of his life when he had become a spiritual leader.

I am with a dark-complexioned woman about my age. I love her, and she has the feeling of being a Sister, also. She becomes attracted to a black man from Africa. From our apartment we can see his; his is above ours. In order to get his attention and insure a date, she sunbathes nude on the small outside veranda. I also am attracted to her and I run my hand over her body. My motive is partly to cover her from the eyes of that man above, whom she wants.

He does take her out. He is a very kind man—a clergyman of some kind, and an intellectual. They go to his apartment. He was going to take her to bed, but he keeps getting distracted by a meeting he has to attend, or some interest or duty. She seems to understand good-naturedly. He throws some things away in a manner that he knows we will find them. They are like items he was leaving behind. One item is a small, framed picture of the Virgin. I can't see it closely. There is a bundle of documents, each bound. They are all dusty. I open one; it represents much meticulous work. He appears from somewhere momentarily and looks like he has fewer clothes on. He also looks older. He has left behind a sort of necklace for me, which makes me want to cry when I look at it. It has square beads and a round ball as the centerpiece. The squares are of different colors, alternating between white and red. The ball is white.

Anselm seemed to be competing here with his past life self over a woman, which is intriguing. While Anselm tried to get her attention, she kept glancing over her shoulder to the "man above her," because he was the one she really wanted. This reminded Anselm of his present-day, short-lived relationship with the Indonesian nun. He had never quite understood why she had broken up with him so abruptly. He felt that the reason she had given him—a conflict of conscience—had not been the real one. We wondered if she had also been his lover in that African life and had hoped that he would be the hero and rebel she had then admired and loved. In his present, more timid incarnation, Anselm might not have measured up to her expectations, at least not at the time when they were lovers.

But now Anselm was beginning to relate to this powerful inner figure. It even appeared from this dream that the black spiritual leader was Anselm's past life representative: the guardian of his personal evolution. In this role he encouraged Anselm to follow his example and do two things. First, to throw away a major icon of the Catholic Church, the Virgin Mary, held up as the apotheosis of womanhood. Second, to send the dust-collecting documents—presumably Church dogmas—after her. To empower Anselm, he left him his necklace as a personal legacy.

Anselm's emotional response to this gift underlined its symbolical significance.

Historically, men used to wear necklaces only in ceremonial dress as a sign of leadership. This tradition still survives in Europe, where town mayors and university presidents wear a ceremonial necklace on official occasions. The necklace in Anselm's dream was clearly of this kind, except that it stood for spiritual, rather than worldly leadership. The value system it represented was symbolically encoded in the shapes and colors and the arrangement of the beads. The necklace's basic design—the strings of beads and the prominent centerpiece—was still based on the rosary, but the rosary's structural elements were significantly altered.

The beads were replaced by cubes, and the crucifix in the center by a round ball. These replacements carry a lot of meaning. The cube stands for earth, or the material world, while the sphere represents the heavens and perfection. Together, they form a superordinate wholeness, uniting the opposites internally and externally. In Anselm's dream, the fact that the black man's necklace had a white ball and not a cross in the center implied that at this time of his life his spirituality was not based on suffering and self-sacrifice anymore. The color combination of red and white underlined the complementary nature of all the structural elements of the necklace. It showed that white, the color of spirituality, is compatible with red, the color of blood and passion. This meant for Anselm that if he was to accept the black man's spiritual legacy, he could turn his back on the dualistic thinking of the Catholic Church and embrace a philosophy where nature and spirit are in harmony with each other.

Since the black spiritual leader had such a distinct personality, I suggested that Anselm establish communication with him through a Jungian technique known as "active imagination." When I described the simple procedure to him, he was already familiar with it. He had learned it in the seminary where it went under the name "Jesuit meditation." It remained an open question as to who had borrowed it from whom, or alternatively, whether these were parallel inventions confirming Jung's theory of the collective unconscious.

More important to me was the fact that Anselm, after following my instructions, came to his next session deeply upset. He had had no trouble getting in touch with the black spiritual leader. When he had asked him for his name, the black man had given it to him quite willingly. He had even volunteered a year, presumably that of his death. With a serious expression on his face, Anselm handed me an index card that had "Abraham Deekel, 1878" written on it. To receive this detailed information at a first attempt seemed like a remarkable success.

So why was Anselm so upset? It turned out that Deekel, after answering his questions, had wanted to know why he had contacted him. When Anselm had replied that he was following his therapist's instructions, the black man had fallen silent and would not speak to him again. Anselm felt certain that Deekel had cut him off because he had not taken responsibility for contacting him. The notion that he had looked like a failure in the great man's eyes was very painful for him. He was also shocked to discover that Deekel apparently had a mind of his own.

A VISIONARY DREAM

Soon after his encounter with Deekel, Anselm turned a corner. An external event helped to bring this about. Every fall he would routinely go to the hospital for his flu shot. This time, while standing in line, he waited anxiously for his customary fainting spell to occur, but when he felt it coming on he reminded himself that he was no longer the little Jewish girl and the moment passed without incident. For the first time in his life, Anselm had gotten through an inoculation without fainting. The sheer physicality of this experience created an opening in his skeptical armor, and shortly thereafter a voice spoke to him in a dream.

I am looking at a sort of display case. There is a form—a claylike form—in the case. A low male voice begins speaking and the form takes many shapes, according to what is being spoken about. At one point the form has three heads, and then one. It simultaneously changes color. The words that are spoken, and the corresponding forms, are so beyond what I have experienced that I couldn't comprehend this display, yet I was gripped by it. At one point the voice says, "This is 950 years old."

Then I see a scene of a world of active volcanoes, all in hues of blue, and I know it was from the origins of this earth. In the middle of this scene, superimposed, is a round aperture, with a scene from another era; a small, hoofed creature (white in color) is very delicately walking in a specific manner through the snow. I know its way of walking in the snow was an adaptation it had made from living in such an environment. The thought comes that this primeval scene presupposes this smaller scene of a highly differentiated and complex creature. From the chaos came this miracle of a creature. Then I see a fawn in the small aperture.

Next, I am walking in an area similar to a small canal road near our house. The low resonant male voice speaks again, as sort of a guide, pointing out all the creatures. Then I see a huge water snake, and the voice speaks of it. The snake—it is very long and thick—comes through the water toward me at an incredible speed and goes right past me, oblivious that I am there. I am mildly disturbed that it might harm me. It goes instead right to a creature half submerged in the water, which looks like an alligator.

This dream, with its powerful archetypes, and even more the omnipresent voice, dispelled Anselm's last lingering doubts about the existence of reincarnation. Although his vision was richer and more elaborate than my earlier vision of the past life container had been, our dreams had important commonalities. We both heard a deep, resonant voice, stood in front of a transparent past life container, and perceived past lives in different colors. We also both knew that the colors represented the four races and that this meant multiracial births for us all.

Apparently, we had encountered the same archetype—the archetype of reincarnation. Yet there were individual differences in the way we experienced the archetype. Whereas in Anselm's vision the past lives were evolving in a linear time sequence, in my vision they were coexisting outside of time. Our past lives also had a different appearance. While Anselm, in accordance with the depiction in Genesis, saw a piece of clay that was being formed and re-formed by an invisible hand, I saw a bunch of deep-sea creatures in lively interaction with each other.

In the second part of his dream, Anselm observed the earth's evolution, which seems to have unfolded in two different stages. In the dream, these stages were represented by two types of landscapes. Our planet's early history was laid out directly in front of him, but he could see the later evolutionary stage only through a small opening at a distance. In the later stage, animal life-forms came into being in response to earth changes that had taken place. Anselm intuitively knew what this grouping signified. He understood that the complex life-forms had evolved from the simpler, primitive ones. For him, this was a timely reminder that all higher development draws its strength from a primitive foundation. As a monk, he had tended to reverse the natural order of things by forcing his instincts into the background and thereby marginalizing them, while making higher soul development his chief priority.

The last part of his dream called attention to the animal kingdom. Animals have a life of their own, but they are also part of our soul. They represent our animal instincts, our animal ancestry. Since Anselm was in conflict with his sexuality, a water snake appeared to him as a messenger of that energy. As a Christian monk, he had taken the biblical seduction story of Adam and Eve, which demonizes sexuality, quite seriously. Thus, to Anselm the snake as a sexual symbol had always represented the devil.

Yet most other religions hold the snake sacred. For the Hindus the snake is a bridge to higher consciousness. They understand that energy so well that snake charmers and yogis—each in their own way—have learned to tame it. In ancient Egypt, the serpent represented cosmic forces. The Aztecs worshipped it—in its feathered form—as wind god and creator god of humankind. In Mediterranean countries in ancient times, it was the animal companion of the Mother Goddess, who was often depicted holding snakes in her hands. Finally, because of its ability to shed and renew its skin, it has always been a symbol of healing and regeneration. Thus the Greek god of healing, Asklepios, was personified as a serpent, and nonpoisonous snakes participated in the healing rituals in his temples. Rudiments of this ancient cult can still be found in the physician's caduceus—a staff with two entwined snakes—and in the medieval wrought-iron guild signs of European pharmacies. The latter shows a rearing snake that lets a drop of its poison fall into a waiting chalice. This emblem recalls the adage "A little bit is medicine; a lot is poison."

It was an important lesson for Anselm that God showed him the snake as a sea serpent and not as a serpent coiled around a tree; in contrast to the snake in the Garden of Eden, the sea serpent has only positive symbolic connotations. It represents the unconscious (water), as well as a primal form of creativity. Although Anselm was afraid of the sea serpent at first, he quickly realized that this primal energy was not out to get him. It did not even notice him as it swept past him in hot pursuit of its archenemy, the alligator.

The alligator is a member of the crocodile family. In Egyptian hieroglyphics, the crocodile represents the principle of evil. It is one of the animal forms of Seth, who is known as the god of chaos, violence, and adversity. In the instinctual realm, the crocodile is an energy form that thrives in murky places of the unconscious, where it lies dormant and hidden until it emerges suddenly and attacks. The archetypal shadow operates in exactly the same way. It seldom overpowers the ego in open confrontation but mounts surprise attacks from a half-submerged—or half-unconscious—place.

Thus, the snake and the crocodile are two antagonistic principles or opposites that manifest as creation and destruction, or light and darkness. The cosmic serpent creates; the crocodile destroys. The serpent makes whole; the crocodile dismembers. Having lived among celibates much of his life, Anselm had seen such half-submerged sexuality wreak havoc on the integrity of many of his fellow brethren.

This was one of the reasons why he was now questioning the value of celibacy.

AN IN-DEPTH EXPLORATION

Although this divinely inspired vision had removed most of his theological doubts, Anselm was still not satisfied. He wanted to know more about reincarnation. One thing he was especially curious about was what makes it possible for us to remember our past lives. The explorations of this question took him "right to the edge of his endurance" in one of his dreams.

My friend Tom and I are exploring in the midst of a beautiful forest and enchanting place. We have stopped and made an encampment. I marvel at Tom, who is not afraid of places so distant and isolated; he never has been. Then I realize that my old fears are not with me either. We are next to a beautiful, flowing, deep stream. I hear something beneath the overhang. I bend over and see some foxes swimming in the stream, trying to elude us. I call Tom, and he looks. The fascination and the beauty of this so move me that I rub Tom's head as I used to do when he and I were young. I feel friendship and warmth toward him.

Then we dive into this clear stream, through some long grass growing and flowing with the current. We come to an area that is qualitatively different; it is suffused in white and it stretches, I think, to infinity. We could not explore it or even enter it because our breath was giving out. Then between us swam a round jellyfish with a white luminous core. It swam into this white area. I knew it was going where few other fish or water creatures go. Tom and I headed toward the surface, and a flash of worry came to me that we would not be able to locate our entry point. We surfaced right at the edge of our endurance.

The dream placed this venture in Anselm's youth, when risk-taking had been more normal for him. Tom represented a fearless shadow aspect, which was about to be integrated. The foxes, which according to folklore are witch animals, represented the magic of an innermost place where everything transcends ordinary reality. The deep, clear river was the river of life, but also, at the same time, the deep unconscious. As Anselm and his companion were exploring this deepest layer of the unconscious, they came across a "qualitatively different" zone that had no oxygen and could not be entered. Suffused in white light and infinite in expansion, it was set apart as an otherworldly place.

In my own dream about "the loft above the loft," (another such otherworldly place), I had not been able to enter it for the same reason; it had been too ethereal for my physical body. Finally, Anselm's encounter with the round jellyfish at the threshold of this white-light zone answered his question about the source of our past life memories. The jellyfish was the missing link—the sacred go-between that carries information to us from other lifetimes and is able to navigate with ease between this world and the otherworld. It seemed to be a representation of an archetype, which Jung calls the Self and the Hindus call the *atman*.

Anselm's dream venture followed almost to the letter the archetypal pattern of the hero's journey, on which the hero embarks to find a treasure or a solution to a collective problem. To win the treasure, the hero must risk his own life. But winning the treasure is not enough; he must bring it back to his community. In psychological terms, the information, knowledge, and wisdom found in the unconscious must be made conscious and translated into practical living. Otherwise the hero's journey has failed. In ancient myths not all heroes succeeded in this task. Some, like Theseus, became trapped in the underworld, while others, like Enkidu in the Babylonian Gilgamesh epic, lost the treasure—the plant that bestowed eternal youth—on his way back.

Anselm only experienced a "flash of worry" that he would fail to find the "entry point" again and would be lost forever in the underworld, but he did find it at the last moment and was able to return to a normal life. In the weeks that followed, Anselm felt a growing need to connect his inner experience to the outer world. This was a clear sign that his return journey had been successfully completed. However, when he tried reading books on reincarnation, he soon got bored. It all felt shallow compared with what he had experienced himself. He then chose another, more challenging way to bring his experience into reality. He told his superior, a wise man he trusted, about his reincarnation dreams. To his surprise, instead of chastising him, the superior confessed that he believed in reincarnation himself. This made Anselm feel less isolated within his order. It also removed some remaining inhibitions from his past life recall so that more challenging, karma-producing lives could emerge.

FACING THE PAST LIFE SHADOW

Anselm arrived with a somber look on his face at his next scheduled session with me. He had had another past life dream, but this time the information had been direct and precise. "I was a revolutionary during the Russian Revolution," he told me. "The year was 1917, and everybody was shooting at everybody. I killed some people, too. One person I shot was a woman dressed in white." He said this experience had been too realistic to be only a dream. He also was quite shaken by it.

The bloodline of rebellion, which stood out so clearly in this Russian revolutionary, had been present to some extent in Abraham Deekel, too. But Deekel had only attacked spiritual principles; he had not attacked real people. The shooting of the woman "dressed in white" deeply upset the peace-loving Brother, but the worst was still to come. A week later, while Anselm was still recovering from the shock of this discovery, he met the executioner in himself.

I am witnessing executions; my perspective is from above, though not directly above the scene. The setting is a huge marble hall. The condemned is led through a door into this hall. This person has already been tried and found guilty. He is followed by his executioner—the person against whom the offense has been committed.

In the first execution, the two men come out. The condemned is in a suit coat. His hands are bound behind him; he stops, and very quickly, the other man shoots him from behind with the pistol.

The next two men come out. The condemned has a black mesh veil over his head that covers his shoulders. As he comes through the door, he begins to run. There are shouts from many voices, as if many spectators are present. The executioner fires and wounds him. The wounded man comes back and wrestles the other for the pistol. The executioner fires again, wounding himself in the process and killing the other. They are both dragged off.

Anselm was not sure where this had taken place. Perhaps in Sicily, he conjectured, but he was quite certain that he had been one of the executioners in the dream. He could tell from the cool detachment with which he had watched the executions and his emotional response as soon as the executioner was wounded. We were both in agreement that this was the karmic counterpart to the little Jewish girl's execution in the German concentration camp. What had seemed like divine injustice before now made sense in terms of karmic law. Although the executioner had brought balance into his past life history, Anselm felt crushed by the guilt of being such a person. As a true Christian, he found it easier to accept the role of a victim than that of a victimizer, yet he could no longer deny the fact that he had not always been as gentle as in his present incarnation. His present serenity and nonviolence was beginning to look more like the result of well-learned karmic lessons than like an attribute of his soul essence. Perhaps an original warrior disposition had gone through an alchemical process, which, in the course of many lifetimes, had turned dark matter into gold.

Yet at this critical moment in Anselm's life it was of the utmost importance that he reconnect with his primitive roots. As he was facing tough choices, he needed to remember that besides being a gentle monk he was also a spiritual warrior who could fight for his beliefs.

This was probably the reason why his unconscious was confronting him now with his violent shadow. However, he could not reap the benefit of this "shadow cure" right away. His immediate response to these revelations was one of shock and retreat. Therefore, in the following session, he requested that we slow down the pace of his therapy. He said our work had given him a depth he had never known before, but he needed time to come to terms with the murderer in himself. I completely understood. The rapid inner changes he had been going through were starting to outpace him. His whole belief system had been turned upside down, and he had accepted it. But now his very sense of self was coming into question, and he needed to stand back for a while and sort out who he truly was. Luckily, his unconscious accommodated him by putting the past life process on hold for a period of two months.

LEAVING THE ORDER

During this slowdown time, which Anselm used to quietly integrate his shadow, the decision ripened in him to leave his order. Because he had allowed the conflict to play itself out, this decision had been a relatively easy one for him to make. He had known for some time that he would never feel complete without a woman's love. Yet to fulfill himself as a man would come at a price. It would cost him the security that the Catholic Church provided. He knew very well what it would mean to face the world alone and unprotected. He would have to train for another profession without the financial support he was accustomed to, and he would have to move to another state, far away from me. Thus his whole support system was about to fall apart at a time when he most needed it.

While he was trying to face these dire prospects he often felt that he was leading a "marginal" life. "I am moving to margins, and I am painfully aware I am alone and moving again to margins," Anselm once dreamed. What he feared most was poverty, which he consciously associated with the terrible destitution he had seen in Bangladesh.

Unconsciously, he also associated it with poverty-stricken past lives of his own, which were soon to emerge in a new dream series.

There is a Korean man and his young son who are engaged in building a house off the shore on a lake, in the water. They are poor, and it seems this place is the only option left them. I can see where he has skillfully taken the wood out from around the base of the house and replaced it with brick. The whole underside and support of the house are constructed of tightly cemented white brick.

Both the boy and the man work extremely hard. I can see the boy work deftly, skillfully, until he is near exhaustion. The father keeps pushing the boy, because the boy has to be obedient to him. They paddle around in a small canoe, putting things into place. The man tells me that if any unknown thing goes wrong, he would probably emotionally collapse because he was so strained by the whole project. He has pushed himself hard.

Although some of Anselm's dreams, like this one, were anxiety provoking, others gave him hope. It seemed that his present crisis was triggering conflicting past life memories in him. What rescued him, in the end, was his spiritual bloodline. This was ancient, multifaceted, and so strong that it overshadowed all his other bloodlines. In our past dreamwork, I had watched this spiritual bloodline meander through many lifetimes, embracing one religion after another. Yet it did not surprise me when the first religion to help him out was the Native American one.

There is a Native American spiritual leader whose name is Iraho Pratet. I am in a little village, looking for a way out. Another person and I are looking for Iraho Pratet to help us find that way out.

What Anselm needed now more than anything was to find spiritual leadership in himself, because he was breaking away from a hierarchical structure that had mediated his relationship with God since his childhood. Native American spirituality had never depended on such mediation. Like other mystical traditions, it had direct access to higher guidance through dreams and visions. Thus if Anselm was to find his way out of the Roman "village"—the Catholic Church—he would have to walk, at least for a while, in the moccasins of Iraho Pratet. Or even better, he would have to tread in the footsteps of a Tibetan holy man who appeared in his dreams two weeks later.

I see a large document; I focus on part of a page. It shows how many incarnations of holy men from a particular (non-Christian) tradition there have been. The section I focus on gives the name of the man and a description of his way of achieving fulfillment or holiness; it even gives where he lived and taught.

Apparently this man was Anselm in a past life, perhaps in an earlier Tibetan incarnation. His next dream confirmed this by giving us more details.

I am a Tibetan in Tibet. I am also a teacher, but I am discriminated against. I apply for permission to take an exam that would entitle me to teach there. I know I would do well in it, but the authorities will not allow it. They are using delaying tactics. Finally, they allow me to take the exam, together with one other person. The exam is several pages long. In the first part we have a beautiful landscape on a stage before us. We are looking down on water from which rock cliffs are jutting out. Our task is to recognize the outlines of whales and sharks on the rock surface. I can distinguish them quite clearly.

Next, a Tibetan dance performance takes place on the stage. One examination question relates to this dance. The two dancers—a man and a woman in traditional Tibetan costumes—mingle with the audience, facing the stage. Mime and quick body movements are characteristic of this dance.

When Anselm dreamed this, he had just asked permission from the Church to "prove himself" in a worldly life. To his surprise, his request had been granted without difficulty. His fears of punishment had therefore been quite unfounded. They had merely been residues of past life experience. On the other hand, having to "prove himself" to the Church had brought back memories of a similar challenge he once had met in Tibet. There his application to teach had been turned down by the ecclesiastical authorities, and he had felt discriminated against. However, when he had persevered, he had been allowed to prove himself. And if this dream and his former dream refer to the same incarnation, Anselm had proved himself so well that he had later been recognized as a spiritual leader in Tibet.

The examinations, which the dream so elaborately described, had, of course, nothing to do with Tibetan traditions or with the academic and spiritual scrutiny that Anselm might have been subjected to on that occasion. Rather, they symbolized the tests of life that Anselm would have to pass in the future. The first thing to be tested was his ability to distinguish between the forces of good and evil in their outer manifestations. These powers dwell deep down in the ocean, in the depth of the collective unconscious according to this dream, but they leave their imprints on the rock—the earth in its most primordial form.

In American Indian animal medicine, the whale is a record keeper and a mediator between heaven and earth. In the Bible, a whale swallows Jonah as a god-defiant man and regurgitates him as a god-fearing man. Thus in the Judeo-Christian tradition, the whale plays the role of a transformational vessel. Whereas the whale is associated with God, the shark is generally seen as an embodiment of evil, like the alligator that appeared in Anselm's creation dream. While the whale swallows his victim whole, the shark dismembers it.

In the world of nature, of course, these are only two different feeding patterns that have nothing to do with good or evil. However, the daunting presence of the shark with its menacing array of teeth on the one hand, and the roundness and largeness of the whale on the other, draw opposite instinctual projections from us. Anselm's dream reflected these opposites, and since the dividing line between good and evil is often blurred, one has to look for the permanent imprints these forces leave behind in the world around us. For Anselm, this kind of discernment was easy. He was, after all, drawing on a vast pool of life experience from many years of service in third world countries.

Anselm's second test was a greater challenge, because it concerned the "dance between the sexes," which to him was still largely unfamiliar. But his unconscious came to his aid by showing him the first steps. As in mating dances in the animal kingdom, the dancer's movements were ritualized. Mirroring and quick response were seen as important prerequisites of a good partnership performance. And although a couple, according to this dream, should play a part in society, it is the quality of their dance together, and not the applause it might earn, that really matters.

On the basis of this dream, it was easy to predict that Anselm would leap over the hurdles that still separated him from an ordinary life with extraordinary ease. Many past life selves had helped birth his new self and had left their gifts of knowledge in its cradle. Because he had so much inner support, it was only a matter of time before an equal amount of outer support would rally around him.

When Anselm came for his last session, I had just built a Medicine Wheel in my front garden. I asked him to bless it for me as a parting gift. As he was praying to the East—the direction of new beginnings— he suddenly became aware of the fact that by blessing the stone circle, he was also blessing his own new roundness. So he turned to me and said, "When I came to you a year ago, I was torn apart. Now I am whole." Then he walked through the front gate and disappeared behind the crumbling high adobe wall, which had protected the privacy of his visits for many months.

When I held a photograph of him and his lovely new wife in my hand a few years later, I knew that the grapes had ripened and his circle had closed.

7

IN THE SHADOWS
OF DACHAU
Purging Collective Karma

Those who cannot remember the past are condemned to repeat it.

SANTAYANA

A LONELY DREAMER

A comprehensive past life recall, like Anselm's, has been an exception rather than the rule in my practice. All that usually happens in past life work is the trauma resolution and integration of two or three incarnations. A good example of this was Marc, a middle-aged, unmarried man. However, what was unusual about his case was the intensity, the focus, and the duration of his integration process. It took him five years and forty-seven dreams to uncover, relive, and eventually accept his most recent lifetime. The reason for this was the heaviness and the collective significance of the karma he carried.

When I met him, Marc was a scriptwriter for the Hollywood

film industry and a college professor. By nature he was what American Indians would call a "dreamer"—a person whose outer reality is created from within. His extraordinary dream recall was unusually vibrant and precise. He also had the rare ability to translate the creative ideas that his unconscious offered him into practical reality and in this regard he was phenomenal. Everything he "dreamed up," envisioned, and initiated professionally sooner or later became reality. Unfortunately, this personal magic did not work in his private life. There his dreams of love and companionship were confined to his fantasy world. Even in his department, he felt isolated. Partly, this was by choice, because he was trying to guard the secret that he preferred men to women. To preserve his "straight" facade, he also abstained from practicing his homosexuality, apart from an occasional clandestine fling. There were other reasons, too, for his abstinence. Not only had he been a celibate in his youth, but he disliked his body for not measuring up to Hollywood standards. His low self-esteem blinded him to the fact that his appearance was impressive, charismatic, and actually quite sexy.

Even outside the bedroom, he related better to men than to women. His relationship with the opposite sex was an endless source of trouble. To some extent this was due to a negative mother complex, but even more so to a peculiar blind spot he had in regard to women's individuality. He experienced women only as stereotypes. This problem, which indicated a disturbed relationship with his anima—his feminine side—was even reflected in his dreams. He only dreamed of three types of women: glamorous movie stars, brainless sex kittens, and dumpy suburban housewives. I featured as the latter in his dreams, although I hardly fit this description in real life. For reasons that were initially not clear, his anima had no personality. The only way she came across in his personal and professional relationships was as a somewhat unpredictable prima donna.

Marc's family background had significantly impacted his personal development, although he had outgrown it completely. He came from a large family of Italian working-class immigrants who didn't have much to offer him except a lot of pasta. As a symbiotic, uneducated family group, they were all grossly obese overeaters. To fit in with his clan, Marc had been a fat boy during his childhood and adolescence. This had given him the feelings of physical inferiority he was suffering from as an adult.

Marc's family had followed Roman Catholic traditions very closely, but this did not explain why he had felt the need to join a monastic order when he was seventeen. There must have been other, less tangible reasons for that. After a year of rigorous spiritual discipline, which had included almost total silence, the Brothers had sent him to college. There he had excelled academically, and after graduating with a master's degree in education, he had served the Church for seven years. When he had finally left the order, his educational credentials and professional experience helped him stand his ground in a competitive labor market. Although his worldly career had taken off like a rocket, his psyche had remained stuck in the old monastic environment. Thus, after twenty years of secular life, he was still in the monastery in his dreams.

Since reentering the secular world, he had experimented sexually and had tried living with both men and women, but neither had ever worked out. Now that he was approaching middle age, he was beginning to feel starved for love and companionship. It was ironic and even tragic that, despite his burgeoning creativity, he had been unable to create for *himself* what he most wanted in life.

Even before he began his five-year analysis, Marc had been able to recognize his past life dreams. Often they would be triggered on his travels abroad, where the *spiritus loci*—the genius of the place— would stir up memories in his unconscious. In Mexico, a country that charmed him and to which he frequently returned, he dreamed about Maximilian (1832–1867), Emperor of Mexico. Most of these dreams revolved around the unfortunate monarch's captivity and execution, but a few also contained brief moments of triumph and joy in that life. He dreamed of a festive ball in Kaiser Franz Joseph's castle in Vienna, of "palace gossip" about Maximilian's impending marriage to Carlotta, and of elaborate preparations for his crowning in Mexico. The many historically verifiable details in these dreams strongly suggested that these were authentic memories. In addition, when I conducted some background research on Maximilian, a soul bloodline came to light that led straight to Marc's writing abilities. Maximilian was a prolific writer, I discovered. When he died, at the young age of thirty-five, he left an impressive oeuvre of seven volumes behind.

During a visit to Rome, another past life emerged. That life went all the way back to the first millennium. Six dreams about this time period were full of nostalgia and melancholic awareness of the impermanence of things. Two of these dreams spoke of past Roman glory, symbolized by Trajan's Column. Marc felt that he had been the emperor himself, but his dreams did not show that. The memories they contained could also have been those of a politician, a military person, or a loyal Roman citizen alive during Trajan's reign. (Trajan was born in 53 CE and died in 117 CE.) On the other hand, Trajan fought and won many battles for Rome, and Marc had a warrior bloodline that was strong enough to follow him all the way into the twentieth century. According to one of his most vivid past life dreams, Marc had served as a German commander in World War I and apparently had died in battle. Although Marc is a peace-loving man in his current life, he still is a natural leader.

Actually, leadership happens to be another one of his bloodlines. In many lifetimes he explored leadership from every possible angle. He learned what it means to be at the receiving end of the populace's positive and negative projections. Yet in order to be able to close this gestalt, he needed to know what it is like to follow a leader. He had already had a taste of that in the fifteenth century when, according to one of his dreams, he had been a courtier of Isabella of Spain. As a member of the queen's entourage, he would have been privy to her and Ferdinand's plans for the persecution and expulsion of the Jews under the Spanish Inquisition.

THE INTERFERING PAST LIFE EMERGES

It was perhaps no coincidence that Marc did another such role reversal precisely at the historical moment when a second European leader hatched a devilish plan to get rid of the Jews once and for all. Quite possibly Marc's soul was working on two polarities at once: leadership versus obedience, and racism versus tolerance. These opposites were being collectively explored by the German people during the Hitler regime. For anyone who needed to work on these issues, Nazi Germany provided the most challenging learning environment. And Marc was one of those brave souls who had chosen to incarnate there for that reason. It was also opportune that Marc was born as a woman in that life. If his lesson was to be about idolatry, the female sex was the best choice.

Anyone who has had the opportunity to study Hitler's effect on German women in the famous Riefenstahl documentary, *The Will to Power,* will understand what I mean. Since watching this film in the mid-1970s, I have been convinced that it was the "army" of German housewives that brought Hitler to power. In order to remain their idolized fantasy lover, he had to keep Eva Braun a top secret. This he did so effectively that it was not publicly known that Hitler had a mistress until he and Eva Braun were dead and the war was over. This secrecy around Eva Braun deeply effected Marc's life in that incarnation as we shall see.

Marc had long suspected that a past life was interfering with his emotional balance. In order to get to the bottom of it, he had undergone a series of past life regressions in Chris Griscom's Light Institute in New Mexico, some years before he came to see me. But even there, the troublesome life had eluded him. Either his attempt had been premature, or more likely, the one-week intensive had not offered him enough emotional security to let it come out. I now understand that it had to be processed slowly or remain untouched. Only the long-term care and steady dreamwork of a Jungian analysis could provide a safe enough environment for such supersensitive material to emerge. The fact that I was born in Germany and had lived there at the same time as Marc in his last incarnation created a common ground between us that inspired his trust and helped me understand this historical material.

For all these different reasons, I found the previously inaccessible Nazi life in the top drawer of Marc's unconscious. By our fourth session, he had dreamed of the German woman's violent death and named her Hilde. Whether that was her real name or not is irrelevant to our story. What matters is that the name was Germanic and common enough during the Hitler era to be representative of the female sex at that time. When, after five years of analysis and forty-seven Hilde dreams, Marc's process was complete, I checked the historical facts in his material against the background data provided by the Encyclopedia Britannica Online and found them all to be accurate.

Of course, the different episodes from this life were not dreamed in chronological order, but after I reorganized them into a story, it read like a diary from that time. Some dreams even had the visual precision of a video. The following dream, which shows the dreamer in search of his missing past life, may serve as an opening to this amazing story:

I am in the storehouse of an antiques shop with my wife. We are looking for clues to something—to a past life. I see an old piano or harpsichord and sit down and start to play it. I play a rag tune—so well that it surprises me; in fact, I look to see whether I am really playing it, or if it might be a piano roll. There is a book on the floor at the side of the piano. I leaf through it—maybe a journal. This is an important clue. Through this, my wife is just as diligent as I am to find information.

I am in an old house, near the front porch, which faces onto an outdoors of lovely autumn flower gardens. The television is on, and

there is an old black-and-white German movie playing. I watch it, mes-
merized. Behind me, Richard Erdoes, who is sitting there, asks me if I
can understand the German. I motion to him that I can understand
about half. There is an auburn-colored dog, maybe a cocker spaniel,
and someone is talking of destroying it.

Now I am back in the antiques shop storage house. I have entered
through a side door that is unlocked, but the place is supposed to be locked
up. I check the main door; it is locked.

Since Marc was single, his "wife" could only be his anima or,
more specifically, a personification of the inborn curiosity he shared
with women. The antiques shop storage house was a symbolic place
where past life memories were stored. It is noteworthy that it was not
accessible through the main door, which, according to this dream,
was "supposed" to be locked. This meant that this memory store is
not open to everyone and can only be entered by those who know
how to sneak in through a "side door." This underscores the difficult access to the past life memory bank that by now we are familiar
with. Once Marc and his "wife" were in the storehouse, they found
several relics of a not-so-distant past: an old piano, a book—which
perhaps was a journal—and a black-and-white film from an earlier period. Since the journal allegedly provided an important clue,
one wonders if Hilde had kept a diary, or even a dream diary, and
whether Marc was now beginning to re-dream her dreams. He had
clearly merged with Hilde for a moment when he surprised himself
by playing a rag tune on the piano, which he had never learned to
play in his present life.

Ragtime music, the forerunner of jazz, was created by black
musicians toward the end of the nineteenth century in the American
South. From there it made its way across the American continent
and into Europe. In German dance halls and bars it would have
been popular between the end of the World War I and when Hitler
came into power in 1933. Toward the end of this period, Hilde must

have been in her teens, which is a time when girls go after the latest fad. Besides, it was expected of so-called higher daughters (daughters of upper-middle-class families) that they learn to play the piano or some other musical instrument. Before musical recordings took over, "house music," performed by family members, had been a long-standing German family tradition.

The television, on the other hand, does not belong in this time period. Although it was invented shortly before Hitler came into power, it did not reach the general public in Germany until a decade after the war. Therefore, we have to see it here as Marc's "inner screen," where forgotten images appeared in projection so they could be mentally processed and emotionally reexperienced.

The black-and-white film also belongs to the Hitler era, and not only in the literal sense. Historically, color film had not been invented yet. But "black-and-white" is also a metaphor. It represents the primitive black-and-white thinking of the Nazi ideology. One was either for or against the *Vaterland*. One was Aryan or non-Aryan. In-between shades did not exist for the Nazis.

It is not clear from Marc's dream whether the auburn-colored dog appeared on the screen or outside the screen in the living room, but there can be no doubt about what he represented. A *bunter Hund* (colored dog), in the German vernacular, means a conspicuous misfit. As a bunter Hund in a conformist society, you can expect to be slandered, physically attacked, or, as in this case, destroyed. In Nazi Germany, the bunter Hund treatment was given to Jews, gypsies, communists, and homosexuals alike. It is noteworthy that here and elsewhere some of Marc's dream metaphors only disclose their full meaning if translated back into German. This seems to imply that a rudimentary knowledge of the German language was preserved in his unconscious. So there was some truth to Marc's statement to Erdoes, a well-known Austrian writer living in Santa Fe, that he understood "half" of the German, despite the fact that consciously he did not know a word of it. The "half" he understood was Hilde's half.

It is a time-honored psychological trick of predatory political systems to dehumanize their victims by turning them into animals. Hitler proclaimed, "The Jews are undoubtedly a race, but they are not human." Calling them "dogs," "rats," "goats," "cows," or "sheep" prepared them for the slaughterhouse. In the following dream series, this is a recurrent theme and will appear in several disturbing variations before a humanitarian breakthrough occurs.

In this dream, Marc was still separate from Hilde; he merged with her only briefly when he was playing the piano. But this separation did not exist in the rest of the dream series where the dreamer consistently took on his past life identity, although he was not always conscious of being a woman. In my experience, this is unusual. Most dreamers go into the observer position at least part of the time in order to protect themselves from the potentially harmful effect of traumatic past life events. Marc, by contrast, was never an observer, but always an actor in this unfolding drama. Why this was so remains an open question. Perhaps there were karmic reasons for that.

I am walking home from a huge rally or event; I can hardly find my way. Everyone is moving slowly—a huge traffic gridlock. I run into Judy, who works at the library, and I ask her about the "speaker" at the event, who must have been someone quite special. She says, "Well, he's an alien," as if that were somehow common. The alien gives talks with his companion, a woman, about the future.

Just before *Past Life Dreamwork* went to print, I came across a passage in Gitta Sereny's biography of Hitler's architect, Albert Speer, that details a speech that Hitler had given in Munich on January 29, 1923.[1] In this speech, Hitler had described his vision of Germany's future. One of the three points he made was that Germany had to "inoculate" itself against the "bacillus" of Judaism. In this speech, Hitler developed his anti-Semetic concept. The date of this speech confirmed our calculation that Hilde must have been six years old when she first heard him speak. (This is assuming that Marc had died during World War I in his previous life.)

When I shared all of this with Marc via e-mail, he replied: "My memory flushed up when I read your letter about the Munich speech, Sabine. I am so sure I was there that night. Herr Hitler was electrifying . . . the air was chill, we were bundled up, we could see our breaths as we walked and talked."

"Alien" has an interesting double meaning in English. It means both foreigner and extraterrestrial. This leads to a comical misunderstanding in the dream: while Hilde thinks he is a space brother, he is only a foreigner in Judy's eyes. It may not be common knowledge that Hitler, as an Austrian citizen, was considered a foreigner in Germany at the beginning of his political career. Some Germans, therefore, regarded him with suspicion until he was able to wipe out the national differences by uniting Germany and Austria into the "Grossdeutsche Reich."

Judy, a librarian and currently a Jewish acquaintance of Marc's, appeared here not only because she was Jewish but also because of her name. It made her into a prototype for all the Jews who were destroyed by this "alien's" plans for Germany's future. Hitler's public appearance in the company of a woman was probably more symbolic than factual. It supported my hypothesis that Hitler's career was "made" by German women.

HITLER YOUTH

In the following dream, the physical distance between Hilde and Hitler was beginning to shrink. This dream recorded a youth group meeting with Hitler. Marc dreamed this during his one and only visit to Germany, which he undertook for the sole purpose of testing his reactions to Munich and Dachau.

I am in an upper room of an apartment house—very bare, hardly fur-nished at all. The focus of the activity is Hitler, who is talking to a woman. We—that is, me and other "children" or young people—are at the other side of the room, near the door. I watch Hitler and listen, notice everything, as if I want to remember all of this. Hitler seems young. He speaks quietly, but with the same cadences as in his speeches; he modulates his voice. Now the woman, who is a painter or performance artist (and we may be part of her troupe), is about to ask Hitler for something—money or support for her work. Hitler interrupts her, insisting that she have faith in God, who has seen her through so many previous periods. She agrees, but still tries to make him see her point of view. She gets nowhere—he is very persuasive—and he is Hitler. "Well, you see?" he says. I stand up, as if the meeting is about to end, but the meeting continues, and I feel ashamed and uneasy about drawing attention to myself. When I stand up I seem very tall, taller that the other "children."

On the morning after this dream, Marc felt disorientated enough to absentmindedly stuff a breakfast roll into his pocket as he left the hotel restaurant after breakfast. Later, he was shocked to discover what he had done. He had acted like Hilde in times of food rationing during the war. This slip, and of course the dream itself, convinced him completely of the authenticity of that life.

In the dream, Hitler must have been in his early thirties, because at that age he was the head of the propaganda branch of the NSDAP (National Socialist German Workers Party) in Munich. It is plausi-ble to see him targeting the school youth like that, for when he later became the Fuehrer he derived much of his power from his indoctri-nated Hitler Youth, a Nazi organization into which every school child aged eleven was automatically drafted. The rest of the dream is equally consistent with what is known about Hitler. It is common knowledge that he patronized the performing arts, yet at this early stage the party would have had no money to spare, so he referred the woman to God. In view of how he later dealt with the Christian Church, this might seem dubious to the reader. Marc even questioned it himself. However, having heard Hitler speak over the radio as a child, I knew this to have been quite typical of him. He always referred to the *Herrgott* (Lord) in his speeches, because he wanted the German people to think that God was on his side.

The next dream is from the same time period, but here Hilde remembered Hitler visiting her classroom.

I am in a classroom with other students. It is very strict here. If we want to move or get up, we have to raise our hands. Now I am sitting at a table with two other students, who sit on the right and left of me. Adolf Hitler is here. He honors the two students I'm sitting with, but he pours a cup of coffee (with milk) over my head. I am embarrassed.

The strict discipline in German classrooms at that time is accurately reproduced. Again, it is very probable that Hitler visited schoolchildren in their classrooms. But he would never have walked around, American style, with a cup of coffee in his hand. The spilling of coffee over Hilde's head was almost certainly a metaphor for being publicly shamed by him in some other way. Again, the German vernacular might help explain this unusual image of getting doused with café-au-lait. The expression *ich kam mir vor wie ein begossener Pudel* (I felt like a doused poodle) is used to describe the feeling of being humiliated in public. This meant that Hilde's second encounter with Hitler had also ended with an embarrassment.

A FATEFUL THIRD ENCOUNTER

However trivial these embarrassing incidents might have been, they had a powerful affect on Hilde. They seem to have left a burning desire to impress the dictator with special achievements. In fact, without these childhood mishaps, a later adult encounter with the dictator might never have occurred. This meeting took place in 1940, in Eva Braun's villa in

Munich, soon after Germany had invaded Poland. Hilde, then in her early twenties, had become a documentary filmmaker. Eva, on the other hand, was a photographer, so the two women probably knew each other professionally. In addition, Hilde must have belonged to Eva Braun's inner circle, because otherwise she would never have been allowed to show a documentary about Poland in her house while Hitler was present.

I am a documentary filmmaker, and I am threading a projector when Adolf Hitler and Eva Braun come into the room. The room is large and well appointed. Eva Braun comes over to me and says, "Don't you ever tell anyone about this. If you do . . ."

I turn on the projector. It is daytime, and some of the drapes in the room are kept open. The "documentary" is apparently a review of the first year of the war. While it is running, Eva Braun tells Hitler, "You should have let them return to their homes." She says this in a slightly scolding voice, adding that a certain Roman general in ancient times allowed the civilians to return to their homes. Hitler tells her that in that general's time there were no automobiles (meaning that the people he is conquering now might have traveled faster and risen up again). Now Hitler and Eva Braun are sitting on a long couch that is in the shape of an "L," with Hitler on one side of the outside angle and Eva on the other, though they are close to each other. They are facing in different directions from each other, however.

Again, this reads like an eyewitness report. The way the room décor was described with the partly open drapes created a distinctly domestic atmosphere, and Eva Braun's open threat, which was intended to keep Hilde from gossiping about the encounter, seemed natural under the circumstances. A disagreement between Eva and Hitler regarding the treatment of civilians in Poland was also credible, because women tend to be more compassionate and home oriented than men. Besides, it is a well-known fact that Eva Braun had no influence over Hitler's political decisions, which presupposes, of course, that her opinions differed from his. The dream showed the couple's opposing viewpoints. It also showed their emotional connectedness. The way they were sitting on the L-shaped sofa (L stands for love) together, yet apart, was a perfect metaphor for the kind of relationship they had.

It looks as if this secret meeting backfired on Hilde. She might have confided in her mother, who confided in her best friend, and so forth until the indiscretion got back to Eva Braun, who then was forced to act on her threat. Something of this nature must have occurred, because in the following dream Hilde and her mother were summoned to Berlin:

My mother and I have come to Berlin—by plane or train, I'm not sure which. We are now inside a large terminal building with marble floors. We have to go through some sort of check-in. We see a sinister-looking man nearby, making negative comments about people, and we are a bit afraid. I tell my mother not to worry, and I hold her hand. Holding hands, together we walk with the others through this hall.

Railway terminals do not have marble floors. This sounds more like the *Reichskanzlei*—the seat of the Nazi government at that time. The scene was bristling with tension for undisclosed reasons, and then, abruptly, the flow of images stopped. This "breaking of the film" is a psychological defense against having to reexperience a traumatic event. This is consistent with the next dream episode where Marc cannot decide if he should clean out the "loft"—the memory storage space—or not. In the end, the prima donna anima comes to his rescue, protecting his ego from a fatal blow:

I am with G. (a film star) in a storage room. The room has a loft, and G. climbs up to sort through some things. She says that the room is almost filled up, and looking around, I see that she is right. In one corner of the loft is a huge pile of my old clothes. I start to go up to the loft, but she says it's not necessary.

Judging from the huge pile of old clothes, which represented Hilde's former social identity, the interview at the Reichskanzlei stripped her of everything—her career as a filmmaker and her private life. To silence her once and for all, she was drafted into the SS where she became a staff member at the concentration camp Dachau.

THE SS TRAINING ORDEAL

In preparation for this unwanted job, she was sent to an SS training camp. She remembered this as an ordeal that she almost did not survive.

I am a young person, maybe a girl, and I am at a training camp. It is the middle of the night, but we are doing exercises. This is very difficult, and I think I might not survive the program. Nazi soldiers are here, watching us and moving us through our paces: calisthenics and running.

The next dream conveyed Hilde's first impression of Dachau when she reported for work there early one morning.

It is just before dawn. I am going into the gate of a chicken farm. This "farm" is actually in the middle of the suburbs. It is a very large lot, around which, in the distance, I see the backs of ordinary houses. Over the gate is a large sign that reads, "Work is good for us Jews," or something like that. Now it's dawn and I see the place begin to come to life. There are chickens all over. I am in a kind of church where a morning service is about to begin. A group of people are here—the people who run the camp. It is the birthday of a woman, maybe one of the owners.

We all gather around her to sing Happy Birthday, and she is shy about the attention. We sing, "Happy Birthday, dear Guggenheimer . . . Happy Birthday to you!"

In the beginning, the concentration camp looked like a chicken farm to Hilde. This was a variation of the dehumanization theme, which had first appeared in connection with the auburn-colored dog that was to be put to death. Obviously, Hilde had been conditioned to see the Jewish prisoners as subhuman. "Chicken," in a derogatory sense, means "coward" in English. The German equivalent *Huhn* is much more diversified when it is used with derogatory attributes. A huhn can be "silly, funny, stupid, weird, crazy," but it can also be "lame and sick." Marc, as I have pointed out before, showed signs of remembering the German vernacular in the dream state. This was another such example.

The environment of the camp, so clearly remembered and described in this dream, Marc later was able to verify on his visit to Dachau. The camp was situated "in the middle of the suburbs," just as he had seen it in this dream. The cynical message over the gate, which he had remembered only approximately, said in wrought-iron lettering *Arbeit macht frei* (Work will make you free).

One could tell from the degree of Hilde's confusion that she was a newcomer to the camp. Was this a church service, or a birthday party? She could not figure it out. And why were they making such a fuss over the birthday of a woman who was quite obviously a Jew? It was all very Kafkaesque. Hilde's initial bewilderment is even more explicit in the following dream:

I am a prisoner in a prison, a new arrival, and I'm being taught the rules of the prison. I hate being here and having to learn all these new things, and I am anxious that I won't remember everything. For instance, what to do when the lights go out or come on, how to make my bed the right way, how to put the games away after we play a game. There is a man who helps me. There are two or three other new prisoners, too, but they seem to know the ropes. Through all of this, I am afraid, and I don't like being here.

According to another dream, Hilde was broken in by her supervisor and coworkers.

It's as if I'm a new worker in a worker's compound—like a prison. The dining hall is full of men. I sit down, and one of the worker-waiters serves me a scoop of rice. It looks very unappetizing. I wait for something else, but nothing else comes. Next to the dish is a piece of dried sausage, but it is rancid and I don't go for it. There is a feeling of danger here, as if the others are "breaking me in." Lots of angry energy.

The man next to me is particularly hostile. I go outside and he follows me. I turn around and he has an empty beer bottle, which he breaks and is about to hit me in the face with. I stand my ground . . . The man seems to be both friend and enemy. I have the feeling that the slightest thing can set him off.

THE SLEAZY UNDERBELLY OF THE CAMP

Hilde's fear of breaking the rules is still palpable in the following dream. But she also had her first experience with the sleazy underbelly of the camp when she accidentally came across secret baths in an "underground cavern" where an eccentric older sergeant kept his "favored young men."

I am newly inducted into something like the military. I don't want to do anything wrong, like forget any of the new rules, but I realize I have forgotten to return the key to one of the "sergeants."

I ask a cadet about returning the key, and he says I can give it to the sergeant in charge. I go to that person—an eccentric older man. His area is a kind of underground cavern with hot baths, and young men and boys are in these baths. They are like the favored young men; the feeling is exclusive and erotic. I give the key back to the man and leave.

These baths were part of a prostitution underground, which operated at the pleasure of the camp's administration. A sadomasochistic branch of it had been "farmed out," probably for security reasons. Marc dreamed of this remote place in the countryside where Hilde had been taken one night, with the intention of getting her hooked on the perversion.

We leave that place at night, and I am driven with others out into the country. I see the headlights on the road, which winds through an abandoned field. Then we come to a barn, where some lights are on. Inside, there are women's screams and moans from men. When I go in, cautiously and somewhat fearful, I see that the place has naked men and women on the hay-strewn floor. They are writhing in pleasure and pain, and now I hear the screams again. A man beside me says I should go closer to watch, because it may be that I can become one of the "teachers." I am curious but also repulsed by the scene.

Although Hilde's repulsion outweighed her curiosity in the end, she seems to have participated in other group sex orgies, described as "amusement park rides." These took place in the basement of one of the staff houses, which Marc consistently called "my grandmother's house" in his dreams. Some of the sleaziest staff activities seemed to have been staged there. But "grandmother" never appeared in person, and Marc had no sinister memories of his own grandmothers. In want of a better explanation, I conjectured that "grandmother" might be a designation for Marc's soul ancestor, Hilde, and that "grandmother's house" was identical with Hilde's living quarters.

The following dream reflected her anxieties before attending the "amusement park ride" for the first time:

There is some sort of party in the basement of my grandmother's house; a part of the basement has been turned into an amusement park ride. At one point I go downstairs in the dark. I am frightened.

Whatever went on in the basement seems to have benefited Hilde's pocketbook, but probably not her soul. She might even have gone to confession afterward (that part of Germany is Catholic), for in the following dream she decided to give the "proceeds" from this enterprise to a charity:

I have come back from a trip, and I want to give some money to a charitable cause. I seem to want the proceeds from the amusement ride to go to help the poor and the sick.

The oversexualized atmosphere in the camp could even make the staff unsafe, as can be gleaned from the following dream:

I am a young woman and I go into a shower room, but I feel pursued by a man. Another man, a young blond man, is there, and I ask him to please stay in the room while I take my shower (because I need protection). I get into the shower, but there is a feeling of uneasiness.

In the beginning of her time at Dachau, Hilde worked as a cook in the staff kitchen. Simultaneously, she carried on a romantic affair with a dark-haired delivery boy.

I am in a kitchen with someone. We are the cooks—not really professional cooks, but it is our job here. Someone gives me a hint on how to make ordinary soup into something very special by putting a dollop of cream mixed with herbs on top. The person who is with me sits at the kitchen table and eats lunch, which is unusual, since we are supposed to eat after, not before, the others have eaten.

A young man comes in with the delivery. He has black hair and is good looking but not "pretty"—a manly young man, probably Italian. The other person leaves, and I am alone with the young man. I go into the adjoining room, which is the back room of my grandmother's house, and I get ready for bed. I struggle to take my socks off, which are tangled, and I peek into the kitchen to see that the young man is also getting ready for bed, which is a large cot. He undresses and I admire his naked body, but I don't seem to be aroused. Now I go to him and sit on the edge of the bed. He has his finger at his eye and says, "I seem to have something in here" (meaning some irritant). I look at it and say, "No, there's nothing," and lower his hand. I have very warm feelings for him.

In an annotation Marc added: *All through this dream, and especially in the last paragraph, I seem to be a young woman.*

Tender moments such as these had to be wrenched from the jaw of hell. Dachau was notorious for its medical experimentation. It officially started under the medical directorship of Dr. Sigmund Rascher and Dr. Klaus Schilling in the fall of 1941 when Hilde was no longer alive. But according to Marc's dreams, it had been going on even before then. On one occasion Hilde was ordered to supply urine for such an experiment. Her vivid recollections of the awkwardness of this procedure are preserved in the following dream:

I am in the back room of my grandmother's house, and there is a large urn set up there. I am to pee into a glass, and that is added to the liquid in the urn. Brother A. is the one adding the urine, and he does it like a ritual. At first I am a bit surprised and somewhat revolted at the idea that other people are going to drink this liquid, which has my urine in it, but he says that it's fine. It is how this special nectar is made.

Between times when I have to pee, I walk through a narrow street in a foreign country, where juices and other things are sold. I look only for water.

When I mentioned urine therapy to Marc, he had never heard of it before. This is a radical nature cure—ayurvedic in origin—which is sometimes applied with astonishing results when all else fails. In classical urine therapy, however, the patient drinks his own urine. On the negative side, urine has traditionally been used for torture, as during the Thirty Years War, when invading Swedish soldiers forced it down the Germans' throats. In Dachau, it might have served both purposes at once—medical experimentation as well as torture. Because the SS, before the liberation, destroyed a substantial part of the incriminating camp records, the whole truth about Dachau will never be known. Marc's past life memories are quite possibly as close as we will ever get to some of its lesser-known secrets.

When Marc had been a Christian monk in this life, one of the Brothers in his order had been Brother A. The substitution of a Christian monk, Brother A., for the SS officer that occurred in this dream was very revealing. It made Marc's time in the monastery appear in a rather sinister light. Also, A. had clearly not been Marc's favorite Brother; Marc had described him as moody, petty, and vindictive. Such personality substitutions are common in dreams. Their function is to point out a likeness between two people. In this particular case, the switch implied that the SS officer in charge of the urine collection had been as moody, petty, and vindictive as Brother A. Yet there was definitely more to that switch. Marc had exchanged one form of communal living for another in two successive lifetimes. This caused some contamination between the two kinds of experience, especially since the SS wore black uniforms and Marc's order wore black robes.

FILMING MEDICAL EXPERIMENTS

After having been a housekeeper for a while, Hilde seems to have taken on additional responsibilities. According to one of Marc's dreams, she was put in charge of a "vacant building," which probably was not as vacant as it looked from the outside. The Nazis were too well organized to let a building on the campsite stand empty, especially under notoriously overcrowded conditions. By putting all the pieces together, I came to the conclusion that the building that Hilde was in charge of was the very place where the medical experiments were being conducted. This would explain how it was possible for her to witness the experiments. Detailed images of one such experiment resurfaced in a particularly chilling and ultrarealistic dream. And again, it was in the "grandmother's house" where these images had been stored.

Now I'm in the back room of my grandmother's house. I am going down to the basement, and I see some books on the shelf above my head. I pull one down. It is very large and a little dusty. It is about Jews, and at first I don't know if it is anti-Semitic or pro-Semitic. It turns out to be a book about the atrocities that were performed on Jews—experiments.

I see that the pictures on the cover are animated. I look at one; it is the picture of a room, like a schoolroom or a shower room. Off in the back, a man is seated, waiting to be experimented on. A man or woman comes up to him. He leans his head back and he/she shoves an object like a large metal comb down his throat. It goes down his throat farther and farther, until the man throws up a thick discharge of mucus and other stuff. The experimenter pulls the comb out of the man's mouth; the man recovers and is given a cigarette butt to smoke. He takes a puff and stares at the camera with a kind of numbed but bemused look. His face looks like someone who is starved, almost Oriental in appearance.

This "close-up" of a torture scene made me wonder how Hilde could have remembered this with such precision unless she had participated in the experiment herself. Only when this thought crossed my mind did my attention focus on the camera in the dream, and then it all fell into place: Hilde, the former documentary filmmaker, had been recruited to film the experiments! What Marc was actually looking at in this large, dusty picture book was his own documentary. When I shared this discovery with Marc, many years after our work had ended, he made a surprising confession. He said that he has always been fascinated by torture and has always wanted to know all the details of it.

Hilde's familiarity with the medical facilities of the camp was apparent from another dream also, in which Marc was flipping through a different picture book. After looking at photographs of a medieval castle—also often a place of torture—he returned to images of Dachau's operating room.

I page through more pictures, and toward the end I get to large photos of articles in an operating room of a clinic: shoes, cloth masks, cleaning tools (brooms, mops), operating tables. Somewhere there are homeless children.

A HUMANITARIAN BREAKTHROUGH

It was, in fact, the "homeless children" that eventually got under Hilde's skin, preparing the ground for a humanitarian breakthrough. In the following dream fragment, she was marveling at the children's innocent play in the middle of starvation and mass executions:

I see children playing—little girls—and one very small girl who has enormous eyes, quite unusual and beautiful.

In the spring of 1942, a concerned citizen took Hilde to one of the side gates where the bodies of older Jewish boys were being loaded into trucks. This was the only time that public relations between the camp and the city of Dachau became an issue in Marc's dreams, although tensions between concerned citizens and the camp are a well-documented fact. The museum catalogue of the concentration camp states that inquisitive citizens who tried to look across the wall were immediately arrested. For Hilde, this was an eye-opening moment; she was beginning to realize that these boys who were being "poisoned like rats" were actually human beings.

It is spring. An order of monks with black hoods has been poisoning very large rats, and the people of the town are very concerned about this;

they don't think the monks should be going to these extremes. One of the townspeople takes me to where one truckload of dead rats (now they seem to be larger, like forest animals) are ready to be transported out, and this is only the last in a long line of trucks. The backs of the trucks are filled with these dead animals with black fur. As the truck pulls out to leave, one of the "animals" gets up and starts to run away; it is an urchin boy in a black coat. Now I see that all of these are poor, homeless boys.

One day, a visitor came in from the outside, wanting to take photographs of the prisoners. He showed Hilde pictures of children's carcasses hanging in a cage. They had been tortured and murdered as part of an experiment in the camp that Hilde was not "entirely in on."

A concentration camp or other "camp" torture center. I am a house-keeper, and I am responsible for a vacant building. There is some secret information I am not entirely in on, something about using children in torture. I am leaving the place for the season; soldiers are coming to take up residence. A man comes in, wanting to take photos. I rush him in but am anxious that he leave before the soldiers get here. We are in the kitchen and I am cooking meat in a skillet on a gas stove. There is an image somewhere of children's carcasses hanging in a cage. Could this be a "farm" for growing and butchering children—a cannibalistic meat-processing center?

Hilde had come a long way from seeing the camp as a "chicken farm." After the "animal" child prisoners had become human in her eyes, the adults were soon to follow. The moment of this final shift of consciousness is clearly remembered and movingly described in the following dream:

We are now upstairs in a large living room, circa 1940. Some people are with me and we are speaking softly, reading newspapers. Into the room, breaking the silence, comes a goat. The man next to me is appalled and motions for me to get the goat downstairs immediately. I take the goat and chase it through the room and down into a place where it hides, frightened.

When I get the goat out of the hiding place, it turns into an old woman. I lift her out and she catches a glimpse out of the windows. I then take her by her shoulders and show her the view out of each window, all around. I tell her to look hard because she is going downstairs again and can use the memory of the views to comfort her later. "It's beautiful, isn't it?" I ask, showing her these vistas of a Bavarian countryside with mountains.

"Yes," she says longingly, "so beautiful."

I now take the old woman down an outside set of stone stairs. It has begun to rain, and the steps are wet. I ask the man next to me what the name of this movie is, and he says, "The Tempest."

The quiet atmosphere in the reading room was that of an ordinary public library. This must have been a safe haven in the concentration camp, where members of staff were acting once more as if they were civilized human beings. The dream placed the reading room on the first floor. In the Dachau catalogue, which Marc deposited in my mailbox before he left Santa Fe to start a new life, I found a photograph of the main entrance building of the camp. Its first floor is built over three wide arches where windows with quaint Bavarian wooden shutters look out onto the city of Dachau. It was there where I pictured the reading room to have been—a Janus-faced buffer zone between two different worlds.

Into this peaceful oasis barged the "goat," as a disturbing and unwelcome reminder that people were starving and dying out there. The "goat" was actually a distraught old woman with some desperate agenda. The animal imagery can again be explained with the German vernacular. "Goat" (*Ziege*) is a derogatory term for woman—an equivalent for "silly goose." At first Hilde saw the intruder only as that, until the woman transformed herself into who she truly was: not a "goat," but a human being in a desperate situation. This awakened Hilde's humanity, and with an act of real compassion she showed her the beauty of the Bavarian Alps once more before the storm of retributions (the tempest) would break loose downstairs.

Although Hilde often felt like a prisoner herself, she was free to come and go. The dream about the photographer's visit showed that her work at the camp was only seasonal. In another dream she was spending time in the city (Munich), which was the target of heavy air raids during the war. Here she organized help for those who had lost their homes overnight.

I am coming back into the city after a disaster. Electricity seems to be running on several generators; there is little light. This is like a subway station, where there are homeless people. I am to take people in and help organize things. There are discussions about sleeping arrangements.

Another emergency—this time in the camp itself—must have made a lasting impression on Hilde, because Marc was able to recall every detail of it in the following dream:

I am in the courtyard of a large government building in what seems like a foreign country—Germany, perhaps. Now something has happened. A prisoner has escaped and the place is being closed down. I am out on the street now. The authorities have called for the trains and streetcars to come and block off all the streets. This is done quickly, leaving some people on the street rather surprised. These blockades go into place like clockwork.

Suddenly, it is clear that the "emergency" is over; the prisoner is in custody. I am in the courtyard again. A government official comes over to me. He is quite nice. He tells me I can be the one to switch the lights back on. The switch is on the wall next to me. When I turn it on, all normal activity will resume. I pull the switch.

By pulling the switch, Hilde restored "law and order" to the camp. In spite of what she knew or suspected, she was still supporting the system. But when the war continued to disrupt life in Germany with a barrage of air raids, evacuations, and food shortages, conditions in the camp also worsened. On Marc's visit to Munich and Dachau, memories of a growing paranoia, which had drastically changed the social climate in the camp, came back to him in a dream.

There are books with black covers and silver lettering on the spines, written in Old German script. These books are directions, rules, laws, and pronouncements. I hear a voice saying that from this point on, such and such a rule is now in effect. There is also a ruling that the rule-breakers are to be punished without their knowing the reason (this goes also for the people keeping the rule books), causing an anxious feeling that rules are changing and people are to be punished.

ARREST AND EXECUTION

It was after these changes had taken place that Hilde began to feel trapped. Fear of punishment was forcing her into obedience, while feelings of shame made her want to dissociate herself from the Nazis. In one dream, she felt embarrassed driving her Volkswagen through Munich on the way to a sports event. The Volkswagen was introduced by the Nazi government in 1937 as an affordable automobile "for the people." It became a status symbol of Hitler's social work. But at the beginning of the war, all privately owned cars were "drafted" into the military, except for those belonging to high party officials. Driving a Volkswagen, therefore, identified Hilde as one of "them." This old embarrassment carried over into Marc's present life as an irrational hate of Volkswagens—a hate that Marc had never been able to explain until he had this dream.

Hilde might have known of a plot against her when she began planning her escape. Apparently, she had reason not to trust her contacts in the underground and decided to rely only on herself.

I am in a foreign country and need a ride somewhere or someplace to keep my things. Someone comes forward to help, but I realize I can do this on my own—perhaps duck into Switzerland, where I can get cleaned up . . . there is something rather sinister about the person or people I'm dealing with, lowlifes who want to "help," but really just want to be paid.

In the later stages of World War II, many Germans dreamed of sneaking across the Swiss border to escape from mortal danger. According to Marc's night dream, Hilde was planning to whitewash herself (get cleaned up) once she got to Switzerland and then apply for political asylum. Her plan might even have worked, because, after having been a Nazi herself, she was on the point of becoming a victim of the Nazis. Unfortunately, before Hilde could realize her plan, the SS caught up with her. The following dream describes the moment before her arrest, late in the fall of 1941:

I am in an old hotel or dormitory building, and I am trying to hide from someone. I wander through the upstairs halls and find a room to hide in. The room has a 1940s décor. A telephone is on the table, and I hope it will not ring. I think I hear footsteps in the hall, and I hide behind the door. (This has the feeling of an old spy movie, a creepy feeling of trying to get away from people who are pursuing me. I am a woman in this dream.)

Here Marc's past life dream recall ended. But he now wanted to know it all. He was determined to find out what had preceded Hilde's execution, of which he had dreamed at the beginning of his analysis. Since his dreams had fallen silent, he decided to try another past life regression—this time with me. In the regression, we were able to access the rest of the story: Another "matron" had denounced Hilde for being too lenient with the women prisoners. On these grounds, she had been arrested. A bald-headed SS officer had conducted the interrogation. He had humiliated Hilde by tearing her blouse open, then threatened her with the women's shed if she did not tell everything. At the end of the interrogation, which had continued into the night, SS officers had loaded Hilde, handcuffed, into an old automobile and had driven her along snowy roads to a remote place in the mountains. There they had ordered her out of the car. As she stood shivering in the snow, she had looked for a split second into the glaring headlights, just as Marc's very first dream had recorded it.

A car's headlights—a bone-cold winter night . . . Headlights on an old Dusenburg or some such large car . . . Snow on the ground . . .

A moment later the SS officers dragged her away from the car, shot her in the head, and pushed her lifeless body down a steep snowbank.

PSYCHOLOGICAL FALLOUT

According to my calculations, Hilde must have been about twenty-four years old when she was executed. She could not have been in Dachau longer than a year and a half, because in the autumn of 1942, Marc was born. But time is relative. For the reader of this story, this year and a half feels like an eternity. It must have felt the same way for Hilde. Time spent in Dachau must have been timeless, like in purgatory, on either side of the fence. Despite Hilde's suffering, probably even because of it, much progress was made on the soul level. Hidden in this horrifying experience were invaluable lessons in the dangers of hero worship and the equality of all human beings. From childhood on, Nazi hate propaganda and Fuehrer worship had befogged Hilde's young, impressionable mind, until in the blackest dungeon of this degenerate collective movement she had been cured of the national psychosis. She had opened her heart in compassion, albeit at a very high price.

Our most recent lifetime seems to have a greater impact on us than others, except for the very traumatic ones. Marc's incarnation as Hilde was both; it was recent *and* traumatic. In his own way a survivor of Dachau, Marc carried a heavy burden of guilt around with him, unconsciously, for most of his life. He carried the collective karma of all those Germans who had shared in the pathological group fantasy of being of a superior race, while projecting all that was undesirable in the national character onto defenseless minority groups. In addition, he carried the group karma of a relatively small Nazi "elite" that had been willing to enact Hitler's "end solution" for these undesirable minority groups. Although Hilde had been coerced to join the Dachau staff, once she had acclimatized herself to her inhumane environment she had made her home in it. Although her contribution to the unspeakable horrors might have been minor, she still was responsible for that minor part.

When Marc befriended a young Jewish man, halfway through his therapy, his guilt started to weigh him down. One night while lying awake in his bed, he had the "clear sense that all the Jews in my life are looking at me, wondering whether I am going to hurt them." Soon thereafter, he broke down in the young man's arms and confessed what he had done to the Jews in his last incarnation. He solemnly promised his friend that he would never hurt him. When the young man, a little bewildered, absolved him, Marc felt comforted but not permanently relieved.

It was indeed fortunate for Marc that his male side was so powerful, for otherwise his broken female side would have completely incapacitated him. In order to remain in control of himself, Marc had to split off his true anima and put a pseudo anima in her place—the Hollywood prima donna who had been so visible to everyone around him and so omnipresent in his dreams. He had paid for this dissociation outwardly with emotional isolation and inwardly with depression and fear. This fear had also been predominant in Hilde's emotional state, as Marc was beginning to realize toward the end of his therapy. "I remember mainly the terrible fear, which I felt almost constantly during this time period, relentless fear—fear of my superiors on the one hand, and fear of the prisoners on the other," he wrote in a personal statement to me. Thinking about how this had affected his life, Marc added, "I have spent the greatest part of my life in fear—often in fear of my superiors, but also, like with the staff I have employed, in fear of my 'subordinates.'"

Unconsciously, he had created a treacherous, hostile work environment in his department not unlike the one he had been part of at Dachau. His fear of his staff was not entirely unfounded either, because at the university where he taught, his staff conspired against him and eventually dechaired him. By doing so, they actually did him a favor because this forced him to give up his old pattern of living in closed communities. He now had no choice but to attend to the unavoidable task of creating a new, more fulfilling life for himself.

When I last saw Marc, this new life was beginning to unfold. There were no further obstacles, because his karma had been cleared. In five years of painstaking dreamwork we had laid the foundation for his personal freedom by throwing light into the shadow that Dachau had cast over his life. At some point in the fourth year of therapy, Marc had grown weary and had wanted to speed up the process. He had tried a shortcut by using rituals. In one of the local Catholic churches he had had a mass read for Hilde, and on Independence Day, under a tree in my front yard, he ritually burned his collection of Hilde dreams. But his unconscious had ignored these Band-Aids completely and continued to empty itself of every sordid and scary image until all of it had been exposed, processed, and released.

Only when this purging was over could Marc progress to the final stage of the healing process and allow love into his life. He chose a much younger but caring and loyal man. They decided to live together, and Marc finally had the courage to come out as a homosexual. The love they have for each other has benefited all his relationships—with men and women alike.

Today, seven years later, Marc is a warm, affectionate, paternal man. His emperor energy has merged with Hilde's nurturing side. He does not care for the distant sparkle of Hollywood film stars anymore, because he now knows true intimacy. Professionally, he is occupied with projects that further consciousness in the collective—the very thing that Hilde had helped to suppress. What has stayed with him from his Nazi life is his fascination with documentary filmmaking. It survived the five-year catharsis period and might well be carried as a bloodline into future incarnations.

There was an eerie sequel to this story. After Marc had assembled all the dream material for this book he dreamed the following:

I am looking at a blank sheet of paper that had only four words written at the bottom:

> *Thank you,*
> *Adolf Hitler*

8

WALKING ON THIN ICE

A Past Life Transference at the Brink of Disaster

For haven't I always known you?
And isn't this house,
This dream we share
Written deep within us both?

ANONYMOUS

A DIFFICULT CLIENT

Usually it is easy for me to keep the appropriate emotional distance from my clients. The empathy I feel for them comes from my own checkered life experience, my familiarity with my shadow, and the mistakes I have made myself. The access I have to my clients' dreams and, through their dreams, to their unconscious is due to the access I have to my own dreams and unconscious. My relationship with my clients is more reflective than projectively identified. Once the session is over, no matter how intense the encounter has been, I do not carry my client's burdens over into my private life. This keeps me sane and

168

prevents a professional burnout. Unfortunately, I had taken my detachment so much for granted that I was not prepared for having it challenged one day. I should have known better, because both Freud and Jung had experienced complications in the so-called transference and countertransference relationship. They had written about uncontrollable emotional enmeshments that may develop during analysis, putting both client and therapist in great danger. What made me think that I alone was immune to such things?

Even my first contact with Eric was different from how such contacts are usually made. Instead of calling me from Santa Fe, he phoned me long distance from New York. He wanted to set up an interview with me in order to find out if I was the right therapist for him. I was one of several Jungian analysts he had selected from the Yellow Pages and intended to meet with once he arrived in Santa Fe. Although to be interviewed in this way made me feel uncomfortable, I agreed to see him.

Eric was in his late twenties. He was medium-blond, well proportioned, and had a boyish Oxbridge look. He had a kind of moody charm that could have gotten him almost anything he wanted under normal circumstances. But presently, things were far from normal for him. After leaving his wife and his five-year-old son on an impulse, he had been immersed in grief and depression.

From the beginning of the interview, Eric seemed determined to be in control. When I asked him for a recent dream, he called this "inappropriate," because he had not "chosen" me yet. I was not offended by this rebuke, because I was, after all, a stranger to him. But I was not prepared for the slap in the face with which he terminated the interview: "I once worked with a woman psychologist for a short time who had unresolved problems," he said. "At the end of our sessions, I always felt that my feet were very far away from my head. I have the same feeling with you now."

With one masterful coup he had reversed our roles. I had become the one with the unresolved problems and he the one who could diagnose them. He seemed to have a good intuition. The trouble was, he was using it as a weapon against me. I knew that it would not do me any good to assert my authority at this moment. In fact, nothing short of a clever repartee would have made an impression on him. But I could not think of anything clever to say; on the contrary, I was speechless. I was even beginning to wonder if there might be some truth to his observation. Yet to give me new insights into myself was clearly not his intention. His intention was to intimidate me in order to gain the upper hand. Thinking of this made me furious, but I managed to keep my emotions under control until Eric was safely out of the door.

If the emotional charge between us was anything to go by, he might be back, I thought later after I had cooled down. He might have a negative mother-complex that I had inadvertently triggered. I was right about his return, although not about the reason for it. A few days later Eric phoned to inform me that he had "chosen" me. With his flight back to New York being only a few hours away, he wanted to come over immediately. Although it interfered with my lunch hour, I agreed to see him.

He was just beginning to relax in my huge, soft leather armchair, which to some clients felt like a womb, when he transformed himself before my very eyes into a cripple with grotesquely distorted features and limbs. Without any warning, he had slipped into a past life self. Although I had seen people change like this in hypnotic regressions on Joy Hinson-Ryder's massage table, I felt alarmed. How was I going to get him out of this state, which I had not induced myself? Uncertain about what to do but concerned about his impending drive to the airport, I ordered him in a stern voice to return to his present self. To my surprise, it worked. His contorted features straightened out, and in a minute or two his body was back to normal.

Intrigued by his impressive impersonation of a past life personality, I asked Eric if he knew that I was the only Jungian in town who worked with reincarnation. He did; he also knew that another local Jungian—a clinical psychologist whom he had interviewed—believed in reincarnation. Unfortunately, this man was convinced that our past lives do not impact on our present one. Since this was contradicted by Eric's own experience, it had disqualified this particular therapist in his eyes. In fact, since his arrival in Santa Fe, he had been so swamped with past life material that it was virtually incapacitating him. Although he had "not chosen" the clinical psychologist for this reason, he had nevertheless accepted his offer to prescribe antidepressants for him.

Seeing how ungrounded Eric was, I only discussed practical matters with him in the remaining part of the session. I told him that we would have plenty of time later to deal with his past and present life problems. As I walked him to the door, he suddenly stopped and turned around. Looking me straight in the eye, he asked, "Who are you?" I did not feel that his intrusiveness was motivated by a desire to dominate me this time, but that he simply wanted to know whom he had "chosen."

I therefore replied, with a twinkle in my eye, "You'll find out." Although my understanding of his question had not been entirely wrong, I still had missed the point. He therefore restated the question. "Do I know you from a past life?" Wondering if he was onto something I was myself not in touch with, I turned the question back at him. "What do *you* think?" I asked.

He responded, "A little voice says 'Of course, of course.'" In the future, I learned to trust Eric's "little voice," because it was always right. But at the time, the only thing that I was prepared to take seriously was his transformation into a cripple. It had looked like an authentic past life to me, but also like a desperate cry for help. This appealed to my maternal instincts, and I instantly bonded with him.

WATCHING THE FLOW OF IMAGES

Two weeks later he was back with bag and baggage in Santa Fe, and the most challenging therapy of all my years of practice began. Previous to his first session, Eric had consulted a local psychic who had informed him of one of his past lives. According to her, he had been a stupid, boisterous Norseman and the second-in-command of a Viking boat that had raided the coast of England. Knowing that I had been abducted by Vikings from the coast of England, with a captain and a second-in-command as instigators, I should have been more alarmed hearing this. Instead, I resorted to convenient rationalizations. There must have been plenty of Viking raids along the coast of England, I told myself. Why should it have been Eric of all people who had abducted me? I had only just started practicing past life therapy and had no idea how purposefully karmic encounters are arranged on the soul level. Had I been more cautious and less defended at the time, I would have managed the transference better later on. At least I would like to think so.

Our first session had already unleashed a flood of unconscious material in Eric. He later showed me his diary, with notes and transcripts of tape recordings he had made while in transit from Santa Fe to New York and from New York to Santa Fe. On his return to New York from his initial visit to Santa Fe, after checking in at the local airport in Albuquerque to await his eastbound flight, he still had had half an hour to spare before his flight was called. As he was sitting in a chair with his eyes closed, an image had started to form. He had seen a long, perhaps endless hallway, hung with pictures on both sides and had intuitively known that's how many past lives a person has. He had seen the same image again in his hotel room in New York later that day, and this time he recorded it.

Lying in bed, watching the flow of images. Many images, can't remember them all. A couple times, feeling just spirit, a black night sky filled with stars.

Also, again, the image of a corridor of pictures, this time like posters on display in a store; these go on and on, maybe forever, but certainly farther than I can see.

In the middle of the night Eric had been woken up by another onslaught of images. He had done an hour-long recording, which started like this:

Image reporting. It's the middle of the night, 3:00. Let the images flow. I want to release . . . I want to . . . Let it go, let it go. What do I see? A sign. A sign with a brown background and a white stag. A lot of background noise. What's that? An ear. A vein of white rock in a cliff side . . . Let's follow that . . . A "T" . . . Hoof prints . . . Deeper, let's go deeper. Yes, yes. Oh, oh. Oh. Another sign. Some stairs going up. A castle? Oh. Mountain lion. Let's go deeper up the stairs. Up the stairs, here we go . . . A castle. Let's go in the castle. Teeth, skull. I see. What is that? What are those things? A tunnel, let's go in there. All right, I'm in the tunnel, going down the tunnel . . . Oh God, I look ugly, deformed! I'm all deformed. Why?! I'm all bent, misshapen . . . Oh, my hands! My left is bent double; the right hand is splayed out. [pain noises] My legs—I'm all curled up. Why? Why? There's a crown . . .

The recording, which he had later transcribed, was a hodgepodge of seemingly unrelated images, but the cripple got my attention because I had met him before. And the crown? Was there a connection between the cripple and the crown? Could Eric have been the infamous Richard III of England, the royal monster portrayed in Shakespeare's play? That he had been King Richard I of England was later confirmed, but this did not rule out that he could also have been King Richard III three centuries later. For it has often been said by experts on reincarnation that we tend to be reborn into the same family.

However, when I first set eyes on this material I was groping completely in the dark. So I concentrated on the only thing I could get a firm grip on, which was the tunnel. The tunnel is an interdimensional link. We can travel through it into the deepest layers of the unconscious and also into the world of the dead. The ancient Greeks, therefore, believed that Hermes, the messenger of the gods, performed a dual function: he took people into the world of dreams and also into Hades.

Although Eric had suicidal tendencies, here he was only searching for lost parts of himself and for deeply buried memories and traumas that were interfering with him today. The medieval castle and the crown turned out to be a memory complex around which more and more images were to form in future dreams and trance sessions.

His transcripts were like nothing I had ever seen. They were meticulous records of self-induced trance states. Although this technique came to him naturally, it was also born out of necessity. It was the only way he could stay in partial control of his turbulent inner world. By allowing the flooding while directing its flow, he protected his ego from drowning in it. The trances were like streams of consciousness, not like cohesive stories. This made it virtually impossible to integrate the past life material. On the other hand, it gave us a panoramic overview of Eric's past life history.

I recently dreamed that past life material cannot be integrated if too much of it comes up all at once. In such a case, the dream stated, the integration work must be done in a future life. Erik was such a case. At the time, neither he nor I were able to keep track of the images, let alone do historical background research on them. This only became possible when, at the end of the therapy, Eric handed over a copy of the transcripts to me. But even then, the transcripts remained untouched until this book was in the planning stage.

The decisive factor to not interfere with the flooding had been Eric's initial dream. This dream, which is diagnostically and prognostically so important, had reassured me from the beginning that he was in no danger of getting swept away into a full-blown psychosis. Quite the opposite, the dream had shown signs of unusual courage, ego strength, and resilience.

Walking with a group of people. There's a body of water, covered with thin ice. The others are cautious of the thin ice, but I go ahead and walk on it and fall through. "Well," I say as I get out of the water, wet and cold, "I guess I'll be going home now."

Then the little boy who's with us falls into the water, too. We get him out and I say, "I guess he better come with me."

Although Eric went where others feared to tread, he could obviously afford to do that. Experience must have taught him that he was tough enough to survive almost any catastrophic event. Even the little boy in him remained unharmed after falling into the icy water. And most importantly, at the end of this wet and cold adventure, Eric remembered just in time to "go home"—in other words, to return to himself.

ACQUIESCENT FEMALES

Despite this innate sangfroid, Eric felt helpless when we began seeing each other three times a week. He knew that his wife, who had stayed behind with his small son, was unpredictable and vindictive. There was no way of telling what she might do to punish her runaway husband. This forced Eric into an almost feminine passivity, which might have been the reason why two of his female lives surfaced first, headed by a primitive African one.

Some very primitive scenes, incomplete; native black women, like Africa, sitting in a row on the ground, working on something, probably preparing food, pounding or grinding.

While this was a dream image, the following pregnancy and birthing process he experienced in a self-induced trance state:

I see a woman from the side. But no! I am the woman, lying on my side. I want him in me. I lift my hips; I feel him inside; it feels good, full. He comes. I don't. I want him to stay, he does as long as he is able; it's warm and nice, I feel cared for, loved. I am amused as his penis grows small and soft.

I want this child, I really do. Then I feel the child—a hard place of my lower body. It's wonderful, good. The child grows; it's a good feeling. I never realized that you still feel your original slim body, even while you grow more and more pregnant; it's as though your original body is still there and the pregnancy is just somehow attached to you. I get heavy with child, feel him stirring. It'll be soon.

I roll on my back, pull my legs up and spread wide. It begins, and I'm excited, scared, almost out of it, passed out. I'm not delirious but rather given in to forces beyond my control. I push down; the pain is there, but it's not great, or maybe I don't feel it. I push more. Then it stops. What happened? I'm not sure; birthing has stopped. I was gone from it. I think I died giving birth. I'm not sure if the child lived or not; I don't have the sense that the child lived, but I'm not sure. I'm sad. But somehow I accept this fate, this end of life. My biggest regret was that I was not able to nurse my child—to breastfeed and nurture the child. I remember how large and swollen my breasts were in that life. The grief I feel is not completely overwhelming; somehow, I accept this end.

This was a very passive person, he commented in his diary. Sweet, but very acquiescent and accepting of whatever happened to her. Very remarkable feeling, being a woman: the absence of aggression and the deep sense—the primeval feeling—of a direct connection to life forces, earth cycles, nurturing and giving life.

MALE WARRIORS

It must have been the separation from his beloved little son that had brought back these memories of a long-ago stillbirth. Eric's inner female—his anima—would have accepted the loss of the child in a spirit of resignation. But feminine passivity was not a healthy attitude for him. Thinking that this acquiescence might contribute to his depression, I pointed out to him that he was unconsciously identified with the dying woman. This elicited an immediate response from his unconscious; he dreamed of a strong male life in Poland during the time of the plague.

A street scene, a Polish man on a grassy hill above the town, his back to the town. The perspective is slightly below so his full figure is visible. Immigrant clothes and a sack over his shoulder. Proud man. Strong, not extraordinarily tall, but sturdy and broad shouldered. In the streets there's a cart carrying a dead body—many bodies. There are many people sick and dying; it seems to be the plague.

This scene put Eric in touch with the survivor in himself. With the "ribbon grass effect," which I have often observed in past life recall, these memories brought more strong male lives to the surface. Most of these were warrior lives—some primitive, others sophisticated—with Eric almost always in a leadership role.

There's a tribe of black people. Very primitive, with spears and shields. They're standing facing me. I might be speaking to them (addressing them), like a chief. There's a very nappy surface; it's the tightly curled hair of a black person.

In another African life, remembered during a trance session, he had been an assassin who cold-bloodedly thrust a knife into a colonial officer's back.

A map, a palm tree, and a knife, then a guy's back. In a white, almost military-like, safari suit [laugh] with a black belt.

In ancient times Eric had been a Roman soldier. The following crucifixion scene came up twice in a self-induced trance state, both times with Eric in the observer role:

I had images of a crossbow, which became the crosspiece of a crucifix, and I could see someone being crucified from the side (the view was from slightly below and from the right side of the person).

The transformation of the crossbow into a crucifix established a causal connection between the two, thus the crucifixion might have been the punishment of a Jew, for using the crossbow on the Romans. Eric's role in the crucifixion scene became clearer when he saw it the second time.

A small figure—on a cross. A guy with a funny—hm, like a soldier, a Roman soldier, but no helmet, it's like the, ah—they must wear something under the helmet. It's like he took the helmet off, and he's got this head covering. He's a young guy; it's like young men these days getting in the military—he just happened to be a soldier. [pause] I suppose this is me.

Twenty centuries later, Eric was a soldier again, this time an American soldier fighting the Germans in France. The following dream described the war scene in the factual style of a newspaper report:

The United States had invaded Germany. At one point, with the U.S. troops in a bad position on top of an expanse of a rocky, urban hilltop, truce and peace talks were convened. We all waited nervously for the outcome of the talks. German and U.S. troops intermingled, nervously. I tried to find a better weapon—an automatic rifle like others had.

Then the truce/peace talks concluded. As a voice incomprehensibly droned on, explaining the outcome of the talks, we marched into the countryside and took up positions in the fields and woods. French soldiers in berets moved with us. There was a movie showing "the men left standing" after Argonne. The movie seemed very real, and we realized, here we are again. Our job was to sweep the countryside.

Earlier, there was a scene of a U.S. soldier almost in slow motion, sneaking up on a group of German officers and assassinating them, shooting each one in the head. One translator type even showed the soldier how to shoot him under the nose to get the fullest effect. Also, another scene, within the U.S. field headquarters. Soldiers were nervously deliver-

ing messages between rooms; they carried weapons, and before entering a room they ducked their heads quickly around the corner to see if it was safe.

As we swept the countryside, we came into a town. We went into a place that was a kind of beer hall; the front room contained a bar on the right and tables on the left, then there was a middle room that was large and open, then there was a smaller room in the back. It seemed that there were some people with guns in the back room. I waved the rest of the guys up to the two doors to the back room. We moved cautiously, ducking behind walls and furniture. I looked into the room; they looked like students, but they were armed—both the young men and young women. I yelled a warning to the other guys, and I yelled to the students to drop their weapons. Because I assumed that they didn't understand English, I stood in the doorway and motioned to them to drop their weapons or we'd shoot. One of the students shot me with a very small caliber rifle (I think it hit me, but I didn't feel anything), and we all opened fire. One German woman, an unarmed waitress, ran to the door and I took her hand. I said to her, "I'm sorry, I'm sorry," but she didn't seem to understand English.

Eric assumed that this was World War II, but this is not consistent with historical facts. In the dream, the armistice agreement was made in France. This was the case in World War I, not in World War II. Also, Argonne was mentioned as the battleground, which was only the case in World War I. Two famous battles were fought in the Argonne between German and American troops at the end of World War I. In the first battle, the Americans were defeated after walking into a trap and being gassed by the Germans, while the second battle was lost by the Germans. It was this first battle in which many American soldiers lost their lives that the "movie" (the remembered scenes) of "the men left standing after Argonne" was referring to. "And here we are again," said the dream. As a survivor of the first battle, Eric thought of the previous bloodshed while he was nervously following orders to "sweep the countryside" once again. He expected to walk into another trap, and they did. In a German beer hall, he and his men were ambushed by German university students and in the resulting conflict Eric was hit by a bullet.

The dream did not spell out what happened to Eric as a result. Why he did not feel anything when he was hit, one wonders? He might have been killed instantly without even realizing it, and his encounter with the waitress might really have been an out-of-body experience. Eric's sincere apology to this simple woman seemed to extend to all innocent civilians who had been unwilling participants in the war. Unfortunately, the waitress did not understand Eric's apology. Or, it might not have been audible to her, because he no longer had a voice. Anyway, there was something so chivalrous about Eric's gesture that I wondered if this was a bleed-through from medieval times. And sure enough, a few days later the related past life emerged in a trance.

RICHARD THE LION-HEARTED

As Eric was getting closer to this past life he noted in his diary, "I must be reverential about this stuff and not let it just feed the ego." He seemed to be warding off an ego inflation even before he remembered the following scene:

There is a group of people with swords at an outside wall of the castle; they are storming the castle, it's like the Bastille. There's sort of a revolution.

And here's a young person, standing before them on a raised platform. I'm seeing this from behind, and slightly to the boy's right. He's dressed in robes, and has a crown—and I almost want to say there's a feather, a feather in his—head (sticking out of his crown). Ah, he's a prince.

Eric later commented in his diary: *I had the feeling the young person may have been a prince in another time, here visiting as a spirit. And yet there's also the feeling that he has inspired the people to act. Then I was startled to remember the dream of December 25 where someone says to me, "There he is! Here's the one who fomented the whole revolution." And I reply lightly, "No, not me, I just sort of helped it along." The boy, the prince, is somehow me.*

The crown had appeared repeatedly in Eric's recordings, but it had never actually been worn by a person before. Here, for the first time, it was worn by a prince whom Eric had been in another life. In order to serve as a role model for the French Revolution, this prince must have lived centuries earlier. Two additional images from the same trance session give us a clue about when that might have been.

I've had this image before: the Christian cross, which turns so easily into a sword. It just goes back and forth, from a very elaborate, ornamental cross to a sword with a very ornamental handle.

Here the Janus face of Christianity was being exposed—one peaceful, the other militant. Eric saw them constantly turning into each other. This transformation back and forth had been particularly striking during the medieval Crusades. The next image belonged in the same cultural and historical context.

Gold embroidery on a purple cloth. It's like the canopy over the throne outdoors. I once had a dream about the same thing.

In a subsequent trance session, the identity of this medieval prince whom Eric had been was all but revealed.

A view from a stone window—I mean a window in a stone wall. It's the castle where the knight came from. A yellow lion on a blue background: King Richard. The view from the window is a very . . . pastoral scene; fields in the foreground, and forest, old low mountains in the background.
The drawbridge, which is way up above me, is open, and there are

many people coming out. Looking at it from below, I'd have to be in the moat, [amused] or whatever is down there.

In retrospect, it appears negligent not to have made an attempt to find out which King Richard this was (there were several), especially since a quick reference to the *Encyclopedia Britannica* would have sufficed. Probably, we were in avoidance of the truth, fearing that it might have given Eric an ego inflation. And for good reason! Fifteen years later, I could easily identify him as one of the most famous kings in European history: Richard I of England, also known as Richard the Lion-Hearted (1157–1199). As a crusader of great renown, he was the hero of many romantic legends. After showing great bravery in combat with the Arab leader Saladin, he was able to negotiate a peace treaty with him, which ended—and saved—the Third Crusade. Thanks to Richard's diplomatic skills, an agreement could be made, which gave the Christians safe access to the Sepulchre from then on.

Another set of romantic legends was woven around Richard's adventurous return from the Holy Land. Having been shipwrecked near Venice, he was taken prisoner by King Leopold I of Austria, who handed him over to his archenemy, Emperor Henry VI, who then incarcerated him. This was the first case of royal kidnapping in Europe, and Eleanor of Aquitaine, Richard's mother, could only set him free by paying a huge ransom to the emperor.

Eleanor had raised her son in the duchy of Aquitaine in Normandy. This was "the castle where the knight came from" in Eric's vision. It was also the castle where Richard died, according to historical records. The yellow lion on the blue background was Richard the Lion-Hearted's coat of arms. As a sixteen-year-old, Richard had joined his brothers in an uprising against their father, King Henry II of England (1133–1189). It could have been this act of youthful rebellion against a parental authority figure that, centuries later, made him a role model for the French Revolution. But Richard was a warrior throughout his life. He lived in conflict with other European heads of state and lay in constant strife with local barons who refused to pay tribute to him. It was in keeping with his adventurous lifestyle that he died in battle, felled by an arrow, at the relatively young age of forty-two. According to a character portrait, provided by the *Encyclopedia Britannica,* Richard was irresponsible, hot-tempered, tremendously energetic, and capable of great cruelty, but he was universally respected as a soldier of unusual capability and as a skillful politician.[1] Privately, he was known as a talented poet, a hero of the troubadours, and a homosexual.

Eric had quite a few personality traits in common with Richard the Lion-Hearted, although he was clearly not a homosexual. His pronounced sangfroid had been apparent from his initial dream, and his rebellion against authority figures had been evident from the moment we met. On the other hand, Eric's transcripts, diary entries, and poems showed very clearly that Richard's gift for poetic expression had also been handed down the bloodline. Thus Eric had inherited both: some of Richard's virtues and talents as well as some of his vices. Once I had ascertained the king's identity, I found Richard's signature written all over Eric's unconscious material. In the following dream, he remembered the sword-fighting lessons he had received as a young prince:

Being trained in sword fighting. The instructor's name was François. I ask him what to do when the point of the opponent's sword is thrust straight at you. According to François, you simply slide your left hand down the blade and push the other sword away.

In the fencing competition, I have one more match remaining. I haven't won any matches so far, but with my wild, unorthodox style, anything could happen. Nevertheless, it takes only a moment for the girl opponent to get me right under the left arm and in the heart.

These past life memories were clearly triggered by Eric's present power struggle with his wife over his son. So far, he had been no match for her in his private negotiations. What still lay ahead of him was a legal battle. He was rehearsing in this dream how he would handle the upcoming dispute. He could always count on the fencing skills that he had developed during the Middle Ages, and if all else failed, he could still fall back on his "wild, unorthodox style," which might influence the outcome. Yet, despite these inner resources, he knew that his love for his son had made him vulnerable, and he anticipated a fatal wounding in this last match with his wife.

Richard was known for his cruelty, and Eric also had traces of that. Not only was this apparent from his unconscious material but also occasionally from his behavior toward me. The following dream, in which Eric was identified with Richard, bears witness to this "inherited" character trait:

One of my servants had lied to me. He had indeed witnessed the event in question, but he had denied it when I questioned him. As the ruler of these people, I can't allow servants to lie to me. He will have to be punished. I tell him quite simply that he must die.

A TERRIFYING MOTHER COMPLEX

Eric's self-induced trance material contained some graphic torture scenes, which were difficult for him to look at. In the following scenes (apparently from a life other than that of Richard the Lion-Hearted) he seemed to have been at the receiving end of the torture, but with Richard the Lion-Hearted as his soul ancestor, it was bound to have been the other way around at another time:

There's someone with his wrists tied over his head, behind his back (pain); he's hanging. (Hanging in this way, the arms would dislocate at the shoulders.) It's a dungeon. I see some hands, as if in prayer, but they're also tied at the wrists with rope. They're white hands (hands of a white person). Scenes of human torture, very repulsive and sickening, chests ripped out, people getting horrible things done in their mouths . . .

What he found most disturbing was that he associated this torture scene with his mother. My first impression that Eric had a negative mother complex was thus confirmed, but not in the usual textbook sense. The kind of mother complex he had was not caused by his mother in his present lifetime but derived from a past life. When I asked him how his present-day mother had treated him as a child, he could not fault her on anything. Yet this irrational fear of her was so overwhelming that he had a hard time being in the same room with her. He had never been able to make sense of this until these past life memories came to the surface.

There's a woman with her left hand over her face, and I have a feeling that if I could see her face I would be very frightened. [noises, breathing, sounds of agitation, fright] Yeah, it would be very, very frightening to see her face. How do you see one eye? [pause] The image was like my mother, about to be very, very cruel . . .

After some unrelated imagery, the recording returned to the same torture scene.

Here's an image of my mother again. And I have the feeling that if I could really see her face I would be—I would see her revealed as a very frightening and cruel person. Who is she really? I've been running away from her, someone she used to be . . . Show me—who was she before? It's worse, not knowing. I see, geez, it's like a human torso with three or four pairs of breasts (the torso was suspended, horizontal, with breasts hanging down). I see clawed hands, heads on sticks—Holy Smokes! [agitation, fear] . . . I think my mother was someone that I was very terrified of in some other time. [pause] . . . There's a head with a long, stretched-out neck. There's a man tied by his neck to a stake. [agitation] . . . Oh, the more I think about that the truer it seems. So who was she? Let me see her face . . . I can't do it. I can't force it to happen.

Here Eric gave up, because he was running into a wall of resistance. The wall was there for a reason, of course: to protect some semblance, however slight, of a "normal" mother-son relationship.

GYPSY NOSTALGIA

A different group of Eric's memories was clustered around a gypsy life. As a gypsy, Eric must have felt as proud and free as a king. This was apparent from the way his first memories of the gypsy life were intermingled with symbolic residues of the king's life.

Here's a group of—like, I don't know—East European gypsies or something. I am sitting on the wagon seat with them. Then there's a large ball, like a huge golf ball, with all the little dents in it, sitting on a huge tee.

In his diary, Eric had sketched a ball surmounted by a cross, not realizing that this was an orb. The royal orb, which is part of the king's regalia, symbolizes the world. The scepter, on the other hand, represents the king's ruling power. Together, they are symbols of the king's global stewardship. By integrating the orb into his gypsy life, Eric united the opposites in himself—the pillar of society and the vagrant outsider.

As soon as the gypsy life surfaced, Eric became very interested. He exchanged his usual nondirective approach to his past life memories for a more directive one. He even went so far as to program his unconscious to show him more about that life. I did not ask him why he was so curious about that life in particular, but suspected that he was searching for a past life connection between us. He had not forgotten his early déjà vu experience with me and was trying to get to the bottom of it.

When his unconscious obliged him by releasing more information, it turned out that he had been on the right track: We had indeed been gypsies together, but not in the way he might have thought. He had been a boy, and I a grown woman. That he had been a member of my band became clear to me when he described the Bavarian landscape where the stoning of our band had taken place. He also remembered a rape scene that must have led to the massacre. I did not know what in particular had provoked the stoning, while he remembered the provocation, but drew a blank on the stoning itself. Thus we were holding two different pieces of the puzzle, and only when we put them together did the whole picture emerge.

Gypsies, East European gypsies. Standing in a grassy area, watching wagons drive past me and away. Wagons are ornate and colorful, one or sometimes two horses, foal tagging along, curved roof...

In a high-altitude place, snow-capped mountains across a valley. Only a couple of wagons. This is not a place we usually go ... strong sudden image of a black cat ... can't decide if I'm male or female ... riding in wagon looking down on horse's back, black harness. I see my hands; they seem to be male, possibly a boy? There's a woman with bright red scarf, black hair, fair skin, white blouse, dark vest, dark red striped skirt that puffs out at the hips.

Eric had drawn a pendant in his diary that was shaped like a waxing and waning moon joined at the apex. This must have been the woman's talisman, designed to protect her fertility and her menstrual cycle. The importance of such a talisman can only be understood within the context of the gypsies' strict sexual taboos. According to Pierre Derlon, even the slightest violation of these taboos had serious consequences, and the rape of a gypsy by another gypsy was punishable by death.[2] This meant that if a gypsy woman was raped by a gadjo, the men of her band had to avenge her.

There's a woman lying on her back on the ground. A man has pinned her down, and he's forcing her to have sex. It is totally a power struggle. She is a very fiery person; she has a knife in her right hand and he has her arm pinned to the ground. Not a pretty scene...

I could easily identify the high-altitude place with the snow-capped mountains across the valley as the lush Alpine landscape around Berchtesgaden. I had worked there for a year as a lexicographer for a German-English language dictionary for the Langenscheidt Publishing House. The village of Berchtesgaden has colorful ethnic traditions, which are religiously observed, but the farmers are narrow minded, gruff, and hostile to strangers. It was not difficult for me to imagine a gypsy lynching having taken place in that part of Germany in the first quarter of the twentieth century, especially since Hitler had already infiltrated Bavaria with his Nazi propaganda and racist doctrines by that time. A few years later, when he became Fuehrer, he built his Eagle's Nest high above this bigoted farming community.

A SHIFT IN THE TRANSFERENCE

The discovery that Eric and I had been relatives not so very long ago created a feeling of kinship between us. A change in the transference relationship was to be expected after that; it should have shifted in the direction of a deepening of trust, but that is not what happened. Instead, the transference became romanticized. When Eric was not sullen, taciturn, and depressed, he openly flirted with me. He often told me that we had been lovers in a past life, which I tried to dismiss as yet another example of his "wild, unorthodox style." Therefore, I only smiled when he asked me at the end of one session what I was doing that night and hinted that he would like to stay on; deep down, however, it unsettled me.

Despite his belief in our amorous past, Eric made no conscious effort to find out more about it. Without persistent nudging from his unconscious, the nature of our past life relationship would never have been revealed. The nudging had actually started even before Eric's first visit to Santa Fe, when he had dreamed one night of a woman named Odessa.

A friend of mine wants to see the third rental video before we must return them. It's called Along the Rio Grande, *and it's narrated by a woman who sounds like she's reading from a novel. I have an insight into the nature of writing, how words are used to create a fictional, but nevertheless solid, world.*

Mother says, "Do you know someone named 'Odessa'?" She's not telling me the whole story, I sense, so I play along to see what's behind her inquiry. "Yes, I do," I say, implying that I know more than what I'm saying. "What do you know about her?" she asks, and I answer, "Why?" "Oh, she called." Mother is a little miffed, as I knew she would be, because I didn't reveal what I knew about this woman. "Odessa called me?" I ask, incredulously. It never comes out what Odessa wanted.

In retrospect, it is easy to recognize all the precognitive elements in this dream. The film, *Along the Rio Grande,* contained all the past life images that would appear on Eric's inner screen during his stay in Santa Fe. The dream predicted a short viewing (given that we didn't have much time to watch it before it had to be returned), which actually did come true: Eric left Santa Fe after only four months, never to look at his past lives again. Up to this point, the precognition only concerned Eric's own future development—something that is not that uncommon in dreams. But with the woman-narrator, the prediction rose to another level, for here Eric was dreaming about me without having met me yet. (I was the woman named Odessa who was calling him.) Obviously, I was to play this double role in his soul drama: I was to be both witness and narrator of his story. He even foresaw the literary style of my writing. It was as if he had time-traveled to the far-distant moment when, after *Past Life Dreamwork* had been published, he would be reading his own story in that book.

But the writing of a book was definitely not "in the cards" almost twenty years ago. I had only just started to practice past life therapy and had no ambition whatsoever to become an author. Therefore, this particular information could not have come to him telepathically, although the symbolism of the telephone call suggested that a telepathic link had been established between us before he even traveled to Santa Fe. Strictly speaking, of course, that telepathic link did not connect him and me, but him and an unknown woman who was no stranger to him in the dream. Unfortunately, this woman's "call" to him had been intercepted by his inner mother who was a sadistic torturer and a source of fear for him. The projection of this female shadow might have contributed to his outrageous behavior toward me during the so-called interview.

At first, I had only a limited comprehension of this dream: I had no idea who the narrator or who Odessa was. All I understood was that the viewing of past life images must have been on Eric's unconscious agenda and that he had been telepathically "called" to Santa Fe by some mystery woman, for whatever reason.

FORBIDDEN PAST LIFE IMAGES

When, at the end of six weeks of therapy, I was beginning to face the fact that a love transference and countertransference was in the making, Eric was instructed in one of his trances to contact a woman named Tessa. Later, he was to realize that Tessa and Odessa were one and the same person. He wrote the following in his diary:

I'm almost asleep, and I heard that I should reach "Tessa" before . . . Who's Tessa?

The "before" was obviously loaded with meaning, because something important was left unsaid. I realized this was a warning dream when I found the following Jung quotation right next to it in Eric's diary:

The images of the unconscious place a great responsibility upon a man. Failure to understand them, or a shirking of ethical responsibility deprives him of his wholeness and imposes a painful fragmentariness on his life.[3]

Eric must have realized that by avoiding difficult past life material he was shirking ethical responsibility and depriving himself of his wholeness. This made him lower his defenses just enough for the first of these memories to emerge.

Now we're, ah, in a remote fjord. Could be like, Arctic (Icelandic? Scandinavian?). In the distance there's a village, with smoke coming up. There are a few guys on the ice. Bet they're cold! No, they're native. Hunters, or—hate to say it, but we got Vikings here. Viking-like people (I realized that I might be confirming the psychic's reading) (sigh). Nice boots! Like caribou skin, big laces. These guys wear a lot of fur. Furry on the outside for trim, but most of the fur is on the inside. They're not Vikings, but some northland people. They've got a spiritual person; he's very upset. He's dressed in brown, he hasn't got a hat on, he has very short, clipped white hair. He's just, like—sobbing. Ah, going somewhere else.

This was, indeed, the Viking life that the psychic had spoken about. A sacred taboo must have been broken, because the priest abandoned his own village. This put Eric in touch with an ancient guilt—a guilt he seemed to associate with me. To demonstrate his feelings, he played me a popular song with an especially tender lyric that expressed his love for me as well as his remorse. When the last notes of the song had faded away, Eric burst into tears.

It was an emotional moment between us, which I will never forget. And only after the session did I become aware of the fact that I had wanted to hear more about Eric's love than his guilt. This told me that I was getting too emotionally involved to be able to function as an analyst. Fortunately, I had admitted this to myself when Eric, only a few sessions later, expressed a need for holding and touching. It did not make it any easier for me that his request was clinically justified. Eric needed the physical contact to counterbalance the intense inner work he was doing, day and night. Yet for me to hold and touch him, while we were both enmeshed in a love transference, would have been courting disaster. Therefore, when Eric tried to argue that the psychological rules could be bent, it had the opposite effect on me. It actually helped me regain my professional composure enough to be able to clearly state that the "psychological rules" could not be bent as long as he was under my care. The intense emotions between us, I told him, had to be used for his healing.

SPLITTING THE TRANSFERENCE

What had strengthened my determination to keep our boundaries intact was a warning dream I had during this critical time. The dream stated in symbolical language that Eric would "trash" my practice if I did not protect myself. But how was I to do that? I could not simply abandon him while he was engaged in a life-and-death struggle with the forces of the unconscious. Neither could I refer him to another psychotherapist; I knew that nobody else in town worked with past life material with Jungian methods. In this professional dilemma, the inclusion of a bodyworker seemed to be the only way out. I thought this would take care of Eric's physical needs, while making the transference more manageable for me.

I deliberately referred him to an attractive woman his own age, hoping that this would divert some of his libidinous feelings to her. And since she was a personal friend of mine, I thought I could count on her professional collaboration. This turned out to be a miscalculation, however. She, too, fell for Eric's boyish charm but did not follow the rules as I did. Also, when the transference split, as expected, it split in a way that was painful for me. Eric's romantic feelings went to the younger woman, while I had to deal with the leftovers—the possessiveness and jealousy that arose in him whenever he suspected that I dated other men. For Eric, the triangulation must have been difficult and confusing, too; he was probably not joking when he said to me one day that he would like to marry us both. On the other hand, having two women doting on him gave him a sense of power, which he abused from time to time by playing us against each other.

One afternoon he came directly from his bodywork session to me. He was unusually animated. With a note of triumph in his voice he told me that he had "touched her" while lying on the massage table. I was trying to compose myself when—sitting across from me in the leather armchair—he placed his unshod feet firmly on top of mine. Experiencing this as a gesture of domination, I froze.

When I addressed the boundary violation in the following session, he said he had felt like a completely different person that day. It had been the bodywork, he explained, that had brought this out in him. I felt that the "completely different person" it had brought out in him was the Viking, and of the Viking in Eric I was deathly afraid. From that moment on, I was on my guard. At first, I tried hiding behind my professional mask, but my unconscious reacted to that very negatively. I dreamed that if I continued wearing "that mask of wax," it would become one with my face, and I would be permanently disfigured. Taking this warning very seriously, I decided to remain open, despite the painful situation I was in. But I protected myself as best I could by not putting my heart and soul into Eric's therapy anymore.

Fortunately, Eric took full responsibility for the estrangement between us. In one of his trances he saw a dog, or wolf—a kind of husky dog—biting the hand that fed him, and he wrote in his diary, "Why am I doing this? I feel like I'm losing Sabine, and there'll be no one to read it (these pages)." Although he often complained about the lack of emotional closeness in our sessions, neither of us could bring it back. Feeling alone and isolated, Eric made another attempt to reach the mystery woman that had been haunting him in his dreams, this time with more success. As the contact with her was made, the dammed up, forbidden images were finally released.

There's a sword. [pause] I'd like to know about Tessa. I really would. Tessa or Odessa. I'm going to wait a minute. [pause] There's a huge crowd of people. Standing. Maybe on the shore of a lake. [pause] What do I need to know? [pause]

Things are shadowy. And elusive. I've been looking for Tessa all night. "You were with her," somebody said. Is Sabine Tessa? [amusement] "Are you George?" Oh, hell, I don't know. "Of course, you do."

Tall boots. Icelandic boots. [laugh] How do I know that?! [pause] There's some gears, meshings, a window, an archway, going under an archway. A very dark place. [pause] I, yeah, I can't see these things. There's a fire that does not give off any light—or warmth. There are some metal objects. [sigh] Where am I? [sighs and irregular breathing, long pause] It's the Chamber of the Dead. Oh, oh. [choking sounds, difficult breathing] No. [pause] There's the Chief Executioner—with his ax, looking down at this—[long, tight inhalation] No! [exhaling in three short puffs] . . . There's a key in a lock. And then outside, there's a vase, a large urn, sitting on top of a wall; there's some trees, and blue sky beyond the branches of the trees. [long pause] Oh, I don't know . . . [pause] Tessa, come here. [pause, sigh] I want to go to sleep.

It was easy enough for me to accept that Eric had been George, and I Tessa. But for Eric, it was much more difficult, which was not that surprising. Who wants to be the villain in a drama of rape and abduction? "A fire that does not give off any light—or warmth" was a perfect metaphor for a rape committed in cold passion. What had followed the rape had been even more brutal. George had axed the girl's father down when he had come to her defense. Then he had carried her off to his boat like a war trophy. In England, the girl had been called Tessa, short for Teresa. But the Norsemen had renamed her Odessa in honor of their god Odin; that's how she ended up with two names. Only George, her captor, had sometimes in tender moments called her by her Christian name—Tessa. Triggered by Eric's memories, I now had memories of my own.

Although Eric's trance experience could hardly have been more credible, he questioned its authenticity. Hoping to get a different answer the next time, he approached his unconscious once more with the same question.

Wish I could focus this. I would like to know about Tessa. And Odessa, are they the same? [pause] No, I don't already know. [said as if in response]

Despite the unwavering honesty of his inner voice, Eric continued to lie to himself. The notion that he had once raped and abducted the woman who was now trying to heal him was simply too strange for him to accept. Unfortunately, his very refusal to face the rapist and kidnapper in himself gave this past life shadow some power over him. And as the therapy was winding down, I felt the Viking's presence more and more. Eric became very critical of the dream analysis and even made an attempt to change the therapy according to his own specifications. At the beginning of one session, he handed me his diary, where he had written down his reform ideas:

> The thought comes to me . . . that it's like pulling teeth in the dream analysis with Sabine because it's not what we should be doing together. Instead, we should be physically involved in acting things out. Some examples come to mind . . .

A list of "wild, unorthodox" examples followed: I was to slap him in the face, ride on his back, exchange clothes with him and so forth. Perhaps, it was a repetition compulsion that was driving Eric to reenact scenes from the past. Or, in the power struggle between us, he was putting my strength to a final test. Whatever his motives might have been, I am convinced that Eric would have backed down himself had his safety net—the therapeutic alliance—not functioned for some reason. Eric was psychologically far too sophisticated not to know that the fine line that keeps a therapy safe cannot be crossed without detriment to both parties. He also was aware of the fact that the karmic purpose of our encounter was at stake. If it was true that I—or rather Tessa—had called him to me in the dreamtime, it could only have been for the purpose of clearing our karma in a safe and protected space. One way of clearing bad karma is not to repeat it, and I do believe that we accomplished this in the push and shove of our deeply conflicted past life transference dynamics.

The fact that our therapeutic relationship survived all these tests and challenges made it possible for us to part on friendly terms. In our last session, Eric gave me two very precious gifts: a copy of his two diaries, and a beautiful poem he had written for me. This poem, which was entitled "Within Us Two Are Many More," showed that he had finally accepted the paradoxical fact that he had come to me for a healing after having wounded me in the past. But this is how karma is cleared, according to Jenny—the victim must always heal the victimizer.

THE OUTCOME

Unfortunately, I could not heal Eric's psyche in such a short time. Transference complications, financial problems, but mainly his pining for his small son contributed to his decision to break off the therapy after four months. Many years later when I read his diaries, I discovered an even deeper reason for why he had thrown in the towel so soon. It basically came down to the question: "If I am an integrator, how can I do this work *and* live in the world?" Some people can; Eric couldn't. His process was far too intense for that. So he put the lid back on Pandora's box and returned to the East Coast to live in the world.

Eric was born with an exceptional talent for communicating with his unconscious. He also was a deeply spiritual man in an unconventional, mystical way. His dreams, transcripts, and drawings were interspersed in his diaries with invocations of the light and love of God and the light of the unconscious. Toward the end of his therapy, he fervently prayed for an answer to his questions regarding the meaning of reincarnation. His prayer was heard—he was blessed with a vision.

Now I see it again. Like people pushing a huge plate, or something like a lazy Susan, but people are much smaller than this plate, and it's turning around. Maybe it would take, oh, fifty or, I don't know, one hundred people to take a space to fill up the whole circumference of this thing, and they're pushing it (turning it) counterclockwise.

Eric understood this to mean that each individual life is only a tiny part of a much greater whole, and that the reincarnational cycle leads, as indicated by the counterclockwise movement, not outward, but inward into the mystical center. The energies that are generated in this inner-directed, dynamic process seem to be food for the soul.

In the end, it was I who got healed in this therapy, although the licensing board would hardly approve of that. However, in my experience the outcome of a therapeutic encounter becomes even more unpredictable than usual if that encounter is, at the same time, also a karmic one. Immediately after Eric's departure, I was too exhausted to notice a change in myself, and later, when I did notice a change, I did not relate it to my encounter with Eric. It was not until many years later, when I was writing Eric's story, that I realized after a dream that I had retrieved a lost part of my soul while I was working with him. In this dream, I was back in England and in the same Victorian house where I spent nine years of my married life in my present incarnation. England had also been my home in the eighth century, before the Vikings abducted me. Thus past life and present life were superimposed in this dream.

I am looking through the bay window of my Victorian terrace house onto Marlborough Avenue where Robert and I used to live. I am watching Miso, my half-grown brown kitten, chase autumn leaves in the front garden. I love this cat. He is exactly the right mixture of independence and affection.

While I am enjoying Miso's capers, a married couple with a little girl walk by. The man grabs Miso and carries him off, holding him like a trophy over his head. Although he does not look like Eric, I know it is him. He is very tall, broad shouldered, and his hair is white-blond. He renames Miso and calls him "the pest." I run after the couple, hoping to catch up with them, but before I can reach them they have disappeared into a department store.

Next, it is many centuries later. I now live in a fancy apartment house that has its own private park. Eric and I have agreed to meet there at a certain time. When I arrive at the park, he is already waiting for me on a bench. As he rises to greet me, I notice that his appearance has changed and that he now looks like himself. I also realize that my old anger about his abduction of Miso has evaporated and that I have only warm feelings for him. We decide to go for a stroll in the park, and as we are walking side-by-side, I put my arm affectionately around Eric's shoulder and ask him to give me Miso back.

Here, I awoke with the happy feeling that Miso had been returned to me. I knew that without the sense of freedom, personified by Miso and Tessa, I could never be whole. This part of my soul had been lost to me until, twelve hundred years later, I was able to reclaim it by standing up to the Viking in Eric.

9

PUTTING THE
PIECES TOGETHER

Past Life Father Meets Past Life Son

*The essential thing is the opus, which leads to the goal:
that is the goal of a lifetime. In its attainment "left and
right" are united, and the conscious and unconscious work
in harmony.*

C. G. JUNG

LEFT-BRAIN DOMINANCE

In 1999 I received a telephone call from a young man whom I will call
Sylvio. Like Eric, he had found me in the Yellow Pages of the local telephone directory. He had just arrived from Switzerland where he had suffered a head trauma two years before. After conventional medicine had
failed to cure him of the aftereffects of this head injury, he had come
to Santa Fe in search of alternative modes of treatment. He wanted to
try a holistic approach that would include psychotherapy, he said. After

making an appointment with me, he surprised me by asking permission to drop off his curriculum vitae before his first session. Since I do not take notes in my clients' presence, I was grateful to receive all his personal data upfront.

On the following morning, I found his vitae, accompanied by a letter, in my mailbox. When I opened the three-page document I initially became disorientated. I thought I had spoken with a young man on the telephone, but what I had in front of me now was the vitae of an older man. And—what was even stranger—this man's life story was very similar to that of the banker Abdullah, my last male incarnation. Like Abdullah, he was a Middle Eastern Jew and a businessman who had fled his homeland due to religious persecution. After moving from country to country, he had settled in Italy where he had joined the workforce of an international trading firm.

Eventually, I identified this as the vitae of Sylvio's father. For some reason, Sylvio had thrown his father's, mother's, and brother's vitae in with his own. He must be overly family orientated, apart from being a perfectionist, I thought. I was certain that he was a perfectionist because of the way he had micromanaged the first session in order to save time on the intake. But the striking parallels between his father's and Abdullah's life stories got my attention. Not knowing what to make of this synchronicity, I committed it to memory for possible future use.

Sylvio's vitae was impressive, although he was only in his mid-twenties. He had traveled all over the world, was fluent in several languages, and had diversified work experience. After graduating from London University with a degree in English law, he had followed in his father's footsteps and interned with a leading international trading firm in Switzerland. He had been one of the rising stars in the corporate office when, in the winter of 1997, his bicycle slipped on a patch of black ice and ejected him, head first, onto the pavement. It had only been a concussion and he had suffered no broken bones, but he had not been able to recover from it. Persistent headaches, dizziness, and nausea had impaired his work performance to such an extent that he had taken a leave of absence. A host of Swiss physicians, neurologists, and chiropractors he had consulted had not been able to improve his condition. "I don't know," he wrote in the letter that accompanied the vitae, "if this is a physical disorder left over from the accident, or a mental condition." And even more lucidly he added, "I feel like there is a voice which is trying to emerge from within."

A few days later Sylvio walked down the brick path toward my office. He was so tall and lanky that he tried to make himself shorter by stooping a little. With his bespectacled, intelligent face, he looked a little nerdy at first sight. But when he began to talk I realized how cosmopolitan he was. Having an Italian father and an American mother, and given his sophisticated education, his cultural background had been too diverse to identify himself with any one nationality. His only identity was that of a human being, he said. When, at a young age, he had been given the choice between his parents' religions, he had chosen neither of them because he had wanted to practice his spirituality outside of any organized religion.

He seemed to have high ethical standards and a caring attitude toward others, but he was also demanding and used to getting his own way. I attributed the emotional detachment that I sensed in him to the divorce of his parents when he was only thirteen years old. Although this had protected him in his teens from being torn apart by conflicting loyalties, it had later delayed his emotional maturation. This explained why his romantic history with the opposite sex was almost nonexistent at this point.

Intellectually, Sylvio was in his prime. His thinking was precise, clear, and reflective, while a childlike curiosity kept it from being dry. At the age of twenty-five he had fine-tuned his left-brain functions so perfectly that no further development seemed possible, even to him. Unfortunately, this had been at the expense of his right-brain functions, which had remained largely undeveloped. Perhaps it was no accident (no pun intended) that his head injury had drawn attention to the right side of his head.

This one-sidedness of Sylvio's also explained his scornful attitude toward my dreamwork when we first met. He made no bones about the fact that he considered dream analysis a complete waste of time. When I asked him why he had chosen a Jungian analyst of all people if that's how he felt about dream therapy, he told me, to my surprise, that it was because I had done my training in Zurich. He had been looking for a therapist, he explained, who would commiserate with him about the Swiss. Although he clearly did not like the Swiss, this reasoning was so far below his intelligence level that I saw it as a mere smokescreen for not having the faintest idea why he had chosen me. In fact, I was almost sure that it was not Sylvio himself who had chosen me, but Sylvio's unconscious. And where the dream analysis was concerned, his childlike curiosity was already winning out by the time he left my office, because he wrote in his diary immediately afterward: "The idea of 'dream analysis' sounds silly, but I am willing to give it a try." The result of his willingness was a "very strange dream," which he brought into the next session, curious about what it might mean.

I'm in an airplane, flying toward Cincinnati, and we are making our final approach to the airport. I'm sitting in the window seat on the left-hand side of the airplane and look down through the window at the Byzantine/Russian architecture of the buildings located on the lake below (the architecture is similar to St. Basil's Cathedral in Moscow). I'm fascinated that such architecture exists in Cincinnati, but since I have never been there before, I really have no way of knowing otherwise.

We land on one of the wooden piers that jut out onto the lake. I get out of the plane and walk along the pier to a parking lot, where there is a woman putting various meats (one of which is prosciutto) into a big white nylon bag that is near a white van. Other similar bags are lying in the van. I open up one of them to help this woman organize the various meats, and I pull out a giant squid and place it into one of the other long white nylon bags.

Sylvio had never been to Cincinnati and had no personal association with it at all. He said it was only a spot of no interest for him on the North American map. Yet in the dream this "uninteresting spot" had surprised him with its ancient, sacred architecture. Thus, while on deeper levels, Cincinnati represented the wondrous realm of the collective unconscious to him, on a more superficial level it was a metaphor for how he had always seen the unconscious—as a place of no interest at all. But this initial dream was beginning to undermine his prejudice by putting St. Basil's Cathedral in Moscow in this "uninteresting" spot. Not only was St. Basil's Cathedral one of Sylvio's favorite churches, it is also known for its mandalic (circular) design, which, as Jung demonstrated, is a universal symbol for psychic wholeness.

The woman at the water's edge who was sorting meat into white nylon bags could have been his anima; she could also have been me. In either case, his unconscious was on the point of getting sorted out. The fact that Sylvio decided to help the woman with the sorting-out work boded well for the therapy, because, as every psychotherapist knows, success or failure in this work depends to a large extent on the client's active participation in it.

Meat could be a symbol for the carnal, the instinctual aspect of the unconscious. The prosciutto, which is especially mentioned here, was taboo for his Italian Jewish father. Thus the Italian ham could have represented an aspect of his father's sexuality that was disallowed or suppressed by his Jewish religion but acceptable in Italy. The squid, on the other hand, was of an entirely different nature—not only as a deep-sea creature, but also as a carrier of a powerful current association.

Sylvio's tai chi instructor had only recently told him that he had to become as flexible as a squid. When I asked him how flexible he was, not physically but mentally, he replied, "half flexible, half not flexible." He further explained that he was flexible toward anything new, but not flexible where personal standards were concerned. This resonated with me, because I am "half flexible, half not flexible" in exactly the same way. Two years later, we both would be able to recognize this as part of a family value system from a shared nineteenth-century life. But when I heard this dream I merely concluded that, judging from the giant size of the squid, Sylvio's flexibility must be huge. Fortunately, this turned out to be true, because he would need every bit of it in the course of his therapy.

A PROPHETIC DREAM

When Sylvio first contacted me, he was receiving acupuncture treatments from a local woman doctor of Chinese medicine. For reasons he could not explain, he did not entirely trust this woman's professional judgment. His intuitive feeling was validated when, during one of his treatment sessions, she suddenly cracked his neck. Because she had not prepared him for this and a chiropractic intervention was too rough for his delicate physical condition, he became retraumatized and suffered a relapse. When we reviewed his dreams from the week before, we found that one of them had predicted this unfortunate outcome. In this dream, the woman doctor had turned into a man before his very eyes. And he had known that this man (in the woman) would be afraid of getting sued.

The dream had therefore foreseen that a malpractice case would arise from a switch-over from a gentle to a more aggressive treatment modality. It had stated in symbolic language that the subtle placing of needles, which is yin (feminine), would be replaced by a forceful cracking of joints, which is yang (masculine). This sudden switch from yin to yang had sent a shock through his whole system.

Thus Sylvio had his first experience with the "absolute knowledge in the unconscious," as Jung called it. The notion that his unconscious might know more than he did threatened him initially, and then later fascinated him. When it began to fascinate him, he turned it into a research project. He did a reality check on every new piece of information he received in the dream state. When these were validated each time, he started to trust his dreams completely.

He remained on a comfortable level with his unconscious, even with the psychic aspect of it, until he saw a ghost one night while he was housesitting for a rich lady in the village of Tesuque, near Santa Fe. At this point, he panicked. It did not help when the returning homeowner frankly admitted that she knew her house was haunted; this only seemed to reinforce his belief that he might be a kook after all. While Sylvio ended up in an identity crisis, I was beginning to wonder if his undeveloped right-brain potential might actually be as big as the squid in his dream.

Fortunately, it did not take him very long to come to terms with his psychic abilities. Subsequently, he spent many analytical hours asking me questions about psychology, parapsychology, and spirituality, while taking notes like an eager student. As my role temporarily shifted to that of a mentor, I felt more and more like a man in the countertransference. I explained this to myself as a psychotherapeutic response to Sylvio's need of paternal guidance until one night, when I was on the point of falling asleep, an unusual idea flashed through my mind. What if I didn't only *feel* like Sylvio's father but actually *was* his father in another life?

Suddenly I was wide awake and my intuition went all over the place, linking seemingly unrelated things to each other. It made a connection between Sylvio's father's and Abdullah's similar life stories and a past life dream I had had two years before this inspired moment. This dream had completely mystified me at the time, because there was apparently nothing that could have triggered it in my present life situation.

I am sitting in a restaurant in London at a little round table with a glass top. Next to me, on my left, sits a small, dark-haired, five-year-old boy. To his left is a dark-haired woman who might be his mother. We are waiting to be served. Glasses of water have already been placed next to each table setting, as is customary in Anglo-Saxon countries.

While we are making polite conversation, the boy puts his mother down with a nasty remark. Infuriated, she raises her left hand to slap him in the face but misses and hits a water glass instead. The glass shatters, sending glass splinters all over the table. Some of the glass splinters penetrate the boy's right eye. Suddenly, there is blood everywhere . . .

Here my dream had snapped like a film, leaving the rest of the story in the dark. In order to protect me from getting retraumatized, my unconscious had taken me to a later time, when I was starting to recover from the shock.

I am walking alone through the streets of London. I am on my way to the restaurant where the accident happened. I am trying to find my yarmulke, which I lost on that occasion. The little round table where we sat turns into a Medicine Wheel, and I pray over it. Afterward, I find my yarmulke all crumpled up under one of the chairs. It is black and has colored embroidery.

The dream had ended on a positive note; the yarmulke had been found, and a healing had occurred. But what was I, a Gentile woman, doing with a yarmulke? As soon as I realized that I had been a Jewish man in the dream, I thought of the banker Abdullah who, according to Jenny, had moved to England later in life. But Jenny had only spoken of Abdullah's relationship with his father. She had never mentioned his wife and children. So this had been total news to me.

When this dream quite unexpectedly became important again two years later, I knew that I would have to make inquiries into the meaning of the yarmulke. Not knowing where else to turn, I called the local synagogue. Thank God, an open-minded rabbi answered the phone! My white lie about a "woman client" who had dreamed of losing her yarmulke in London intrigued the rabbi enough to invite "her" and me to the temple's upcoming Hanukkah celebration. He also explained that the yarmulke symbolizes respect for God and confirmed that some yarmulkes do have colored embroidery. This particular type, he informed me, was worn by liberal Jews.

This explained why I had lost my yarmulke in the dream after my son had been blinded by his own mother. I must have been so devastated by the accident that I had temporarily lost my faith in God. When I had later recovered it, it had not been in its original pristine condition. According to this dream, it had not even been the Jewish religion that had helped me restore my faith in God, but an inborn belief in the divine order of things, as represented by the teachings of Medicine Wheel. In other words, during this spiritual crisis, on completely unconscious levels, the spiritual resources of my previous American Indian life had come to my rescue.

After my intuition had made these connections, I took a waiting attitude, because, so far, all of this was only a hunch. However, a few nights later, a dream responded to the hunch. It came in the form of a brief, cryptic message.

Sylvio's baggage comes from an ancient stream. Your karma is a white lily.

The dream clearly stated that my karma with Sylvio was lily white. However, by doing so, it also implied a past life connection between us. It even reassured me that Sylvio's "baggage"—his karmic burdens—had nothing to do with me, but was caused by his wrongdoing in ancient times.

Since I knew that my personal unconscious, and even the collective unconscious, could not have access to this kind of information, I had to assume that it came from the Akashic Records themselves. This meant that this information was important and intended not only for me but also for Sylvio. Thus, when I subsequently had some doubts whether to share the dream or not, the question was quickly decided in favor of sharing it.

CROSSING PSYCHIC BOUNDARIES

After I had told Sylvio the dream, I added that I suspected a past life connection between us. His immediate response was defensive. He said he wanted to find that out for himself; a dream he had the following night showed had he had felt intruded upon.

I am leaving your office, but I forget my notebook, so I go back and get it. As I do, it turns into a plate with meat and vegetable stew on it. I sit down (uninvited) at a picnic table in your backyard to have some of the stew. Meanwhile, you are sitting there giving a woman German language lessons . . . then you take a fork from my plate and take a scoop of my stew . . . I'm offended by this (but I may just be feeling how you felt when I trespassed into your German class).

It might have been a sign of Sylvio's inner connection with me that he addressed this dream to me in his diary. More likely, though, it was intended to make his accusation more direct: I had helped myself to his "dream food," he complained through his dream. At the same time, he admitted to having crossed *my* boundaries, too. For even before I had taken the food off his plate, he had come into my backyard uninvited, like a family member, to eavesdrop on my professional past as a German language teacher. Thus, boundaries had been crossed both ways on unconscious levels, while our conscious relationship had remained strictly professional. On Sylvio's side, this did not remain an isolated incident, either. In the following months, his dreams repeatedly showed him spying on me in the dream state. During one of those dream visits, he had entered my bedroom and could later accurately describe the floral pattern on my bedspread.

After three months of therapy, Sylvio decided to stop seeing the doctor of Chinese medicine who had hurt his neck. Trying to avoid negative karma with her he had written her a letter, which he wanted to run by me before sending it off. "I have always been afraid of being hit in the face for speaking my truth," he wrote. Knowing that Abdullah's son had lost his eye for the same reason, this took my breath away. But before I could mark this up as evidence for our past life connection I had to rule out that Sylvio had been physically abused as a child. So I asked him where he thought this fear was coming from. He did not have a clue. There had been nothing in his childhood that could have caused this; it could only go back to a past life experience, he said.

Determined to stay on the track while it was still hot, I asked him, "Which side of your face do you expect to be hit on?" Without hesitation, he pointed to the right side of his face. This pretty much settled it for me, but there was one more thing I needed to find out before I could turn this into a working hypothesis. That was the date of Sylvio's accident. Something told me that I would find another synchronicity here, and I did. When Sylvio confirmed that his accident in Switzerland had happened in the week before Christmas in 1997—the same week I had dreamed about the little boy's accident—I had all the evidence I needed. In addition, I had finally found the trigger for my past life dream.

The implications of this discovery were mind blowing, although hardly surprising for followers of quantum field theory. It meant, in fact, that when Sylvio had been injured, I had dreamed thousands of miles away of the heartbreaking moment when some one hundred and forty years ago, and in another body, he had been injured on the same side of his head. Not only that, in order to heal his new injury, which was complicated by his old injury, Sylvio had crossed the Atlantic to get help from his past life father who was now a woman and a psychotherapist.

And he believed he had chosen me because I had studied in Switzerland!

AN INDEPENDENT INVESTIGATION

It was not easy to keep this to myself, but I had promised not to interfere with Sylvio's independent investigation. This meant that it was now his turn to find this out. In order to speed up his past life recall, I introduced him to my strobic colored light instrument, the Photron. The Photron had been designed for optometrists and had been successfully used in the treatment of a wide variety of eye conditions before it was found to be equally effective as a psychotherapeutic tool. The instrument is equipped with twelve color filters, a two-inch lens, and a small computer box where the flicker rate can be adjusted. Depending on the flicker rate, alpha, theta, and delta brainwave patterns can be induced in the viewer without a hypnotic induction simply through optical stimulation. In addition, the colored light has healing properties of its own that filter down to cellular levels, clearing the body of old trauma residues and negative energies.

Sylvio, whose squid was alive and well, agreed to use the Photron to explore this irrational fear of being slapped in the face. At first he did not seem anxious at all, but two days before the appointed time, he phoned and asked me to analyze some dreams that might refer to the upcoming color therapy. The dreams—three in number—reflected his anxiety. The first dream predicted the failure of the "experiment" due to "technical difficulties."

I am in a hotel in the Dominican Republic, and I am on the edge of a swimming pool. I am given scuba equipment, and as I gear up, I look down into a very large, deep pool and see other people there, which comforts me. However, the gear malfunctions, then the air tank slips out of its harness. We replace the air tank in its harness, but I never make it into the water; the gear is messed up and not functioning properly.

In the second dream, Sylvio was driving his Honda into the Bay of Hong Kong Harbor, and it began to sink. Again, he was using the wrong piece of equipment to get to the bottom of his fear. I had my own associations with Hong Kong Harbor: according to Jenny, I had lived there as a beggar woman on a houseboat with many children, and we had all drowned during a storm. Whether Sylvio had been one of those children or not, he definitely associated the Bay of Hong Kong with drowning for some reason.

In the third dream, he was hiding under the bedcovers of an old girlfriend, looking for warmth and protection. This told me that he was so terrified that he was regressing to early childhood.

For me, these were clear indications that the Photron was the wrong tool to use if I wanted to gain access to Sylvio's past life memories. I was therefore ready to cancel the color session when Sylvio, to my surprise, insisted that we go ahead in spite of his dreams. Although I had reservations, I went along with his plan because I trusted his inner guidance. On the day of the session, I darkened the room, put the blue-green filter in the slot, and set the flicker rate to alpha. One of the psychological effects of the blue-green color is that it bypasses the intellect, which was very necessary in Sylvio's case. As soon as he looked at this color in the Photron lens, a clear image started to form in front of his eyes. He reported seeing "saloonlike doors, which might lead into a bar." Behind the doors, he saw a middle-aged man with dark hair that was thinning on top. The man was wearing a white tunic and a head cover.

At this point I got nervous because I had the uncanny feeling that Sylvio was describing me as Abdullah. My hunch proved to be right; a few years later, I found a picture of Abdullah in a family biography and he looked exactly as Sylvio had described him. The saloon door, on the other hand, I immediately recognized as the entrance to the restaurant where—in my dream—the accident had occurred. It therefore made perfect sense to me when Sylvio could not open the door, no matter how hard he tried. And when, at the end of the color session, the "experiment" seemed to have failed because the door would not open, only I knew how successful it had actually been. It had also prepared the ground for a dream that would complete the past life recall during the night. When Sylvio told me this dream, I instantly understood why he had not been able to look at these images during the color session: they were so disturbing that he could only face them in the privacy and safety of his own bed.

I'm in an airplane, Sabena Airlines, and we are in our final landing approach. We descend into a channel-like formation, where we have trees on either side of the plane and below us, but the trees below us are maybe half as tall as the ones on either side of the plane (hence the channel-like formation).

My dad and I are on the plane. We land, I go ahead and leave him a little behind, go down some escalators, and behind them to a quiet and hidden area. I want to have a few moments alone before he arrives down at the baggage claim area as well. I end up on a table (like a masseur's table) and my body is lying flat on the table, with my spirit standing over it, massaging my body, tranquilizing it. Meanwhile, the body is experiencing severe muscular spasms, and is writhing all over the table. It is barely staying on the table . . . there is also blood in both my eyes.

We both smiled at the mention of "Sabena Airlines," because the pun (Sabine-Sabena) was obvious. Although Sabine had taken him into the past, Sylvio had made his own landing, which was typical of him. First, he had flown through a "channel-like formation"—this time a pun for channeled information. Then—after leaving his father behind—he had gone down an escalator, which had taken him quickly into the unconscious. From there, he had retreated to a "quiet, hidden area" in order to remember the rest of that scene. Like myself, he had seen blood in his eyes, but his dream had continued beyond my dream. It had made him live through an epileptic seizure and a terrifying out-of-body experience. The seizure suggested that the eye injury must have gone deep enough to cause brain damage. Although the loss of the yarmulke had pointed toward a catastrophic event, the damage to my son's eyes must have been much more serious than I could ever have imagined on the basis of my own dream.

LEARNING TO TRUST HIS KNOWING

By now it had become very clear that our memories fit together like pieces of a jigsaw puzzle. This made me less cautious in my responses. Thus, after discussing this dream, I briefly mentioned that I had dreamed something similar two years prior. This had a profound effect on him, which he later described in his diary.

> I have my first big emotional breakdown . . . I spend four hours crying, hyperventilating, and experiencing severe muscular spasms/convulsions. I have absolutely no control over my body, and yet feel that somehow I am okay and that I am being protected through this "experience." An incredible release of pain and energy takes place.

This was the beginning of a trauma-healing process, which was to continue for about a year. Acupuncture, deep tissue massage, and gentle chiropractic manipulations accompanied and supplemented my psychological work. Sylvio found new evidence for his past life injury when he consulted another doctor of Oriental medicine for the first time. When she was examining him she spotted a problem with one of his eyes. She called it "lazy eye," which is a condition where one eye moves more slowly than the other eye. And again, it was his right eye, which was the slower one. When Sylvio asked his mother if she knew about the lazy eye, she said yes, he had been born with it. To Sylvio, this meant that the past life injury had left a visible residue in his body.

The connection between the past life eye injury, the epilepsy, and his present lazy eye became even clearer when the doctor placed needles around his right eye and his whole body went into convulsions. Sylvio was deeply shaken by this experience, because it made him realize how present this so-called past life still was. And soon after that, a dream pointed out that the memories of that lifetime were also more accessible to him than he had ever thought.

I'm in a room with S. L. and another man, who is also a therapist, and he says that he will bring in another person who can give me more past life information. I blow up at him and ask him, "Who the hell gave him the right to decide how the therapy sessions should be run? It's my money, and I make the decisions on how the sessions are run". . . nonetheless, I eventually give in to this man's suggestions.

Sylvio was relieved when I told him that "the other person" in the dream was not a new therapist but actually part of himself. This also meant, of course, that the ball was now in his court. Thanks to our noninterference agreement, Sylvio had very little information at this point. He only knew about the blood in his eyes (from being slapped in the face?), the out-of-body experience, and the subsequent seizure. He also realized that the saloon door and the Middle Eastern man had something to do with that. But after this dream, things began to change. Because he was putting more trust in his abilities to access these memories on his own, he began to have frequent and spontaneous flashbacks. When this happened, Sylvio broke his own rules by asking me to validate these flashbacks. In one of these, he remembered having been a Jew who lived in Golders Green, a suburb of London. I could confirm the Jewish part, but not the Golders Green part, because I knew nothing about that. But my confirmation of his Jewish life alone had such a profound effect on him that he had another flashback immediately after the session, which he noted in his diary.

S. L. confirms that I was Jewish in a past life. After I leave the session, I'm feeling a little upset and down, and sit in the car outside her house. Two words pop into my head: *Shiva* and *yeshiva*. Then all of a sudden I have this feeling that I was a teacher of the Torah in my past life. I don't know where the information is coming from, but it seems to come from within and feel right.

The Shiva association was important because of the Hindu god's connection with India. Having spent most of his life in Bombay, Abdullah must have had many Hindu servants, so his son must have grown up with Shiva, although he was raised as a Jew. I even vaguely remembered now that the servants had told the boy after the accident that Shiva had taken his right eye, and that I had been very angry about that. Much less credible, on the other hand, were Sylvio's memories of having been a Yeshiva teacher. Unless these were memories of a different lifetime, they could only have been a daydream of Abdullah's son of what he would have liked to be had he not been brain damaged and stricken with epilepsy. In such a case, he might have felt that Shiva had not only taken his eye but also his dream of becoming a yeshiva teacher. This would explain Sylvio's upset and "down" feelings when these two words popped into his head.

PUTTING THE PIECES TOGETHER

Soon after the flashbacks had started, at the beginning of a session Sylvio announced that he wanted to give the Photron another try. He wanted to see what would happen if he relaxed, rather than strain for images as he had done before. Of course, to relax in front of the Photron was easier for him now that the edge had been taken off his trauma. I exposed him again to the blue-green color, but this time at his own request I took him all the way down to the brainwave state known as theta. Theta produces a hypnagogic state that allows unconscious images to come to the surface. As soon as Sylvio looked into the lens, he saw the saloon doors again. But this time he had no problem going inside the bar, and as he entered this is what he saw:

I see a chair. I see people circling around me while I lie on the floor. I see a left hand moving toward my face.

Sylvio was seeing one of the images that I had seen in my dream two years before—a left hand moving toward his face. But again, he saw more than I had seen. He also remembered having come from a wealthy family with parents who had doted on him; and he recalled that his name had been Seph. While he was remembering all this, he flinched, sobbed, and squirmed in his chair.

I had expected some emotional fallout from this past life regression with the Photron, but nothing as dramatic as Sylvio later described; he had cried for days and had literally "fallen apart." However, once the catharsis was over, he had reached a plateau of greater inner composure. Thus, at our next meeting, he seemed calm and resolved. He also proudly produced a vision and two important dreams, which he had retrieved from his "dark night of the soul."

I have a vision where I see an older man standing next to a woman who is about twenty years younger, with a little boy of about five years of age, dressed in a dark suit and bow tie, standing before them. Everyone is dressed very formally, and we are in a hallway made of marble. It's as if we are posing for a picture. The building we are in exudes incredible amounts of wealth, which would be almost impossible for a single person to amass in just one lifetime (Buckingham Palace?).

Yes, this was almost certainly Buckingham Palace. Since Abdullah was knighted some years later, a reception at Buckingham Palace was a likely event. But Sylvio did not know that his past life father was knighted, which gave his vision even more weight.

The vision had been followed by two short dreams. In the first dream, a five-year-old Indian boy led Sylvio up the Orinoco River in South America, all the way to its source. Sylvio had no choice but to follow him. He associated this with a trip up the Orinoco River that he had taken a few years before. There, too, he had had to rely on the local knowledge of a young Indian guide. And although there had been many obstacles along the way, they had safely reached their destination. This augured well for the outcome of Sylvio's present inner journey. It was also a timely reminder that if he wanted to get to the source of his present problem only his five-year-old past life self could take him there.

The second dream, unlike the first one, had a nightmarish quality. He saw a woman's face come at him in great fury, and then, quite suddenly, the dream stopped in the familiar self-protective manner. Even though Sylvio had no idea whose face this had been or what had followed, he still did not want me to give him any information about it. I was growing tired of this one-sided poker game, which required that I pretended to know nothing while he was groping around in the dark. I was therefore greatly relieved when, at the beginning of the next session, he formally announced that he had to come to the end of his "independent investigation." Would I mind telling him now "the whole once-upon-a-time story?" When I had finished telling it, Sylvio asked, "What's next?" But before I had a chance to reply, he answered his own question. "There is lots more to come," he said with a tone of finality in his voice. After the session, he made a closing statement in his diary about the outcome of his experiment, which had been concluded to his satisfaction. Perhaps appropriately, he addressed it to me.

> I finally give up on trying to figure the whole story out, so I ask you to tell me the whole story of this particular past life. I feel secure enough in the information I received by myself, and that you have confirmed, and I know that there is a high degree of truth to it. I definitely needed this time to try and find some information by myself, though, in order to believe the information you give me.

But was there really "lots more to come"? All of the cards were now on the table. Sylvio had discovered his past life more or less on his own, and not only were his findings consistent with the information I had, but they even added to it. But—what was most important—his head trauma now had a chance to heal because the underlying past life trauma had been released. So what else was to come?

THE MISSING SHADOW

After thinking about the particulars of Sylvio's case for a while, I realized that his shadow was missing. After being identified as a victim, he had started to feel like one. Yet the question of what he had done to deserve this had never been answered, or even raised. I thought of my dream about Sylvio's "baggage" and the "ancient stream," wondering what that had been referring to. Concerned about Sylvio's present "victim" identity, I decided it would be better for him to face the dark underbelly of his soul than to be stuck in this helpless role for the rest of his life. I therefore suggested that he ask for a dream that would take him to the karmic cause of little Seph's suffering. We still had to locate the "ancient stream" where this particular "baggage" was coming from, I told him.

Unfortunately, my instructions coincided with Sylvio's switch to a different form of physical therapy that became very time-consuming in the following months, so much so that I rarely saw him. I had almost given up hope that we would ever be able to give proper closure to the psychological work we had done when Sylvio phoned me one morning with the exciting news that he had had the dream we were looking for. I found it to be fragmented, enigmatic, and in need of decoding, but also, at the same time, surprisingly specific:

It is the fifth century, or 550 CE. I am talking with a Caucasian man with a face painted black . . . a natural shift has taken place on some (cosmic?) level, and either I have come back or the "white" man has come back. M., a Danish friend of mine, is in the dream. She represents purity, innocence, good-heartedness . . . possibly an anima representation.

I was a white magician in the fifth century. The word "magi" keeps appearing in the dream, or is spoken often in the dream, meaning magic/king (?) I seem to ask what it is that I should be doing now, and the answer is to stay grounded and follow the path as indicated . . . follow what feels right, and you will be safe. There was a feeling in

*the dream that as long as I was lying on the right side of my body, with
my right hip connected to the mattress, I would continue to receive this
"information" . . . if I moved my right hip, I would lose the connection.*

The magi were a powerful priesthood in Persia during the fifth century CE. At that time the Orient was saturated with magic. The magi,
in particular, practiced this art extensively. Our word "magician" is
therefore derived from this Persian root. On the other hand, the Three
Wise Men from the Orient were also called magi. This suggests that
the magi performed a dual function: they were wisdom carriers on the
one hand and practitioners of magic on the other. During the period of
Persian history that Sylvio's dream was referring to, the magi, as keepers
of the traditions, had become involved in politics. Some of them might
have used magic to eliminate political opponents under the pretext that
the end justifies the means. Yet as my own past life history shows, the
abuse of spiritual powers carries a heavy karmic penalty, regardless of
the worthiness of the cause or the severity of the provocation.

Sylvio's dream stated in symbolical language that in 550 CE he had
been a white magician who had turned black (that is, used his spiritual powers for evil ends). But a "natural shift" on cosmic level—some
kind of purification process—had taken place between incarnations, so
that his original goodness could be restored. What he was like in his
next incarnation can be gleaned from the presence of a benign anima
figure whom he describes as pure, innocent, and good. Yet despite this
apparent purification, his psychic powers and right-brain functions had
been taken away until such a time when he would be spiritually mature
enough to be trusted with them again. Similar dynamics are at work in
the fairy tale of *Sleeping Beauty,* or *Briar Rose,* as it is sometimes called.
In the enchanted castle, everyone is frozen in motion, and no prince
can cut through the hedge of thorns or break the sleeping spell of the
princess until the hundred years are over.

For Sylvio, "the hundred years" were now over. This was the only
reason I was able to restore his right-brain functions to him through

the therapeutic work we did together. Unfortunately, the temporary loss of these functions had been the lesser price to pay for the black magic crimes committed in ancient Persia. The more costly one had been karmic. It became very clear to us in the end that Seph's suffering was only the tip of an iceberg of many tormented male incarnations. Sylvio's most recent life, which had been in Russia (therefore the reference to St. Basil's Cathedral in his initial dream), came up in a nightmare two months later. That life had ended with false imprisonment and electrical torture. When I tried to process it with the Photron, Sylvio went into such severe convulsions that I had to discontinue the treatment.

Fortunately, the return of his psychic powers, the healing of the traumas, and the return of the magi in his latest dream were clear indications that the karmic debt had been paid off. The magi dream, which—not unlike Mozart's *Magic Flute*—derived some of its power from Zoroastrian traditions, gave Sylvio a sense of inner certainty that he had been given a second chance. He felt once more protected and guided by the magi—a highly evolved soul group that still seems to exist on another level of reality. But Sylvio was only on probation it seemed. His connection with the magi was dependent on his commitment to the right-handed path, which was symbolized by the right hip in his dream. The magi gave him three practical guidelines to follow: stay grounded, follow your conscience, and listen to your inner voice.

A week later Sylvio had a second magi dream, which was clearly a sequel to the first one.

S. L. and I are somewhere . . . it is 4:10 p.m. and our session ends at 4:30 p.m. We have been catching up on the last month, but without getting into the heavy stuff . . . she suggests delving into some dreams with the time we have left . . . "Let's work!" . . . so I say okay . . .

I start to tell her the dream, and S. L. is awed by the information related in the previous magi dream, but S. L. feels that we do not need to go back that far. There is no need to visit every lifetime; nonetheless I express that I feel that the "baggage from an ancient stream" information is not related to Russia, but possibly to something far older. The fifth century information seems to be a better fit, so I recommend that we take a look at this stuff. S. L. says "okay . . ."

We move and are now downstairs somewhere and people are passing by; I think I may know them (relatives?). My arms are stretched out in front of me, and with my two hands I am holding a round cardboard container, similar to the Quaker oatmeal ones. The lid is off, and it contains vibrating white crystals, or salt rocks. The friction, due to the vibration of these pieces, creates a lot of noise. I pull my hands into my chest, place the container against my sternum, and wrap my arms around the container, and state that I am a white magician. At this point, the vibrations and the noise stop, absorbed by my body. I move the container away from me so it's about a foot and a half in front of me, and the vibrations and noise start again. I bring the container back to my chest and state that I am a white magician again, and they stop. I try to test the theory and see if saying "I am a red magician, or a green magician" will stop the crystals from vibrating and making noise, but it doesn't; they only stop when I say that I am a white magician. S. L. is stunned. I start to cry because the information/experience is overwhelming.

In this second magi dream, Sylvio explored his returning magical powers by entering into a relationship with the crystals or salt blocks inside the cardboard box. Crystals are energy amplifiers in the spiritual realm. They can be programmed in every which way and used for good or evil. Salt, on the other hand, had been a soul symbol for the alchemists. In this dream, these symbols intersected in a place that could be defined as amplified soul power. This was what Sylvio was now exploring.

At first I felt that the cardboard box was an unworthy container for such sacred contents and wondered if this was a residue of Sylvio's former disrespect for the unconscious. But I remembered just in time that Jung had kept a carved manikin, also a soul symbol, in a wooden pencil box as a little boy. Perhaps great things have to come in humble wrappings, I finally concluded.

In his interaction with the salt crystals, Sylvio made an important discovery: his amplified soul power caused trouble if he held it at arm's length, projected it outside, or denied it in any way. He had to enter into a personal relationship with it and hold it literally close to his heart. And even then, its vibrations only came to rest if he clearly defined himself as a white, versus a red or green (not to mention a black) magician. Thus, certain conditions were attached to the return of his magical powers also, the major one being that—this time—he could only use them for good.

Sylvio's experiment with the red and green magician was so typical of him that it made me smile. It was driven by the same scientific curiosity that had caused the tension and timed the rhythm of our therapeutic encounter from beginning to end. What Sylvio took away from this experiment was a very personal understanding of the need to take responsibility for whatever happens to us in life. Only he knew how badly this lesson was needed, because he said to me in our last session that he would have been a broken man for the rest of his life had he walked away from the therapy before it was time.

10

DISCOVERIES OF
A PAST LIFE DETECTIVE
Opening and Closing Pandora's Box

In Old Baghdad we'll call a halt
At the Shashun's ancestral vault;
We'll catch the Persian rose-flowers' scent,
And understand what Omar meant.

ROBERT GRAVES

THE SEARCH FOR ABDULLAH DAVID

This could have been the end of the story, but while I was writing this book surprises happened and synchronicities occurred. After Sylvio's therapy had officially ended, he went on an extended European vacation. The last thing he told me before he left was that he would try to find records of Abdullah David in London. Skeptical by nature, he needed documentation to be completely satisfied that our reconstruction of Seph's life had not been merely a telepathic *foli à deux*. I felt uneasy about his plan, because a previous attempt by an English friend to trace Abdullah in London had failed. I feared that if Sylvio's

223

new "independent investigation" should fail as well, he would start to question everything, including the results of his therapy. But all my objections would have done was make him suspicious; so I gave him my blessings instead.

For two months I heard nothing. Not even a postcard arrived. But one morning during the third month I found a large, brown manila envelope stuck in my mailbox. It was addressed to Sir Albert Abdullah David Sassoon, care of my home address. "Sassoon" was underlined twice to draw attention to the previously missing family name. I laughed at Sylvio's joke; I also finally understood why the name of the British hair stylist Vidal Sassoon had so obstinately stuck in my mind after only one haircut in a fancy salon in Bond Street. When I opened the fat envelope, a huge amount of biographical material fell out: photocopied excerpts from three family monographs, an article from the *Jewish Encyclopedia,* and a long obituary from the *London Times* dated October 26, 1896, for Sir Albert Abdullah David Sassoon. Jenny had either left out the family name, or I had not heard it. It was that simple.

The biographical material was accompanied by a tightly written two-page report about Sylvio's exploits in London. Because we had wrongly assumed Abdullah's family name to be David, it had taken Sylvio three full days to track down the banker. He browsed through the archives of the British Museum Library and visited the Guild Hall Library, where the names of knighted persons are kept; he even inspected the headstones in Jewish cemeteries, without finding a trace of the David family. Discouraged but unyielding, Sylvio took the subway to the old Jewish quarters of London. There, as he put it, he interviewed several "Jewish looking persons" in the streets.

One man he questioned was a Jewish textile merchant from India. The merchant had heard of an Indian rabbi by the name of David, in connection with the Odyoseph Chai Synagogue in Golders Green. So Sylvio took the underground to Golders Green, but it turned out that the Odyoseph Chai Synagogue was not located there, but in Hendon. So he took the next subway to Hendon. But by the time he arrived at the synagogue it was already late afternoon and the rabbi had gone home for the day. Luckily, Sylvio was able to obtain the rabbi's home phone number from the caretaker and called him from a nearby telephone booth. Rabbi David, although no relation of Abdullah David, turned out to be very helpful and knowledgeable. And although he knew of no family with the surname of David (apart from his own), he knew of two Jewish families who were originally from Baghdad—the Sassoons and the Koreshs—who had come over from India and settled in London in the mid-nineteenth century. The rabbi suggested that Sylvio contact these families.

The Odyoseph Chai Synagogue is only a few blocks away from the London School of Jewish Studies on Albert Road. Sylvio took the synchronicity of Albert Road and Sir Albert (Abdullah's name after the knighting) as a sign that he should give the institute's library a try. An hour-long search of the reading room again produced nothing, but at the very end of his search the book title *Victorian Jews through British Eyes* "jumped out at him," as he put it. He pulled the book off the shelf and opened it to a chapter on the Sassoons—one of the families the rabbi had mentioned. There he found Sir Albert's life story, as he had heard it from me. In his letter, Sylvio wrote:

> The rest, as they say, is history. I saw the words "David Sassoon," then "Sir Albert Sassoon," and suddenly realized that this was the family that I had been looking for—only that I had been missing a piece of the puzzle. The last name was not David. It was Sassoon! I started to read about this man's life, and saw that it pretty much matched everything you told me about him.

After collecting and photocopying everything he could find about Abdullah Sassoon, Sylvio spent an extra day looking for records of his own past life. According to the genealogical tables, Abdullah had two sons; the eldest was named Joseph. When Sylvio realized that Seph can be a pet name for Joseph, he knew that he was on the right track.

Unfortunately, that right track went nowhere. Apart from Joseph's date of birth and a brief obituary in a local newspaper, no other records could be found. The obituary simply stated that Joseph Sassoon had died of apoplexy, aged thirty-one, in Brighton. Apoplexy is either a stroke or a sudden hemorrhage into one of the body organs. According to Sylvio's dream, Seph's eye injury had led to hemorrhaging in the brain, thus Joseph's death by apoplexy and Seph's eye injury seemed to be directly related.

THE FORGOTTEN FIRSTBORN SON

One of the biographies that Sylvio sent me excerpts from promised to be very interesting—Stanley Jackson's family monograph, *The Sassoons,* published in 1968.[1] So I ordered it over the Internet from an antiquarian in Israel. In his foreword, the author mentioned that the Sassoon family had given him access to private papers and business correspondence, because they found "excessive reticence" unnecessary at this point. This made it possible for Jackson to paint lively character portraits of the various family members. It also enriched his book with a wealth of colorful anecdote. Despite the special resources that were available to him as a biographer, Jackson hardly ever mentioned Abdullah's firstborn son, Joseph. In the index of his book, Joseph is not even listed, and genealogical tables in Jackson's biography, Cecil Roth's biography, and the *Encyclopedia Judaica* contradict each other in regard to his family status. While, according to Jackson's table, he remained single, Cecil Roth and the *Encyclopedia Judaica* have him married to a Rebekah Hayyim. To confuse things even more, Jackson then contradicts his own genealogical table by explaining why Joseph had been absent from the opening of the dock in Bombay (the dock being Abdullah's pet project): Joseph had been getting married in Calcutta. Then he lets Joseph die "not long afterward" (after the wedding, that is) although, according to Joseph's obituary, he lived nine more years.[2]

Considering the high quality of Jackson's book, this does not make any sense, unless one assumes that certain facts about Joseph's life were being distorted or deliberately withheld. According to a time-honored family tradition of the Sassoons, Joseph, as firstborn son, should have represented the firm at public events before replacing Abdullah as chairman after his death. Instead, this lot had fallen upon his younger brother, Edward Albert. To break with a family tradition was so completely out of character for Abdullah that only highly unusual circumstances could have forced him to do that. These circumstances were never made public, however. A dream I had after reading Jackson's biography might throw some light on the family policies, especially in regard to Joseph's so-called wedding.

There is a large family gathering taking place in a spacious room. We are all standing like at a sherry party, and I am presiding over the meeting as a man. An engagement has been broken off in the younger generation, and we have decided not to make this public. There is an overall feeling of many strictly guarded family secrets.

If it was Joseph's engagement that my dream was referring to, there might have been different versions of the cover-up story in circulation, which would explain the inconsistencies in the genealogical tables.

A NOBLE LINEAGE

Family secrets were a necessity for the Sassoons to protect an impeccable public image. *Candide et Constanter* (honest and reliable) was the motto in their coat of arms. In England, they moved in upper-class circles that included the royal family. In Baghdad, their place of origin, they were considered Jewish aristocracy. Apart from being descendents of King David, they had traditionally held the high office of Nasi, which means "Prince of the Captivity." The Nasi was the chief treasurer and financial advisor to the Pasha, and, at the same time, his liaison to the Jewish community. As a liaison, the Nasi collected taxes from the Jews and looked after their secular welfare.

Whenever he rode to the palace of the Pasha, he wore gold tissue, according to Jackson, and the people in the streets and outside the bazaars stood with bowed heads until he and his retinue had passed. I was stunned when I read that the original family name had been Shoshan, meaning "lily," because this gave a whole new meaning to my lily-white karma with Sylvio in my dream.

The Sassoons enjoyed these privileges while the Ottoman Empire was in bloom (see Robert Graves's verse on page 223). During this time period, Baghdad was the hub of the trade from east to west, and a noted center of culture and learning. While the economy flourished, Jews and Arabs lived peacefully together, and the Jews honored their hosts by speaking their language and wearing native Arabic dress. But already in Abdullah's grandfather's generation, the social climate in Baghdad was starting to deteriorate, together with the economy.

The Arabs blamed the economic decline on the minorities and began to target wealthy Jewish families. The persecution of the Jews culminated under the dictatorship of Daud Pasha, a former slave who rose to power in 1818, the year when Abdullah was born. During Daud Pasha's reign of terror, many Jewish families fled the country. Some went to Australia, but the majority immigrated to India, where they could expect religious tolerance and free trade under the protection of the British Crown. Jews in high offices who remained in Baghdad were thrown into prison and had to pay huge ransom monies if they wanted to come out alive.

Abdullah's father, David Sassoon, had been one of those blacklisted Jews. After complaining to the Sultan about the rampant corruption under Daud Pasha's administration, he was arrested by the police and incarcerated until his father paid off the authorities. Knowing that the persecution would continue, David Sassoon boarded the next ship to Persia as soon as he was released from prison. After that, it had taken him two full years before he was able get his wife and children safely out of Iraq.

Abdullah had been ten years old when his father was imprisoned. Two years earlier, when he was eight, his mother had died in childbirth. The twelve-year-old girl his father had married after a year could not have been a mother substitute for him. And when—after years of separation—he had been reunited with his father, he had whisked Abdullah away to India, a country with very different cultural traditions. These early losses and anxious separations must have contributed to Abdullah's emotional dependency on his father, which was to last a lifetime.

DAVID AND ABDULLAH

Jenny, after accurately describing the family's escape from Baghdad to Persia, and from Persia to Bombay, had given this charismatic father figure a lot of attention—with good reason, as I was to discover. According to Jackson, David Sassoon was both an exceptional human being and a brilliant businessman. He was also a deeply spiritual man. In Baghdad, he had offered financial aid to orphans and the poor in the Jewish community, and later in Bombay he extended his charitable work to all of the poor, irrespective of race, caste, or creed. He built a synagogue and a Mechanical Institute in Bombay, and in Poona, his second residence, he founded a hospital where lepers and the poor could receive free medical care.

In the course of his life, David Sassoon funded some of the most important cultural and civic institutions in India. Yet he had very few needs of his own and was content to lead a simple life, in obeisance to his Orthodox Sephardic Jewish religion and out of loyalty to the Arabic culture he had been raised in. Although he swore allegiance to the British Crown, he did not speak a word of English and continued wearing his native Baghdad dress with turban, tunic, and pointed slippers until his death. His eight sons refrained from wearing Western clothes as long as he was alive, out of respect for him. In a family photo, taken in 1858, a year before Seph's accident must have occurred, Abdullah and two of his brothers are shown wearing a white tunic and a black head cover, exactly as Sylvio had seen and described it.

In 1840, David Sassoon founded a banking house in Bombay, and after his death, Abdullah became chairman of the bank, just as Jenny had said. My feeling that the name of the bank was "Bank of Bombay" was later validated by Jackson. My other hunch, that the bank had folded under Abdullah's chairmanship, was also confirmed. Like the rest of the private banks in India, it did not survive when the English started buying their cotton supply from Alabama (instead of from India) after the American Civil War. On the other hand, my assumption that the folding of the bank had been Abdullah's financial ruin was very far from the truth.

By the time the Bank of Bombay had gone under, David Sassoon & Sons had diversified their Oriental trade so extensively that they emerged "intact, indeed more powerful," according to Jackson.[3] As one contemporary observed, "silver, gold, silks, gums and spices, opium and cotton, wool and wheat—whatever moves over sea or land feels the hand or bears the mark of Sassoon & Co."[4] The main strength of this oriental firm was that they were strictly a family business. "David Sassoon & Sons meant precisely that," notes Jackson.[5]

The eight sons that David Sassoon fathered with two different wives in thirty-five years were all raised and personally trained by him to conduct the family business in compliance with his exceptionally high ethical standards. As soon as they came of age, they were sent out to establish branches of the firm in the Far East and the Middle East. They grew up speaking Arabic and Hebrew; by the time they reached manhood they were also fluent in Turkish and Persian—the business language in the Orient during the nineteenth century. Later, English, as well as some Hindi and some Chinese, were added to their impressive language repertoire.

With the numerous offspring of David's eight sons, the Sassoons were in a position to recruit their staff almost entirely from family members. When in exceptional cases outsiders were hired, disloyalty was never forgiven, and no mercy was shown to Gentiles or Jews who embezzled money. On the other hand, Sassoon & Sons paid the best wages and pioneered welfare plans for workers and their families at a time when nobody else did.

Abdullah appears to have been first and foremost his father's loyal son. During his chairmanship, he faithfully upheld all of David Sassoon's main principles and ideas. He was close enough to his father in temperament and ability to be able to continue his life's work. "He inherited his father's commercial ability and reputation for personal integrity, as well as his benevolent tastes," writes Cecil Roth in his biography.[6]

Like his father, Abdullah combined audacity with a stern, uncompromising traditionalism. This did not mean, however, that he was a slave to his father's ideas. In fact, in some ways, he was a creative innovator. He had a keen eye for new business opportunities and was willing to give them a chance, as long as they did not involve speculation or risk. He boosted the Indian economy by building the first dock in Bombay and by starting a home industry in spinning and weaving. Previous to this innovation, raw materials such as silk and cotton had to be exported from India to England, where they were woven into textiles and then imported back to India. This made textiles in India very expensive. By eliminating the exportation/importation step in the manufacturing process, Abdullah killed two birds with one stone: he made the textiles more affordable and provided work for the poor. Cecil Roth calls this "the most important development in the history of Indian industry in the nineteenth century."[7]

Despite these major achievements, Abdullah never seemed to be working very hard, according to Jackson. Reportedly, he was never in a hurry and always wore a smile on his face—a smile that was replaced in later years by a serious, tense expression in his photographs. A lot of his time seems to have been spent in coffeehouses and clubs. This makes him—in modern terms—an excellent public relations man. In fact, his time in coffeehouses and clubs was so well spent that he managed to double the family fortune during his lifetime and expand his father's philanthropy in the bargain.

Roth lists his many benefactions to the city of Bombay. He founded scholarships at the university and the art school, donated large sums to the rebuilding of the Elphinstone High School, supported the Institute for Mechanics that his father had established, and presented the Town Hall with a world-class organ, and the city of Bombay with a marble statue of Prince Albert. His philanthropy extended even beyond India to Persia and Great Britain. The knighting of 1872, which Jenny had mentioned, was only one of many honors bestowed on him by different countries. Between 1867 and 1880 he was awarded the "Star of India" by India, the "Order of the Lion and the Sun" by Persia, and the "Freedom of the City" by Great Britain. The "Freedom of the City," which is a rare honor, had never been bestowed upon a Jew before. When Abdullah was in his late fifties, Queen Victoria made him a baronet for using his influence on foreign politics to England's advantage.

Abdullah deviated from his father's lifestyle and philosophy in only two important ways: His religious orientation seems to have been more liberal than that of his father, although it is not clear how liberal it actually was. A liberal orientation would certainly have been suggested by the embroidered yarmulke in my dream. On the other hand, in one of Sylvio's dreams, Abdullah was wearing a half-black, half-embroidered yarmulke. This would place him halfway between a liberal and an orthodox Jew, which might actually be closer to the truth.

The main difference between father and son was in lifestyle. While David Sassoon was content with leading a simple life, Abdullah had luxurious tastes. "He had superb villas at Garden Reach, Poona, and at Mahabaleshwar high on the hills above it, where he lavishly entertained fellow-fugitives from the summer heat of the plains," writes Cecil Roth.[8] Yet his main residence was in the outskirts of Bombay. It was named somewhat pretentiously Sans Souci, after Frederick the Great's retreat in Potsdam, and was modeled on an Italian palazzo of the Renaissance. This is where Abdullah received his distinguished guests. In 1872, the same year he was knighted, he gave a ball in Sans Souci in honor of Lord Northbrook, the newly appointed viceroy of India. This feast was so spectacular that it was still remembered in Bombay a quarter of a century later. Judging from Jackson's following description, the ball had all the magic and splendor of the *Arabian Nights:* "From 10:00 P.M. onward, over a thousand guests drove up to the mansion through an avenue of lamps and colored flares that bathed the flowerbeds and fountains in a glow visible for a clear mile from the top of Mount Road."[9]

THE LONDON CONNECTION

Apart from being a joint celebration of the viceroy's appointment and his own knighting, this ball was also Abdullah's parting gift to the haut monde of Bombay, because he was on the point of moving to England. This relocation did not come out of the blue; it had been in preparation for many years. As early as 1858, David Sassoon had sent one of his younger sons to London to establish an English branch of the firm. After that, Abdullah had taken occasional business trips to England. His first visit to London on record had been in 1859, when he had represented his father at the opening of the London office. This had coincided with the critical time when Joseph had been between five and six years old. Although Jackson makes no mention of it, Abdullah must have taken his wife, Hannah, and his firstborn son, Joseph, along on this overseas journey to show them the British metropolis.

According to Sylvio's vision, they had attended a reception at Buckingham Palace before Joseph was injured. Jackson states that Abdullah had left England "in a great hurry" on that occasion, which, as we know, was out of character for him. On his subsequent journeys to England, Hannah never accompanied him—always excusing herself with ill health. This could be interpreted as an avoidance of guilt-provoking memories. She also seems to have gone through a radical personality change later in life. As was customary for middle-aged orthodox Jewish women of that time, she shaved her head and wore a wig; she reportedly no longer enjoyed hosting Abdullah's parties and became obsessively involved with Jewish schools.

I strongly suspect that, after his son was maimed for life, Abdullah had maintained his marriage only as a matter of form. As a man of principle, he would have argued that his wife, Hannah, who had a bad temper, could not be trusted to raise more children. Thus, after 1859, there were no more offspring, although Hannah was still of childbearing age, and the Sassoons were known to be fruitful. When Abdullah left this wife fourteen years later to move to England, the relocation ostensibly was for business reasons. However, the fact that on subsequent visits to India he only spent a minimum of time in his beloved Bombay speaks for itself.

In London, Abdullah bought a millionaire's mansion in Queen's Gate, not far from Hyde Park, where I had imagined him feeding the ducks. But instead of being a lonely retiree, he continued to be the chairman of Sassoon & Sons. In his new mansion he lavishly entertained foreign ambassadors, Oriental princes, and members of the royal family. He bought a second residence in Brighton, a seaside resort, where some of his half-brothers and their families had settled. Joseph must have joined him there at some point, because that's where he later died. As Joseph's illness progressed, the skills of English doctors might have been required to keep him halfway sane and alive.

Epilepsy has a strange history. Folklore ascribes a demonic origin to this mysterious illness, and whole superstitious belief systems have grown up around it. In antiquity epilepsy was thought to be infectious, and people spat out in front of the epileptic in order to protect themselves. In ancient Rome, whole assemblies had to be broken up if someone in the crowd suffered an epileptic seizure. And in medieval times, the Christian Church believed epilepsy to be of demonic origin and treated it with exorcism.

Even today, people are terrified of witnessing epileptic attacks. Apart from the old superstitions that are still alive in the collective unconscious, the illness itself produces personality changes that tend to isolate the epileptic. Extreme egocentricity, pettiness, a highly inflammable temperament, and often an obsessive preoccupation with imaginary tort tend to alienate the people around them. Since Joseph had symptomatic epilepsy, caused by brain trauma, he was probably also suffering from chronic headaches. In the nineteenth century this was treated with opium, which happened to be one of the commodities that Sassoon & Sons traded. According to Sylvio, who remembered this in a flashback, Joseph had been an opium addict in the later stages of his illness. The opium addiction, in addition to the epileptic seizures and the epilepsy-related personality changes, would have been more than enough to keep image-conscious family members at a distance. And—as Sylvio began to remember in London—Abdullah had been one of them.

HAVING IT OUT WITH FATHER

After receiving the letter from Sylvio with the past life documentation in October, I heard nothing more from him. It was actually not until the end of November that I ran into him at the Marketplace, a Santa Fe health food store. He was pleasant but somewhat distant. I was surprised to hear that he had already been back for a month. I would have considered a phone call normal after what he had uncovered in London and instinctively knew that something was wrong. For personal and professional reasons, I needed to know what was causing his emotional withdrawal. Since it would have been inappropriate for me to suggest a therapy session after our professional relationship had ended, I invited him over for tea.

I was relieved when Sylvio did not find an excuse not to come, and when we were sitting together in my living room, drinking English tea by candlelight, he began to open up. After my phone call, he said, a huge surge of old anger and hurt had welled up in him. He still could feel it there, he added, pointing at his sternum, the seat of old pain. He said that in Brighton he had felt abandoned by the whole family. He and I, in particular, had been—even after his move to England—emotionally whole continents apart. Also, according to him, I had given him everything materially, but nothing emotionally. Why, for instance, had I bought him a house instead of taking him into *my* home? And why had I never taken him for walks on the seaside promenade?

As I listened to his accusations, I felt more and more like Abdullah; I was going on the defensive. "I gave you everything I had to give," I stiffly replied. "I was not an emotionally demonstrative man. My father didn't raise me that way." While we were arguing back and forth, I was trying to make sense of this insane dialogue and decided that we were in the middle of some reincarnational housecleaning. Unfortunately, every rational argument I brought forth to justify my actions as Abdullah seemed to make little impression on him.

Yes, yes, he said, he knew all that, but it made absolutely no difference to the way he was *feeling*. What he wanted to hear from me was that Abdullah knew what it had been like for him (Joseph) to be hidden away in a closet for most of his life. I replied that I was quite sure that Abdullah could have imagined that, considering that he had spent many lifetimes as a woman in the same situation.

But why did I bring him to Brighton, if I did not want to be seen with him in public? And why had I not been able to help him, despite all the money and power I had? Sylvio's accusations were becoming unreasonable and repetitive and, as Abdullah, I was beginning to feel utterly frustrated and helpless. I remembered now that our arguments in Brighton had always ended the same way and that this had been one of the reasons why I had withdrawn from him. Besides, I did not know how to respond to some of Sylvio's accusations, because I did not remember why I had acted the way I did. I finally said that in order to be able to continue this conversation, I needed to look inside or wait for a dream. This put an end to the argument for the time being. When I walked Sylvio to the door, we were our present selves again. And although he gave me a conciliatory hug, we both knew very well that the father-son conflict between us was far from over.

Later that night, using a form of active imagination, I got in touch with Abdullah. I was surprised to hear that the decision to keep Joseph's injury a secret had not been made by Abdullah himself, but by his father who, at the time of the accident, had still been head of the family and chairman of the firm. Yet, Abdullah had never, at any time, questioned the wisdom of his father's decision. Abdullah also informed me that Joseph had been quite ill by the time they had moved him to Brighton for better medical care, and that, in this last stage of his illness, he had been raging at everybody.

Of course, quite apart from the anger, which is symptomatic of epilepsy, Joseph had had plenty of things to be angry about. After becoming a victim of physical abuse, he had been hidden from public view like a shameful family secret. The privileges of being the firstborn son had passed on to his younger brother, while he had been doomed to a marginalized existence for the rest of his life.

Since I could not change Sylvio's past, I wondered what I could do for him in the present. So, as soon as I had recovered from our afternoon tea, I phoned and asked him how he was. He had been having a rough time, he told me. After confronting me in my living room, he had been flooded with old anger. When I asked him if there was anything I could do to make him feel better, he turned the question back to Abdullah. He wanted him to admit that he had emotionally abandoned him and wanted an apology from him. Since I felt that Sylvio's accusation was unfair, I did not want to apologize for Abdullah. But I readily admitted that Abdullah had felt helpless vis-à-vis Joseph's illness. It had been too painful to see him suffer, so he had often avoided him altogether.

This confession made no impression on Sylvio at all. In fact, everything I said only provided him with new ammunition for his next attack. Seeing him stuck in a vicious circle of anger and blame, I diplomatically ended the phone call while leaving the door open for a continuation at a later time.

Ironically, I found myself benefiting from these confrontations, because they were forcing me to get acquainted with an inner figure that had felt like a total stranger to me before. No wonder, for during his lifetime, Abdullah had also been an enigma to the people around him. Even the British, who are known for their reserve, had found his professional and personal secrecy as noteworthy as his sense of humor. But now, cornered by Sylvio's attacks, Abdullah was starting to drop his mask.

While this conflict between Sylvio and myself was going on, I often found myself, in my dreams, in Abdullah's very alien world. Although I could never remember any details in the morning, I always awoke with an uncomfortable feeling of having been in public view all the time. Another insight I brought back from my dream excursions into Abdullah's life was that I had been terrified of my son's rages, and even more so of his seizures. On several occasions, Joseph's angry outburst at me had brought on an epileptic seizure in him. I had already been in my sixties then and had been suffering from asthma and bronchitis. I had rightly feared that these highly emotional scenes between us would affect my health and hasten Joseph's death. So I had listened to the doctors' advice and had discontinued my visits to him. While Joseph had been abandoned by the whole family, as Sylvio correctly remembered, a host of doctors, nurses, and domestic servants had waited on him day and night. At age thirty-one, he had very suddenly died, unreconciled with me and the rest of the family and full of self-pity.

This unresolved ending explained the present angry energies between us. I was even beginning to suspect that it had been at least as much Joseph's enduring wish to have it out with Abdullah as Sylvio's desire to be healed that had brought him into my practice. Although his father's karma might have been lily white, it had not looked that way in Joseph's eyes. While we were both involved with the therapeutic process, Sylvio's vengeful, unconscious agenda had remained in the background. But now that his recovery was well on its way and our past life history was an open book, the moment had come for it to emerge. This could have been the chance of a lifetime to heal the son-father relationship, but presently it looked as if Sylvio was getting stuck again in the same old vicious circle of anger and blame. I knew if he chose to stay in that place there was nothing I could do about it. Since Abdullah's offense had only existed in Joseph's imagination anyway, Sylvio would have to work this out with another father in another lifetime; but I, personally, would be off the hook.

I had just come to this conclusion when Sylvio launched another attack on me over the telephone, only this time I was better prepared. Since I had been communicating with Abdullah in the meantime, my words had more substance and carried more weight. Sylvio might have felt this, because in the course of the argument his rigid mind-set began to soften and he began to listen to me. As soon as I saw an opening, I made a bold move: I offered him a free Photron session as a personal gift from Abdullah. When Sylvio accepted this offer, I knew that half the battle was won.

WHITENING THE LILY

When Sylvio called two days later to make an appointment with me for the color session, a major shift had taken place in him. He said that he had come to realize that he had been stuck in a vicious circle of anger and blame in his two most recent incarnations and that he was ready to get unstuck. We deliberately scheduled the Photron session for New Year's Day, because of the symbolical meaning of it.

When he arrived the afternoon of the first day of the New Year, he was mentally and emotionally wide open. He told me upfront that, since our last contact, more insights had come to him. He had realized that even Joseph had had choices but had settled for the lesser ones. He had been thinking a lot about Helen Keller and how she had coped with her blindness. She was living proof to him that even under the most difficult circumstances it is possible to lead a meaningful life. The life of an invalid did not have to end in self-pity and envy, as Joseph's had done. Sylvio had also finally understood that Joseph would have received much more love and support from his family had he not driven everyone away with his anger.

I thought only the magi could have worked such a miracle in only a few days. I became even more convinced of a transpersonal intervention when he told me his dream from the night before. In this dream, he had been given detailed instructions for how to orchestrate the color session: We were to create a sacred space with candlelight and use the colors blue-green, yellow, and violet—in this exact order. I was amazed at the astuteness of the color choice, because blue-green is the gateway to past lives; yellow instills hope and self-empowerment in the viewer; and violet facilitates the relinquishment of past memories. Sylvio had even been shown some pressure points on the soles of his feet, which I was to hold if a Reiki treatment should become necessary at the end of the session. (I had been clearing the energy field of my clients with Reiki at the end of past life regressions until I discovered that the colored strobic light of the Photron gets even better results.) He had made a sketch of the soles of his feet with the pressure points penciled in, which he handed over to me before we started.

It goes without saying that I followed these instructions religiously. While Sylvio lay down on my blue carpet, with his head under the Photron, I lit a candle and darkened the room. I turned on the Photron, set the flicker rate at theta, and placed the blue-green color filter in the slot. As soon as the turquoise light shone into Sylvio's eyes, his head began to twitch and the energy release began. After a few minutes of releasing, a surge of emotions swept over him. In the voice of a little boy, he complained of feeling alone and unsupported by his father.

Here is where I came in. Speaking softly on behalf of Abdullah, I explained that I had not been a free man; my hands had been tied by conventions, traditions, and family obligations. I said that Joseph's accident had destroyed my marriage, and that I had never completely recovered from the shock of seeing my happy family life destroyed in one single moment. This time Sylvio heard me. There was a moment of silence between us, while he was absorbing what I had told him.

Then he said, "I can now see it all as a mistake, an accident."

Then the process shifted back to his physical body. As the dark energies that had been held in place by Sylvio's negative thinking were forced out, his twitches turned into convulsions. From a state of deep trance, he reported that the physical damage was being repaired, and that old and new traumas, which had now merged, were being released together. From an even deeper place, Sylvio informed me that Joseph had just recovered his eyesight. But seeing was still scary for him, he added, and he needed time to adjust. I thought how wonderful it was that the past was being changed. After that, his body stopped twitching and went limp. This called for a color change, so I exposed him to yellow, which effected his mood dramatically. Laughing joyfully, he said that the separation between Joseph and Abdullah—him and me—was gone, and that we were "all one." After a few minutes of silence, while asking for inner guidance, he solemnly declared, "The journey is complete!"

This would have been the perfect moment to end the session, but I dared not ignore the dream instructions to finish the process with violet. Since violet opens the mind to higher consciousness and relinquishes past memories, this color choice made sense. Sylvio later made the analogy that being exposed to violet at the end of the session was similar to spraying a fixative on a finished painting. When I switched off the Photron at the end of the session, his body was humming with energies, and no Reiki treatment was needed. When we looked at the clock, two hours had passed in what had seemed like a much shorter time. We were both so full of wonder that Sylvio felt the need to lighten things up by saying—tongue in cheek—that we did have a Hollywood-style happy ending, after all.

Another Hollywood-style happy ending was that I could finally integrate my least understood inner figure—the millionaire Abdullah Sassoon. Without Sylvio's "independent investigation," his negative past life father complex, and our reincarnational housecleaning this would never have happened. And yet, as a final dream told me, Abdullah and I are in need of each other—not only as male and female counterparts but also as complementary opposites.

I am approaching a long, cast-iron fence that partitions off a huge estate. The property has two front entrances—an elaborately crafted, cast-iron two-wing gate, large enough to let carriages through, and a small side gate for the servants.

I sneak in through the servants' gate, while the host is seeing off another guest at the main entrance, but he has noticed me right away. "I like to come in through side doors or back doors," I tease him, as if we were old friends. Although I have come in through the servants' gate, he is treating me like royalty. He takes my arm and clasps my hand and shows me around his estate. Two huge, impressive Renaissance-style build-ings take up most of the grounds. While I am admiring them, I secretly look at my host's profile. He has an artistic flair that I had not expected to see in him. His features are bold and aquiline; his energy is strongly male. Although he is elderly, and I am, too, I feel attracted to him. While we are walking, arm in arm, I seem to be taking on some of his physical symptoms; I am suddenly wheezing, and my joints are creaking at every step. Pointing at his palaces, I say to him, "Do you think that God has a business anima? How could he have given you all this?"

Yes, God's business anima had given Abdullah material wealth in abundance, but God's emotional anima had been less generous with him. We are all both rich and poor, like Abdullah, in different areas of our lives. But as eternal souls, we can take comfort in the fact that, within the reincarnational cycle, we will all experience life to the full-est, and everything will balance out in the end.

EPILOGUE

An epilogue is something like a *rite de sorti*—a closing ritual. A book like this needs it, because it draws its strength from the "dreamtime," as the Australian Aborigines call it. Although all of our stories are true and have been assembled with great care, they cast a spell over the reader, which at this point must be broken. Otherwise, some of the lessons they carry might slip away like the lizard, the medicine animal of American Indian dreamers.

So let's go back and gather up the bits and pieces of information that we have come across on our journeys to that hard-to-reach, numinous, sacred place in the deep unconscious where the memories of all of our lifetimes are stored. This will give our stories a practical value, in addition to the emotional and spiritual value they already have.

The five main case studies in this book, including my own, revolved around a "new" archetype, which is as old as humanity. To distinguish this new archetype from Jung's archetype of rebirth, which only applies to psychic renewal, I have named it "the archetype of reincarnation." Like all archetypes, it is surrounded by a symbolic field, which our dreams were staking out. As we were covering this staked-out ground, it became increasingly clear that the unconscious knows a great deal more about reincarnation than we know consciously. In fact, the unconscious seems to take the rebirth process for granted. This explains why those

243

religions that are based on mystical experience and meditation practices all have the belief in reincarnation in common.

In the process of our therapeutic work, some of us had visionary dreams about reincarnation itself. Although we experienced this process from different angles, its quintessence can be summed up like this: Reincarnation seems to be a creative, dynamic process that runs in circles of simultaneous existence, with each incarnation being only part of a much greater whole. Within each of these circles, basic existential and philosophical issues such as justice, leadership, or spirituality are explored. Although our incarnations seem to be simultaneous, they represent different evolutionary stages within the reincarnational cycle, characterized by life forms of increasingly greater complexity and lighter energy bodies.

According to Jungian theory, the human psyche is organized in pairs of opposites. The reincarnational cycle seems to follow the same pattern. Each life situation is explored first from one side, then from the other, until eventually a union of opposites is achieved. This means that victims and victimizers will switch roles at some point and that lives of material affluence will be either preceded or followed by lives in poverty. Karma seems to be the great equalizer in this process. It balances the opposites by arranging that "what goes around comes around." Since reincarnation is a simultaneous process, it is of no importance, karmically speaking, if the balance is restored today, tomorrow, or many centuries later. Like everything else on this planet, karma has a light and a dark aspect. On the one hand, it is the guardian of our wholeness, and on the other, the arm of justice that will catch up with us in the end.

Occasionally we caught a glimpse of how karmic "appointments" are made in the dreamtime. We seem to be part of a trans-incarnational telepathy network, through which we communicate with each other whenever we are ready to come together again. The purpose of these karmic encounters is always to work things out. Unfortunately, the repetition compulsion, discovered by Freud, carries over from one lifetime to another and often manages to force the partners to repeat negative patterns over and over again. This appears to be one of the reasons why human evolution, in contrast to technical evolution, is so tediously slow.

Two stories in this book describe a karmic encounter between client and therapist. In both of these cases the karma could be resolved, but only with great difficulty. Theoretically, the safe and protected space of a therapist's office should be an ideal place to work these things out, but psychotherapists are human, and like other unconscious manifestations, repetition compulsion tends to intensify in the therapeutic encounter. My case studies demonstrate, each in its own way, that past life transference and countertransference is emotionally highly charged and deeply enmeshed, because here the emotional dynamics of the transference are not determined by projection and response, but by unconscious, often disturbing memories from a shared past life.

This can put the therapist under so much pressure from within and without that the professional boundaries may collapse. Yet a breach of the sacred healing contract will not only harm the client emotionally, and the therapist professionally, it will also have serious karmic consequences for both. What saved me in these cases was my awareness of the nature of the transference, my concern both for the client and myself, and a fierce determination to clear the karma at any price.

The self-regulating function of the psyche, first noted by Jung, is very active in past life dreams, particularly around trauma issues. In one case, a past life trauma healing occurred spontaneously in a dream series. In the rest of the cases, the dreams protected the dreamer from getting retraumatized whenever disturbing past life memories surfaced. They did this by either putting the dreamer in the "observer" position or by letting the "film" snap just in time.

Every past life dream had a correlate in the present life situation. Dreams were triggered either by a similarity of past and present events, or by a visit to a past life locale, or by a need to access past life knowledge. In two cases they were set off by a telepathic communication between past life partners who were ready for another encounter.

The stories in this book present convincing evidence that we are not one, but many all at once, and that we inherit certain talents, idiosyncrasies, and life themes and injuries from our soul ancestors. This multiplicity is a weakness, insofar as it causes inner tensions, but it is also a source of strength, because it has the potential of putting powerful inner resources at our disposal. In a certain sense we are all "old souls," although some of us, admittedly, are a little older than others. Having evolved from simpler life-forms, we are already "old" by the time we have made it into a human body. This is why the spiritual masters keep telling us—which is sometimes difficult to believe—that a human birth is a privilege.

GLOSSARY

Active Imagination

A visualization technique, developed by C. G. Jung, where, in a meditative state, one focuses on a dream image, allowing it to change and unfold. This technique can also be used to enter into an inner dialogue with a dream figure.

Abaissement du niveau mental

A term first used by Jung's teacher, the French professor Pierre Janet. It describes a mental state in which the intensity of consciousness is reduced, allowing unexpected contents from the unconscious to come to the surface.

Akashic Records

From Sanskrit *akasha,* meaning "boundless space"; also called "the book of life." The Akashic Records are like a supercomputer system of the universe. They are considered the central storehouse of information about every human being that has ever lived. Some psychics seem to have direct access to these otherworldly records.

Anima/animus

The contrasexual archetypes (see *Archetypes*) in the human psyche, according to Jung. In dreams they appear personified as a woman (in men's dreams) or as a man (in women's dreams). In waking life, they are often projected onto desired love objects.

Archetypes

Timeless images shared by all humanity, which are representative of universal human experience, such as mother, father, child, birth, death, trickster. They are located in the collective unconscious, according to Jung, and can be traced in dreams, fairy tales, myths, and world literature.

Catharsis

From Greek *katharsis,* meaning "purgation"; a powerful emotional release that sometimes occurs in therapy, leading to greater emotional balance.

Collective unconscious

Jung distinguished between the personal and the collective unconscious. While the personal unconscious contains personal memories that have either been repressed or forgotten, the collective unconscious comprises racial memories that are universal and eternal. It is a fount of ancient wisdom, symbols, and archetypes.

Complex

Complexes are emotionally charged psychic fragments that have split off under the impact of traumatic experience. We all have complexes ("buttons" in popular language) of different kinds, of which the most commonly known is the inferiority complex. If a complex is hit (or a "button" gets pushed) we become irrational and flustered; we overreact and make bad decisions. Some complexes that cannot be explained otherwise, might have their origin in traumatic past life experiences.

Ego inflation

A pathological ego identification with material from the deep unconscious (usually of an archetypal nature), leading to an overblown sense of self. An ego inflation can either be accompanied by an immense sense of power and uniqueness, or by the very opposite—a sense of total worthlessness.

Flashback

The spontaneous resurfacing of forgotten memories.

Initial dream
A dream, often observed at the beginning of psychotherapy, containing valuable diagnostic and prognostic information.

Integration
The assimilation of previously unconscious or unrecognized personality parts into the conscious personality. There is a fine line between integration of such material and becoming possessed or dominated by it.

Karma
From Sanskrit, meaning "deed, action, work"; the spiritual law of cause and effect, which ordains that we must experience what we have done to others.

Parapsychology
From Latin *para,* meaning "beyond"; a branch of research psychology, which investigates psychic phenomena associated with the paranormal.

Past life bleed-through
A momentary, unconscious identification with a past life personality, which leads to inappropriate behavior in terms of the person's present life situation.

Past life recall
The ability to remember past lives. Past life memories can either surface spontaneously in dreams and flashbacks (see *Flashback*), or be induced in past life regressions.

Past life takeover
Contrary to a past life bleed-through, where the conscious ego becomes only temporarily identified with a past life personality, in a past life takeover such identification becomes a permanent condition. Under this influence, the individual may display unrealistic, unadapted and often grandiose behavior and has a self-image that is distorted in the direction of the dominant past life self. In the resulting state of "possession," the original blueprint for the present life is obscured.

Past life transference

A subdivision of transference/countertransference that may well be defined here for the very first time. It differs from ordinary transference in some significant ways: For here, the feelings are not transferred from a relationship with another person, but from a reciprocal relationship between two souls from another lifetime. Unlike an ordinary transference relationship, a past life transference relationship is based on unconscious memories rather than on a fantasy. It is a relationship that is real and represents an enmeshment in which both client and therapist are equally involved. In a past life transference, karmic healing is always the ultimate unconscious purpose. Unfortunately, this purpose is interfered with and often aborted by a mutual compulsion to reenact destructive relationship patterns of the past (see *Repetition compulsion*).

Repetition compulsion

A universal, compelling tendency, discovered by Freud, to repeat painful and traumatic experiences of the past. In Freud's opinion, it is driven by the death instinct. According to my own observations, this tendency or compulsion carries over from one lifetime to another.

Shadow

One of the major archetypes, according to Jung. It has a personal and a collective aspect. On a personal level, it represents all the unrecognized or repressed character traits that an individual might have. These are mostly negative, but can also be positive if parental or social value systems are distorted and defective. On a collective level, the shadow represents pure evil. In mythologies, fairy tales, and dreams, it appears personified as diabolical deities and demonic beings of different kinds. In past life psychology with a Jungian orientation, the shadow represents morally unacceptable past life selves that have produced negative karma. Like the personal shadow, these past life selves are usually deeply repressed.

Transference/countertransference

Concepts originally developed in psychoanalysis. They signify certain psychodynamics that typically occur in psychotherapy. In a transference and countertransference relationship the client "transfers" his or her feelings for significant others, usually parental figures, onto the therapist. The therapist responds with a countertransference, which represents his feeling reaction to the client's transferred emotions. For the therapist, both transference and countertransference are useful tools to uncover unconscious childhood problems and trace destructive relational patterns back to their original source. Since the feelings transferred to the therapist have usually little to do with the psychotherapist as an individual, the transference/countertransference relationship is in essence an illusionary one.

NOTES

CHAPTER 1. DREAM INITIATION

1. Erlo van Waveren, *Pilgrimage to the Rebirth* (York Beach, Maine: Samuel Weiser, 1978).
2. Z'ev ben Shimon Halevi, *A Kabbalistic Universe* (York Beach, Maine: Samuel Weiser, 1977).
3. Jane Roberts in a letter to the author, dated October 27, 1979.
4. C. G. Jung, *Psychology and Alchemy* (Princeton, NJ: Princeton University Press, Bollingen Series XII, 1970), 482.
5. Mircea Eliade, *Shamanism: Archaic Techniques of Ecstasy* (Princeton, NJ: Princeton University Press, Bollingen Series LXXVI, 1974).
6. Ibid.; van Waveren, 23.
7. Alberto Villoldo, *Shaman, Healer, Sage: How to Heal Yourself and Others with the Energy Medicine of the Americas* (New York: Harmony Books, 2000), 73–75.

CHAPTER 2. WOMEN ON THE FRINGE

1. Gehlek Nawang Rimpoche, *Good Life, Good Death: Tibetan Wisdom on Reincarnation* (New York: Riverhead Books, 2001).
2. Edgar Evans Cayce, *Edgar Cayce on Atlantis* (New York: Warner Books, 1968).
3. The Encyclopedia Britannica Online, *Nell Gwynn*.
4. Roger J. Woolger, *Other Lives, Other Selves: A Jungian Psychotherapist Discovers Past Lives* (New York: Doubleday, 1987).
5. Arthur Guirdham, *The Cathers and Reincarnation* (Saffron Walden, England: The C. W. Daniel Company, 1970).

6. Pierre Derlon, *Unter Hexern und Zauberern—Die okkulten Traditionen der Zigeuner* (Basel, Switzerland: Sphinx-Verlag, 1982).

CHAPTER 3. MEN OF POWER

1. Woolger, *Other Lives, Other Selves,* 331.
2. Charles Francis Jenkins, *Button Gwinnett: Signer of the Declaration of Independence* (New York: Doubleday, 1926), 22, 48.
3. Ibid., 183.
4. Ibid., 184.
5. Ibid., 229.
6. Ibid., 136.
7. Ibid., 128.
8. *The I Ching or Book of Changes,* Wilhelm/Baynes Translation, Bollingen Series XI (Princeton, NJ: Princeton University Press, 1987), 121.
9. Manley P. Hall, *The Secret Teachings of all Ages: An Encyclopedic Outline of Masonic, Hermetic, Qaballistic and Rosecrucian Symbolical Philosophy.* (Los Angeles: The Philosophical Research Society, 1977), 200.
10. Jenkins, *Button Gwinnett,* 209.
11. Hans Läng, *Kulturgeschichte der Indianer Nordamerikas* (Breisgau, Germany: Walter-Verlag, Olten und Freiburg im Breisgau, 1981).

CHAPTER 4. INTEGRATION

1. Peter A. Levine, workshop brochure.
2. J. E. Cirlot, *A Dictionary of Symbols* (London: Routledge & Kegan Paul, 1971), 29.
3. Cayce, *Edgar Cayce on Atlantis,* 131.
4. J. A. Hadfield, *Dreams and Nightmares* (Middlesex, England: Penguin Books, 1973).
5. Harry Wilmer, "Combat Nightmares: Toward a Theory of Violence," *Spring Journal* (1986): 122.
6. Johann Wolfgang von Goethe, *Faust I. Teil, Goethes Werke* (Hamburg, Germany: Christian Wegner Verlag, 1954), 29.
7. *The I Ching or Book of Changes,* 49–50.

CHAPTER 5. WITCH MOTHER AND EMPEROR FATHER

1. Lynn Andrews, *Medicine Woman* (New York: Tarcher, 2006), 153–54.

CHAPTER 6. CLOSING THE CIRCLE

1. Sylvia Brown and Lindsay Harrison, *Past Lives, Future Healing* (New York: Dutton, 2001).

CHAPTER 7. IN THE SHADOWS OF DACHAU

1. Gitta Sereny, *Albert Speer: His Battle with Truth* (New York: Vintage Books, 1996), 58–59.

CHAPTER 8. WALKING ON THIN ICE

1. Encyclopedia Britannica online, *Richard I (known as Richard Coeur de Lion)*.
2. Pierre Derlon, *Unter Hexern und Zauberern,* 133.
3. C. G. Jung, *Memories, Dreams, Reflections* (New York: Vintage Books, 1989), 193.

CHAPTER 10. DISCOVERIES OF A PAST LIFE DETECTIVE

1. Stanley Jackson, *The Sassoons* (London: Heinemann, 1968).
2. Ibid., 56.
3. Ibid., 44.
4. Ibid., 30.
5. Ibid., 20.
6. Cecil Roth, *The Sassoon Dynasty* (London: Robert Hale, 1941), 74.
7. Ibid., 76.
8. Ibid., 84.
9. Jackson, *The Sassoons,* 53.

BIBLIOGRAPHY

Andrews, Lynn. *Medicine Woman.* New York: Tarcher, 2006.

Brown, Sylvia, and Lindsay Harrison. *Past Lives, Future Healing.* New York: Dutton, 2001.

Cayce, Edgar Evans. *Edgar Cayce on Atlantis.* New York: Warner Books, 1968.

Cerminara, Gina. *Many Mansions.* New York: Signet, 1988.

Cirlot, J. E. *A Dictionary of Symbols.* London: Kegan & Paul, 1971.

Derlon, Pierre. *Unter Hexern und Zauberern: Die okkulten Traditionen der Zigeuner.* Basel, Switzerland: Sphinx-Verlag, 1976.

Eliade, Mircea. *Shamanism: Archaic Techniques of Ecstasy.* Princeton, NJ: Princeton University Press, 1974.

Guirdham, Arthur. *The Cathars and Reincarnation.* Saffron Walden, England: The C. W. Daniel Company, 1970.

Hadfield, J. A. *Dreams and Nightmares.* Middlesex, England: Penguin Books, 1973.

Halevi, Z'ev ben Shimon. *A Kabbalistic Universe.* York Beach, Maine: Samuel Weiser, 1977.

Hall, Manley P. *The Secret Teachings of All Ages: An Encyclopedic Outline of Masonic, Hermetic, Qaballistic and Rosecrucian Symbolical Philosophy.* Los Angeles: The Philosophical Research Society, 1977.

I Ching or Book of Changes. Wilhelm/Baynes Translation. Princeton, NJ: Princeton University Press, 1987.

Jackson, Stanley. *The Sassoons.* London: Heinemann, 1968.

Jenkins, Charles Francis. *Button Gwinnett: Signer of the Declaration of Independence.* New York: Doubleday, 1926.

Jung, Carl Gustav. *Psychologie und Alchemie*. Olten und Freiburg im Breisgau, Germany: Walter-Verlag, 1972.

Läng, Hans. *Kulturgeschichte der Indianer Nordamerikas*. Breisgau, Germany: Walter-Verlag, 1981.

Lucas de Javanne, Sabine. *The Medicine Wheel: An American Indian Model of Psychic Wholeness*. Zurich, Switzerland: Diploma Thesis, C. G. Jung Institute, 1987.

Mills, Antonia, and Richard Slobodin. *Amerindian Rebirth: Reincarnation Belief among North American Indians and Inuits*. Toronto, Canada: University of Toronto Press, 1994.

Nawang Gehlek, Rimpoche. *Good Life, Good Death: Tibetan Wisdom on Reincarnataion*. New York: Riverhead Books, 2001.

Roberts, Jane. *Seth Speaks: The Eternal Validity of the Soul*. Upper Saddle River, NJ: Prentice Hall, 1972.

Roth, Cecil. *The Sassoon Dynasty*. London: Robert Hale, 1941.

van Waveren, Erlo. *Pilgrimage to the Rebirth*. York Beach, Maine: Samuel Weiser, 1978.

Villoldo, Alberto. *Shaman, Healer, Sage: How to Heal Yourself and Others with the Energy Medicine of the Americas*. New York: Harmony Books, 2000.

von Goethe, Johann Wolfgang. *Faust I. Teil, Goethes Werke*. Hamburg, Germany: Christian Wegner-Verlag, 1954.

Wilmer, Harry. "Combat Nightmares: Toward a Theory of Violence." *Spring Journal* (1986).

Woolger, Roger J. *Other Lives, Other Selves: A Jungian Psychotherapist Discovers Past Lives*. New York: Doubleday, 1987.

INDEX

BOOKS OF RELATED INTEREST

Creating the Soul Body
The Sacred Science of Immortality
by Robert E. Cox

Immortality and Reincarnation
Wisdom from the Forbidden Journey
by Alexandra David-Neel

The Dreamer's Book of the Dead
A Soul Traveler's Guide to Death, Dying, and the Other Side
by Robert Moss

Dreamways of the Iroquois
Honoring the Secret Wishes of the Soul
by Robert Moss

Toltec Dreaming
Don Juan's Teachings on the Energy Body
by Ken Eagle Feather

Don Juan and the Power of Medicine Dreaming
A Nagual Woman's Journey of Healing
by Merilyn Tunneshende

Kabbalah and the Power of Dreaming
Awakening the Visionary Life
by Catherine Shainberg

The World Dream Book
Use the Wisdom of World Cultures to Uncover Your Dream Power
by Sarvananda Bluestone, Ph.D.

Inner Traditions • Bear & Company
P.O. Box 388
Rochester, VT 05767
1-800-246-8648
www.InnerTraditions.com

Or contact your local bookseller